ILLUSTRATED DICTIONARY OF
ARCHITECTURE

SECOND EDITION

Illustrated Dictionary of
Architecture

Ernest Burden

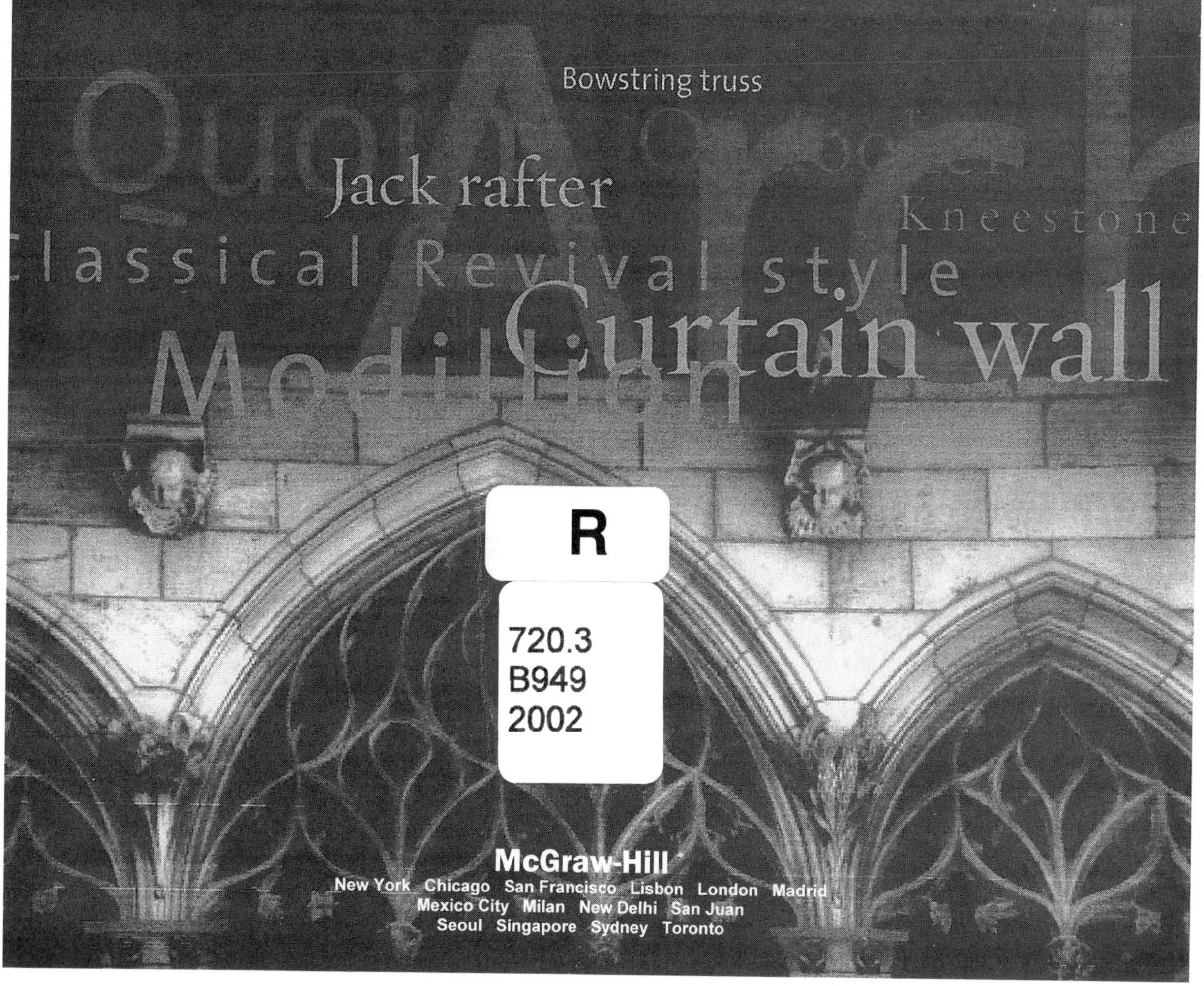

Bowstring truss

Jack rafter

Kneestone

Quoin

Classical Revival style

Curtain wall

Modillion

McGraw-Hill
New York   Chicago   San Francisco   Lisbon   London   Madrid
Mexico City   Milan   New Delhi   San Juan
Seoul   Singapore   Sydney   Toronto

Library of Congress Cataloging-in-Publication Data
Burden, Ernest E.
Illustrated dictionary of architecture / Ernest Burden.-- 2nd ed.
p. cm.
Includes index. ISBN 0-07-137529-5

1. Architecture -- Dictionaries. I. Title.

NA 31.B83 2002

720'.3--dc21   2001034558

McGraw-Hill

A Division of The McGraw-Hill Companies

1 2 3 4 5 6 7 8 9 0 DOC/DOC 0987654321

ISBN 0-07-137529-5

The sponsoring editor for this book was Scott Grillo, the editing
supervisors were Penny Linskey and David E. Fogarty, and the
production supervisor was Pamela A. Pelton.

Printed and bound by R. R. Donnelley & Sons Company.

 This book is printed on recycled, acid-free paper containing a
minimum of 50% recycled, deinked fiber.

McGraw-Hill books are available at special quantity discounts to
use as premiums and sales promotion, or for use in corporate
training programs. For more information, please write to the
Director of Special Sales, McGraw-Hill, Professional Publishing,
Two Penn Plaza, New York, NY 10121-2298. Or contact your
local bookstore.

PREFACE

Architecture throughout the ages has provided shelter from the elements, refuge and safety from intruders, palaces for royalty, shops for merchants, and shrines for religions. Throughout history all of these structures have been constructed with different materials, components, forms, and architectural styles. These items were all part of an integrated system of building, which represented the current customs of each culture.

The Egyptians had a relatively integrated system of building using simple parts. This produced a monolithic style, which featured extensively carved ornamentation on the otherwise simple, massive forms.

The Greeks developed an architecture derived from wooden prototypes, which consisted of a "kit of parts." It is this system which became the standard adopted by western civilizations, and modified by many succeeding generations into infinite variations of these basic forms.

Other civilizations, such as those in China, Japan, Thailand and India, developed similar stylistic features indigenous to their culture and religions. This dictionary describes these styles, and illustrates many of them with photographs of their typical structures.

The number of individual building components has not increased significantly over the past centuries of building. In fact, the number of building components has decreased as building designs became simplified. On the other hand, buildings have become more complex on the technical and functional aspect of the interior. Many of these new technical terms have been included here.

Architecture is a tangible product, and the numerous photographs herein add a dimension that is not possible using word definitions alone. However, there are many intangible aspects involved in contemporary practice as well, and these have also been listed. They include not only aspects of the design and building process, but many new terms relating to building renovation and restoration that are so prevalent in today's practice.

The typical function of a dictionary is to isolate and define individual elements, and to provide specialized information. This dictionary carries it to another level, by illustrating many of the definitions with photographs of these elements in their position within the structures. In addition, this dictionary illustrates several variations of the same element, including historical and contemporary examples.

The photographs in this book were selected from building sites around the world. Some examples are well known, while others provided the clearest illustration of the definition. No attempt was made to identify any of the subjects by building type, location, date, or architect, except the listings of the architects themselves.

Another distinctive feature of this dictionary is the clustering and cross-referencing of similar elements. There are over 40 grouped categories of definitions, where one can find many related definitions. This includes specific types of arches, doors, joints, moldings, roofs, walls, or windows. These grouped subdefinitions are listed alphabetically following the main definition.

INTRODUCTION

The format throughout the book is structured so that it can be used as an easy reference guide, consisting of two main categories; definitions that are illustrated, and those that are not illustrated.

ILLUSTRATED DEFINITIONS: The definitions that are illustrated are shown in a narrow column adjacent to the first illustration; as shown in the following example.

Abacus
The flat area at the top of a capital that divides the column from entablature; consisting of a solid block, or one enriched with moldings. In some orders the sides are hollowed and the corners are truncated.

DEFINITIONS ONLY: Definitions that are not illustrated are shown in a wide column, as in the following example.

Acropolis
An elevated stronghold or group of buildings serving as a civic symbol; those of ancient Greek cities featured the temple of a deity, such as at the acropolis in Athens.

HISTORIC STYLES: All historic styles are set in a wide column, whether they are illustrated or not, due to the lengthy descriptions of those entries; as shown in the following example.

Absolute architecture
A proposal by Hans Hollien and Walter Pickler (1962) for a pure, nonobjective architecture. It was regarded as the antithesis of functionalism: its form would be dictated by the architect's individual taste and not by any utilitarian requirement.

ARCHITECTS: Abbreviated biographies of well-known architects and their major works and dates are listed in the wide column format, as in the following example.

Alvar Aalto (1898-1976)
Finnish architect, who designed the Viipuri Public Library with an undulating timber roof (1929). His design for the Paimio Sanitorium was the first hospital to be built in the International style. Later work includes Baker House at Massachusetts Institute of Technology, Cambridge (1948) and the Public Library, Rovaniemi (1963).

CROSS-REFERENCES: All subcategories, or types of a main category, are listed alphabetically and referenced to the item under which they appear. All cross-referenced listings are also listed alphabetically in the index

SUBCATEGORIES: The cross-referenced definitions included in the grouped subcategories are listed using all lower case letters. They follow under the main listing of that category in alphabetical order, as shown in the following examples.

Arch
A basic architectural structure built over an opening that is made up of wedge-shaped blocks, and supported from each side.

acute arch
A sharply pointed arch with two centers, which are located farther apart than the opening.

All cross-referenced subdefinitions are listed under the main item in strict alphabetical order, whether they are one word, two words, a compound, or hyphenated.

A a

Alto, Alvar (1898–1978)
Finnish architect who designed the Viipuri Public Library
with an undulating timber roof (1929). His Palmio
Sanitorium was one of the first hospitals to be built in
the International style. Later work includes Baker House,
Massachusetts Institute of technology, Cambridge (1948),
and Public Library, Rovaniemi (1963).

Abacus
The flat area at the top
of a capital; dividing a
column from its entabla-
ture. It consists of a
square block, or one en-
riched with moldings. In
some orders the sides are
hollowed and corners
are truncated.

Abadie, Paul (1812–1889)
Designed Sacre-Coeur Church in Paris and is best known
for French Neo-Romanesque churches.

Abat- jour
A skylight in a roof that
admits light from above:
any beveled aperture.

Abat-vent
A louver placed in an
exterior wall opening to
admit light and air, but
offering a barrier to the
wind.

Abbey
The monastic buildings of
religious bodies governed
by an abbot or abbess.

Abramovitz, Max (1908–1963)
American architect educated at the Ecole des Beaux Arts
in Paris. He was a partner to Wallace K. Harrison.

Absolute architecture
The opposite of Functionalism: as its forms were to be
created by imagination rather than by consideration of
need. It was proposed as a purposeless architecture by
Walter Pickler and Hans Hollien in the 1960s, and was
used by Bruce Goff to describe his investigations of
structure and the enclosure of space.

Abstraction
The omission or severe simplification of details in a
drawing, leaving only massing, form and solids, so that
the basis of the design can be explained.

Abutment
A masonry mass, pier, or solid part of a wall that takes the lateral thrust of an arch.

Abutment arch See **Arch**

Academy
A place of study to advance the arts or sciences; named after the place Akademia in Athens where Plato taught.

Acanthus
A common plant of the Mediterranean, whose stylized leaves form the characteristic decoration of capitals of the Corinthian and Composite orders. In scroll form it appears on friezes and panels.

Acanthus

Accent lighting
Any directional lighting that emphasizes a particular object or draws attention to a particular area.

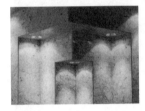

Accessibility (handicapped)
The provision of access to and through a building or site for physically impaired individuals.

Accolade
A rich ornamental treatment made up of two ogee curves meeting in the middle, as found over a door, window, or arch.

2

Accordion door See **Door**

Accouplement
Pairs of closely spaced
columns or pilasters:
typically the abacuses
of the capitals touch
each other without being
joined.

Achromatic
Having no color, a neutral such as black and white.

Acorn ornament See **Ornament**

Acoustic plaster
Plaster with a high degree of sound absorption.

Acoustical door See **Door**

Acoustical tile See **Tile**

Acropodium
An elevated pedestal
bearing a statue that is
raised above the sub-
structure.

Acropolis
An elevated stronghold or
group of buildings serving
as a civic symbol: those of
ancient Greek cities usually
featured the temple of a
deity, such as at Athens.

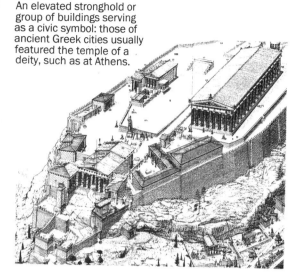

Acroteria
A pedestal for statues and
other ornaments placed
on the apex and the lower
angles of a pediment; or
often refers to the orna-
ment itself.

3

Acrylic
A plastic which in solid form is rigid, clear, and transparent.

Acrylic fiber See **Plastic**

Active solar energy
A method of using solar energy through collectors, or requiring the use of electricity, as opposed to passive solar energy, which uses only the fabric of the building.

Acute angle
Angle of less than 90 degrees.

Acute arch See **Arch**

Adams, Robert (1728–1792)
British architect; whose designs returned to the Classical forms of antiquity, not their Renaissance-derived imitations. Adams excelled in using the natural early Classical forms in domestic settings.

Adams style
An architectural style (1728–1792) based on the work of Robert Adam and his brothers, predominantly in England and strongly influential in the United States and elsewhere. It is characterized by a clarity of form, use of color, subtle detailing, and unified schemes of interior design. Basically Neoclassical, it adopted Neo-Gothic, Egyptian, and Etruscan motifs.

Adaptive use
Changing an existing building to accommodate a new function; the process may involve removal of some existing building elements.

Addition
Construction that increases the size of the original structure by building outside the existing walls or roof.

Addorsed
Animals or figures that are placed back to back and featured as decorative sculpture over doors, in pediments, medallions, and other ornamental devices.

Addorsed

Adjacency
The placement of elements in a planning diagram, ranked according to their importance and inter-connections.

Adler, Dankmar (1844–1900)
German-born engineer, moved to Chicago in 1854, and became a partner of Louis H. Sullivan. The Auditorium Building, Chicago (1886), was their first joint commission. In 1889, the firm employed the young Frank Lloyd Wright.

Adobe
Large, roughly molded, sun-dried clay units consisting of varying sizes.

Adobe brick See **Brick**

Aedicule
A canopied niche flanked by colonettes, intended as a shelter for a statue or a shrine; a door or window framed by columns or pilasters and crowned with a pediment.

Aegricranes See **Ornament: animal forms**

Aeolic capital See **Capital**

Aerial photo-mosaic
A composite of aerial photographs depicting a portion of the earth's surface; basic mapping information such as the name of towns and cities is usually added.

Affleck, Raymond (1922–1989)
A Canadian architect whose best multipurpose building is the Place Bonaventure, Montreal (1968), a vast complex with many internal spaces, but overall becomes a forbidding example of Brutalism.

Affronted
Figures or animals that are placed facing each other, as decorative features over doors and in pediments.

A-frame
A house constructed of wood, with a steep roof that extends down from the ridge to near the foundations; the roof is supported by a framework in the shape of the capital letter A.

Aggregate
Any of a variety of materials, such as sand and gravel, added to a cement mixture to make concrete.

Agora
An open public meeting place for assembly surrounded by public buildings, or a marketplace in an ancient Greek city: the Roman forum is a typical example.

Agraffe
The keystone section of an arch, especially when carved with a cartouche or human face.

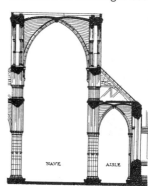

Air-conditioning
Artificial ventilation with air at a controlled temperature and humidity; often implies cooling and dehumidification.

Air-inflated structures
Same as pneumatic structures.

Air lock
A lobby or small room with self-closing doors to allow access between two other spaces while restricting the amount of air exchanged between them.

Aisle
The circulatory space flanking and parallel to the nave in a church, separated from it by a row of columns: a walkway between seats in a theater, auditorium, or other place of public assembly.

5

Alabaster See **Stone**

Alberti, Leon Battista (1404–1472)
Italian Renaissance architect and author who designed the marble facade of San Maria Novella, Florence (1456–1470), which contains Classical details in an otherwise Gothic church. From Vitruvius, via Alberti, came the concept that buildings should be in proportion to the human body, and all their dimensions related. In 1452, Alberti wrote *De re Aedificatoria,* the first architectural treatise of the Renaissance.

Alcove
A small recessed space, connected to or opening directly into a larger room.

Alhambra
One of the most exquisite, elaborate, and richly ornamented of all Moorish palaces in Spain; consisting of a series of joined pavilions with two great courts set at right angles; channels of water, linking pools with fountains, add to the overall effect.

Alignment
An arrangement or adjustment of forms or spaces according to a specific line.

Allegory
A figurative representation or sculpture in which the meaning is conveyed by the use of symbols.

Alley
A passageway providing access to a rear yard or central courtyard.

Alteration
Any physical change to an existing structure or building.

Altarpiece
A panel, sculpted or painted, situated above and behind an altar.

Alto-relievo See **Relief**

Aluminum See **Metal**

Aluminum door See **Door**

Aluminum foil
A thin sheet of aluminum; commonly used for reflective insulation.

Amalaka
A type of capital found in Hindu architecture.

Ambient lighting
The general background lighting, excluding the effects of task lighting.

Ambulatory corridor
A passageway around the apse of a church, or for walking around a shrine; the covered walk of a cloister.

Amenities
The activities provided by a facility regarding comfort and convenience.

American Order

A capital resembling that of the Corinthian order, with the acanthus leaves replaced with corncobs, corn ears, and tobacco leaves; invented by Benjamin Latrobe for the U.S. Capitol in Washington, D.C.

American School style

This style (1940–1959), characterized by the later work of Frank Lloyd Wright and the early work of Bruce Goff, represents the association of organic principles, such as: relationship of the part to the whole, self-sufficiency, rejection of tradition, freedom of expression, and passion for the land.

Amorini

In Renaissance architecture and derivatives, a decorative sculpture or painting, representing chubby, usually naked infants; also called putti.

Amorini

Amorphous

Those forms that do not have a definite or specific shape: or a distinctive crystalline, geometric, angular or curvilinear structure.

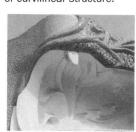

Amortizement
The sloping top portion of a buttress, or projecting pier that is designed to shed water.

Amphiprostyle
A temple featuring porticos at both ends.

Amphitheater
A circular, semicircular, or elliptical auditorium in which a central arena is surrounded by rising tiers of seats; originally for the exhibition of combat or other public events.

Analglyph See **Relief**

Anamorphic image
A distorted image that must be viewed in a special mirror in order to become recognizable.

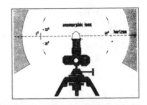

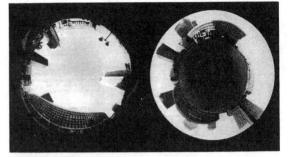

Anchor
A metal device fastened on the outside of a wall and tied to the end of a rod or metal strap connecting it with an opposite wall, to prevent bulging; often consisting of a fanciful decorative design.

Anchor bolt
A bolt with its head embedded in the structure; used to attach a structural member, such as a sill to a foundation wall.

Anchor plate
A metal plate on a wall that holds the end of a tie rod; used in masonry construction.

Anchorage
A device used for permanently securing the ends of a post-tensioned member, or for temporarily securing the ends of a pre-tensioned member during hardening of the concrete.

Ancone
A scrolled bracket or console in classical architecture, which supports a cornice or entablature over a door or window.

Ando, Todao (1941–)
Internationally recognized Japanese architect; largely self-educated, who founded his office in Osaka. He uses traditional materials, vernacular style, and modern techniques of construction. Works include Church of Light, Osaka (1989); Japan Pavilion, Seville Expo (1992), and Naoshima Contemporary Art Museum, Kagawa Prefecture, Japan (1995).

Andrews, John (1933–)
Australian-born architect who made his name with Scarborough College, University of Toronto (1964), a megastructure using the raw materials and the chunky forms of New Brutalism. He designed the George Gund Hall, Harvard University, Cambridge (1972). He also designed the CN Tower, Toronto (1975).

Angle brace See **Brace**

Angle bracket
A bracket at an inside corner of a cornice; usually presenting two perpendicular decorative sides.

Angle buttress See **Buttress**

Angle capital See **Capital**

Angle cleat
A small bracket formed of angle iron, which is used to locate or support a member of a structural framework.

Angle column See **Column**

Angle iron
A steel section, either hot-rolled or cold-formed, consisting of two legs, almost always at a right angle.

Angle joist
A joist running diagonally from an internal girder to the corner intersection of two wall plates; used to support the feet of hip rafters.

Angle niche See **Niche**

Angle of incidence
The angle that an incoming ray of light makes with the reflective surface.

Angle of reflection
Angle that a reflected ray of light makes with the surface that is reflecting it. The angle of reflection is the same as the angle of incidence.

Angle post See **Post**

Angle volute
One of the four corner volutes of a Corinthian capital; with an axis at 45 degrees to the face of the abacus.

ngled bay window See **Window**

Anglo Saxon architecture
The pre-Romanesque architecture (800–1066) of England before the Norman; it is characterized by its massive walls and round arches and by timber prototypes later translated into stone.

Angular
Areas formed by two lines diverging from a common point, two planes diverging from a common line, and the space between such lines or surfaces, whether on the exterior or interior of a structure.

Annulet
A small molding, usually circular in plan and angular in section, encircling the lower part of a Doric capital above the necking: a shaft or cluster of shafts fitted at intervals with rings.

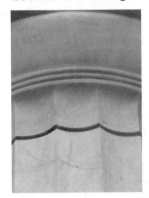

Anshen, Robert
Partner in the firm of Anshen and Allen, San Francisco, California. Designed the Chapel of the Holy Cross, Sedona, Arizona (1956).

Anta
A pier or pilaster formed by a thickening at the end of a wall, most often used on the side of a doorway or beyond the face of an end wall.

Antechamber
A room that serves both as a waiting area as well as an entrance to a larger room.

Antefix
A decorated upright slab used in classical architecture and other derivatives to close or conceal the open end of a row of tiles that covers the joints of roof tiles.

Antepagment
The stone or stucco decorative dressings enriching the jambs and head of a doorway or window; a door Jamb.

Anthemion
A common Greek ornament based on the honeysuckle or palmette, used in a radiating cluster, either singly on a stele or antefix, or as a running ornament on friezes.

Anthemion band
A Classical Greek style decorative molding with bas-relief or painted anthemion leaf clusters; often, two alternating designs are used along the band.

Antic
A grotesque sculpture consisting of forms of animals, humans and foliage incongruously run together; used to decorate molding terminations and parts of medieval architecture.

Apadana
The hypostyle hall of Persian kings, such as at Persepolis, in Iran.

Apartment
A room or group of rooms designed to be used as a dwelling: usually one of many similar groups in the same building.

Apartment hotel
A building with multiple dwelling units that do not have private kitchens and are usually rented on a short-term basis.

Apartment house
A building containing a number of individual residential dwelling units.

Apex
The highest point, peak, or tip of any structure.

Apex stone
The uppermost stone in a gable, pediment, vault, or dome, usually triangular, often highly decorated.

Apophyge
The concave curve formed where the base or top of a classical style column curves inward to meet the shaft; tangent to the shaft and perpendicular to the fillet above.

Applied trim
Supplementary and separate decorative strips of wood or moldings applied to the face or sides of a frame.

Applique
An accessory decorative feature applied to a structure. In ornamental work, one material affixed to another.

Apprentice
A young person who is legally bound to a craftsman for a specified period of time in order to learn the skills of a particular trade.

Apron
A flat piece of trim below the interior sill of a window, limited to the width of the window.

Apse
A semicircular or polygonal space, usually in a church, terminating an axis and intended to house an alter.

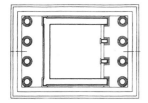

Apteral
Classical building with columns across the width of the portico at one or both ends, but without columns on the sides.

Aqueduct
An elevated masonry structure with a channel for carrying water that is supported on arches; it was invented by the ancient Romans.

Arabesque
Generic term for an intricate and subtle ornate surface decoration based on a mixture of intermixed geometrical patterns and natural botanical forms used in Muhammadan countries.

Arabesque style
An imitation of the Moorish architectural style of Spain, characterized by masonry walls with multicolored Mooresque decoration in plaster, precious stones, or glazed tiles on most surfaces; horseshoe arches, interior courtyards surrounded by colonnades; pointed dome roofs, wide horizontal stripes, and stalactite ornaments.

Arbor
A light open latticework frame, often used as a shady garden shelter or bower.

Arboretum
An informally arranged garden: usually on a large scale, where trees are grown for display, educational, or scientific purposes.

Arcade

A line of arches along one or both sides, supported by pillars or columns, either as free-standing or attached to a building. Applies to a line of arches fronting shops, and covered with a steel and glass skylight, usually running the length of the arcade.

blind arcade

A row of continuous arches applied to a wall and used as a decorative element.

intersecting arcade

Arches resting on alternate supports in one row, meeting on one plane at the crossings.

Arcaded arch See **Arch**

Arcading

A series of arches, raised on columns, that are represented in relief as decoration on a solid wall.

Arcature
An ornamental arcade on a miniature scale.

Arch
A basic architectural structure built over an opening, made up of wedge-shaped blocks, keeping one another in position, and transferring the vertical pressure of the superimposed load into components transmitted laterally to the adjoining abutments.

abutment arch
The first or last of a series of arches next to an abutment.

acute arch
A sharply pointed two-centered arch, whose centers of curvature are farther apart than the opening.

arcaded arch
An arch that occurs where a vault intersects a wall.

back arch
An arch that supports an inner wall where the outer wall is supported in a different manner, such as a brick arch behind a stone lintel.

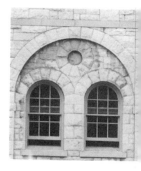

barrel arch
An arch that is formed by a curved solid plate or slab, as contrasted with one formed with individual members or curved ribs.

basket handle arch
A flattened arch designed by joining a quarter circle to each end of a false ellipse; a three-centered arch with a crown whose radius is greater than the outer pair of curves.

bell arch
A round arch resting on two large corbels with curved profiles.

blind arch
An arch within a wall containing a recessed flat wall rather than framing an opening. Used to enrich an unrelieved expanse of masonry, or to fill an existing arched opening.

blind Arch

blunt arch
An arch rising only to a slight point; struck from two-centers within the arch.

broken arch
A form of segmental arch in which the center of the arch is omitted and is replaced by a decorative feature applied to a wall, above the entablature over a door or window.

camber arch
A flat segmental arch with a slightly upward curve in the intrados and some-times also in the extrados.

catenary arch
An arch that takes the form of an inverted catenary, i.e., the curve formed by a flexible cord hung between the two points of support.

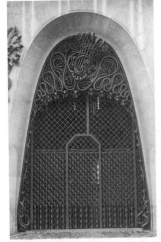

cinquefoil arch
A five-lobed pattern divided by cusps; a cusped arch with five foliations worked into the intrados.

circular arch
Arch whose intrados takes the form of a segment of a circle.

composite arch
An arch whose curves are struck from four centers, as in the English Perpendicular Gothic style.

compound arch
An arch formed by concentric arches set within one another.

corbel arch
A false arch constructed by corbeling courses from each side of an opening until they meet at a midpoint; a capstone is laid on top to complete it.

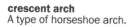

crescent arch
A type of horseshoe arch.

cusped arch
An arch which has cusps or foliations worked into the intrados.

cusped arch

counterarch
Arch that resists the thrust of another arch.

depressed arch
A flat-headed opening with the angles rounded off to become segments of circles; often used in the perpendicular style.

diminished arch
An arch having less rise or height than a semicircle.

discharging arch
An arch, usually segmental and often a blind arch, built above the lintel of a door or window to shift the weight of the wall above the lintel to each side.

drop arch
A pointed arch which is struck from two centers that are nearer together than the width of the arch so that the radii are less than the span; similar to a depressed arch.

elliptical arch
A circular arch in the form of a semi-ellipse.

equilateral arch
A pointed arch with two centers and radii equal to the span.

extradosed arch
An arch in which the extrados is clearly marked, as a curve exactly or roughly nearly parallel to the intrados; it has a well-marked archivolt.

false arch
A form having the appearance of an arch, though not of arch construction, such as a corbeled arch.

flat arch
An arch with a horizontal, or nearly horizontal intrados: with little or no convexity; an arch with a horizontal intrados with voussoirs radiating from a center below.

flat keystone arch
Flat arch with a distinctive keystone at its center.

Florentine arch
An arch whose entrados is not concentric with the intrados, and whose voussoirs are therefore longer at the crown than at the springing, common in Florence in the early Renaissance.

foiled arch
An arch incorporating foils in the intrados, such as a two-cusped or trefoil arch.

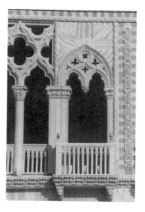

French arch
A flat arch with voussoirs inclined to the same angle on each side of a keystone.

gauged arch
An arch of wedge-shaped bricks which have been shaped so that the jambs radiate from a common center.

Gothic arch
A pointed arch, especially one with two centers and equal radii.

groin arch
An arch formed by the intersection of two simple vaults: an arched extrusion of a cross vault.

half arch
One half of a full arch; usually used with a quarter round window or in the lower part of a flying buttress.

haunch arch
An arch having a crown of different curvature than the haunches, which are thus strongly marked; usually a basket-handle or three-centered arch.

horseshoe arch
A rounded arch whose curve is wider than a semi-circle, so that the opening at the bottom is narrower than its greatest span.

inverted arch
An arch with its intrados below the springline, especially used to distribute concentrated loads in foundations.

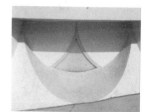

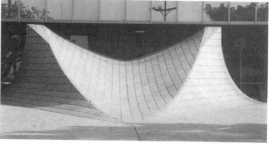

19

lancet arch
Same as an acute arch.

Mayan arch
A corbeled arch of triangular shape common in the buildings of the Maya Indians of Yucatan.

miter arch
A structural support over an opening in a masonry wall formed by two stones that meet at a 45-degree angle and form a right-angle miter in the center; technically not a true arch.

Moorish arch
The Islamic arch of North Africa and of the region of Spain under Islamic domination.

multi-centered arch
An arch having a shape composed of a series of circular arcs with different radii, making an approximate ellipse.

obtuse-angle arch
A type of pointed arch, formed by arcs of circles that intersect at the apex; the center of the circles are nearer together than the width of the arch.

ogee arch
A pointed arch composed of reversed curves, the lower concave, the upper convex; a pointed arch, each haunch of which is a double curve with the concave side uppermost.

parabolic arch
An arch similar to a three-centered arch, but whose intrados is parabolic with a vertical axis.

20

pier arch
An arch supported by piers rather than columns.

pointed arch
Any arch with a point at its apex, characteristic of but not limited to Gothic architecture.

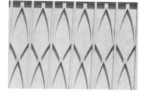

proscenium arch
Large opening in a proscenium wall that surrounds the stage; may be rectangular or in the shape of an arch.

rampant arch
An arch in which the impost on one side is higher than that on the other.

rear arch
An inner arch of an opening which is smaller in size than the exterior arch of the opening and which may be a different shape.

recessed arch
An arch with a shorter radius set within another of the same shape.

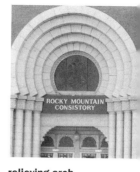

relieving arch
A discharging arch.

ribbed arch
An arch composed of individual curved members or ribs.

rigid arch
An arch without joints that is continuous and rigidly fixed at the abutments.

Roman arch
A semicircular arch in which all the units are wedge-shaped.

rough arch
An arch constructed with rectangular bricks and tapered mortar joints; usually found on relieving arches.

Round arch
An arch having a semi-circular intrados.

round horseshoe arch
A horseshoe arch with a totally circular entrados, instead of one resting on straight legs.

rowlock arch
A segmental arch composed of full rowlock bricks; especially when formed with concentric rows.

rustic arch
An arch laid up with regular or irregular stones, the spaces between them filled with mortar.

segmental arch
A circular arch in which the intrados is less than a semi-circle.

semi-arch
An arch in which only one half of its sweep is developed, such as in a flying buttress.

semicircular arch
A round arch whose intrados is a full semicircle.

shouldered arch
A lintel carried on corbels at either end: a square-headed trefoil arch.

splayed arch
An arch opening which has a larger radius in front than at the back.

squinch arch
A small arch across the corner of a square room, that supports a superimposed mass above it.

stepped arch
An arch in which the outer ends of some or all of the voussoirs are cut square to fit into the horizontal courses of the wall at the sides of the arch.

stilted arch
An arch whose curve begins above the impost line; one resting on imposts treated as a downward continuation of the archivolt.

surbased arch
An arch having a rise of less than half the span.

Syrian arch
A round arch with the spring line almost at ground level; common in Richardsonian Romanesque style doorways.

three-centered arch
An arch struck from three centers: the two on the sides have short radii, the center has a longer radius, and the resultant curve of the intrados approximates an ellipse.

three-hinged arch
An arch with hinges at the two supports and at the crown.

three-pinned arch
An arch with two pin joints at the supports and a third pin at the crown.

transverse arch
An arched construction built across a hall or the nave of a church, either as part of the vaulting or to support or stiffen the roof.

trefoil arch
An arch having a cusped intrados with three pointed foils.

triangular arch
A structure composed of two stones laid diagonally, mutually supporting each other to span an opening; a primitive form of arch consisting of two stones laid diagonally to support each other over an opening.

trussed arch
An arch-shaped truss with radial posts between the parallel arched top and bottom chords.

Tudor arch
A four-centered pointed arch, common in the architecture of the Tudor style in England; a four-centered arch whose inner pair of curves is greater than that of the outer pair.

two-centered arch
An arch struck from two centers, resulting in a pointed arch.

two-hinged arch
An arch with two hinges at the supports at both ends.

Venetian arch
A pointed arch in which the intrados and extrados are further apart at the peak than at the springing line.

Arch order
A Roman architectural style characterized by a series of arched openings with an entablature above the head of the arch and engaged columns that appear to support the entablature between adjacent arches.

Archaic
Antiquated or old-fashioned, but when used in connection with Greek architecture the term refers to a specific period, c. 600–500 B.C.

Arched
Shapes formed by the curved, pointed, or rounded upper part of openings or supporting members.

Arched dormer See **Dormer**

Arched impost
An impost block with
moldings that continue
around the archivolt.

Arched truss See **Truss**

Archigram (1960–1975)
Group formed by Peter Cook, Ron Herron, Dennis
Crompton, and others, who publicized their ideas through
seductive graphics, exhibitions, and the magazine
Archigram.

Architect
An individual who is engaged in the design of buildings
and who supervises the construction.

Architectonic
Related or conforming to technical architectural
principles.

Architectural
Pertaining to architecture, its features, characteristics,
or details; also to materials used to build or ornament
a structure such as mosaic, bronze, wood and the like.

**Architectural
conservation**
The process of maintain-
ing and/or repairing the
materials of a building or
structure to reduce or
reverse the physical
deterioration; it includes
cleaning, repointing of
masonry joints, and
reattaching any loose
elements.

Architectural design
A process which includes analysis of a program that
results in the creation or alteration of a building or
similar structure.

Architectural element
Portion of a building or its
ornamentation.

Architectural engineering
The art and science of engineering functions that relate
to buildings or structures.

Architectural historian
Specialist in the history of the built environment, with
special expertise in architecture.

Architectural history
The field of study of architectural style, including the
theoretical basis of design and the evolution of design
vocabularies and construction techniques.

Architectural Review Board
An appointed local body that reviews proposed new
construction and alterations to existing buildings in a
historic district for conformance to established design
guidelines and/or good design practice.

Architectural significance
The importance of a particular structure based on its
design, materials, form, style, or workmanship; particularly if used for a National Register nomination.

Architectural style
The overall appearance of the architecture of a building, including its construction, form, and ornamentation;
which may be a unique individual expression or part of
a broad cultural pattern.

Architecture
The art and science of designing and building structures,
or groups of structures, in keeping with aesthetic and
functional criteria.

Architrave
The lowest of the three divisions of a classical entablature, the main beam
spanning from column to
column, resting directly on
the capitals.

Architrave

Architrave cornice
An entablature in which the frieze is eliminated and the cornice rests directly on the architrave.

Archivolt
The ornamental molding running around the exterior curve of an arch, around the openings of windows, doors, and other openings.

Archway
A passageway through or under an arch, especially a long barrel vault.

Arcology
A conception of architecture (1969) involving the fusion of architecture and ecology, proposed by Paolo Soleri, an Italian architect living in America. Arcology is Soleri's solution to urban problems. He proposed vast vertical structures capable of housing millions of inhabitants. One of Soleri's' visionary projects, Arcosanti, is being constructed in Arizona.

Arcuated
Based on, or characterized by, arches or arch-like curves or vaults; as distinguished from trabeated (beamed) structures.

Arena

A space of any shape surrounded by seats rising in tiers surrounding a stage; a type of theater without a proscenium.

Armory

A building used for military training or for the storage of military equipment.

Arquitectonica

High-style designers in the Post-modern style, such as the Atlantis apartments in Miami (1982), their first major project. Their latest is the e-walk hotel and commercial development in Times Square, New York City (2000).

Arris

An external angular intersection between any two sharp planar or curved faces, as in moldings; or between two flutes in a Doric column.

Art Deco style

Stimulated by an exhibition in Paris, this new style (1925–1940) drew its inspiration from Art Nouveau, Native American art, Cubism, the Bauhaus, and Russian ballet.

The stylistic elements were eclectic, including the use of austere forms. It was characterized by linear, hard edge, or angular composition with stylized decoration. It was the style of cinemas, ocean liners, and hotel interiors. It was called "modernistic," and reconciled mass production with sophisticated design.

Facades were arranged in a series of setbacks emphasizing the geometric form. Strips of windows with decorative spandrels add to the composition. Hard-edged, low-relief ornamentation was common around door and window openings and along roof edges or parapets.

Ornamental detailing was either executed in the same material as the building, in contrasting metals, or in glazed bricks or mosaic tiles. The style was also used for skyscraper designs such as the Chrysler building in New York City.

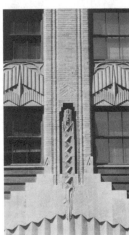

Art glass See Glass

Art metal
Decorative metal elements, such as sheet-metal cornices or pressed tin ceilings.

Art Moderne
A design style characterized by horizontal elements, rounded corners, flat roofs, glass blocks, smooth walls, windows that wrap around corners without posts, and asymmetrical massing, all intended to look streamlined. Also known as Streamline Moderne and Style Moderne.

Art Moderne style
A modern style (1930–1945), characterized by rounded corners, flat roofs, and smooth wall finishes devoid of surface ornamentation. A distinctive streamlined look was created by wrapping curved window glass around corners. Ornamentation consisted of mirrored panels and cement panels with low relief. Aluminum and stainless steel were used for door and window trim, railings and balusters. Metal or wooden doors often had circular windows.

Art Nouveau architecture
A movement (1880–1910) in European architecture and applied arts, developed principally in France and Belgium, characterized by flowing and sinuous organic and dynamic forms, naturalistic ornament and a strict avoidance of any historical traits.

Other names for the style include, Le Modern Style (France); Jugendstil (Germany), after the German term for youth style; Stile Liberty (Italy), named after the Liberty and Company store in London; Modernismo (Spain); and Sezession (Austria), named after its proponents seceded from the Academy of Art In Vienna.

The style drew primarily on Baroque, Gothic and Moorish traditions, but was mainly unbounded by rules. Art Nouveau exploited the machine and reveled in the possibilities of decorative tiles and wrought iron. This was a deliberate attempt to put an end to imitations of past styles. In its place was a free type of architecture that integrated arts and crafts and architectural forms.

Articulation
Shapes and surfaces that have joints or segments which sub-divide the area or elements; the joints or members add scale and rhythm to an otherwise plain surface.

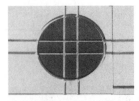

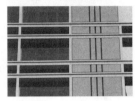

Artifact
Individual product of human manufacture, such as cutlery, glassware, pottery, textiles, tools, and weapons.

Artificial light
Light produced by electrical processes or the burning of fuel.

Artificial sky
A hemisphere or ceiling painted and illuminated to imitate the natural sky. Lighting effects can be used to simulate any time of day or night.

Artificial stone
A mixture of stone chips or fragments, usually embedded in a matrix of mortar, cement, or plaster; the surfaces may be ground, polished, molded, or otherwise treated to simulate natural stone.

Artificial wood See Wood

Arts and Crafts movement
A movement (1880–1891) which restored creativity to the decorative arts and indirectly to architecture. Architects such as Henry Van de Velde, Joseph Hoffman, and Charles Rennie Mackintosh had a very strong influence on this movement. It abandoned the stylistic imitation of the nineteenth century and laid the groundwork for the creative works of the Art Nouveau styles that followed.

Asam, Egid Quirin (1692–1750)
One of two brothers who created a distinctive Baroque style in Bavaria, Southern Germany. They designed church interiors in Munich and Regensberg, using fresco and stucco to create fantastically rich effects.

Asbestos
A noncombustible, flexible fiber that is able to withstand high temperatures; it is fabricated into many forms, either alone or mixed with other ingredients.

Asbestos abatement
Removal of material that contains asbestos which is considered a potential health hazard, in a manner that minimizes risk to the abatement workers and the public.

Asbestos shingle
A roofing shingle composed of cement reinforced with asbestos fibers, manufactured in various shapes and sizes.

Asbestos slate
An artificial roofing slate manufactured with asbestos-reinforced cement.

Asbestos-cement board
A dense, rigid board containing a high percentage of asbestos fiber bonded with portland cement, noncombustible, used in sheet or corrugated sheathing.

As-built drawings
Plans that incorporate the changes made during the construction to record accurately the actual construction of the structure, as opposed to the initial construction documents.

Ashlar masonry See Masonry

Aspect
The point from which one looks, a point of view: a position facing a given direction, an exposure.

Aspect ratio
In any rectangular configuration, the ratio between the longer dimension and the shorter dimension.

Asphalt
A mixture of bitumens obtained from native deposits or as a petroleum by-product used for paving, water proofing, and roofing applications.

Asphalt roofing
A roofing material manufactured by saturating a dry felt sheet with asphalt, and then coating the saturated felt with a harder asphalt coating, usually in roll form.

Asphalt shingles
Shingles manufactured from saturated roofing felt that is coated with asphalt, with mineral granules on the side that is exposed to the weather.

Asphalt tile
Resilient floor tile that is composed of asbestos fibers with asphalt binders; set in mastic and installed over wood or concrete floors.

Asplund, Eric Gunnar (1885-1940)
One of the most eminent of Swedish architects; he adopted Neo-classicism and designed the City Library, Stockholm (1920), which had architectonic shapes reduced to basic rectangles and cylinders.

Assembly room
A room in a hotel or town hall, where social gatherings can be held.

Assyrian architecture
Large palaces and temple complexes with ziggurats characterize this style (900–700 B.C.); the exterior walls were often ornamented in carved relief or polychrome bricks. Doorways had semicircular arches with glazed brick around the circumference; windows were square-headed and high up in the wall.

Interior courts were filled with slender columns with high molded bases, fluted shafts and capitals of recurring vertical scrolls. The bracket form of the topmost part was fashioned with the heads of twin bulls. They were widely spaced to support timber and clay roofs.

Astragal
A member or combination of members, fixed to one of a pair of doors or casement windows to cover the joint between the meeting stiles and to close the gap in order to prevent drafts, passage of light, air or noise.

Astylar
Buildings that have classical features, but do not have any of the traditional orders, or pilasters.

Asylum
An institution or facility for the care of ill or destitute persons, or mentally ill or insane.

Asymmetry
Not symmetrical, with the parts not arranged correspondingly identical on both sides of a central axis.

Atlas
A figure of a man used in place of a column to support an entablature; also called Atlantes and Telemon.

Atrium
The forecourt of an early Christian basilica, with colonnades on all four sides; and usually a fountain in the center. It was derived from the entrance court or hall of a Roman dwelling, roofed to leave a large opening to admit light. Rain was received in a cistern below. The modern version is a common space with skylights in an office or hotel complex.

Attached house
House which shares one or more common walls with another house, including row houses and semidetached houses.

Attic
The top story or stories of a building: the structure's termination against the sky.

Attic base

A circular Ionic column base with an upper and lower torus joined by a concave scotia molding bordered with a pair of quadra fillets.

Attic ventilator

A mechanical fan in the attic of a house, which removes hot air from the roof space and discharges it to the outside.

Auditorium

That part of a theater, school, or public building that is set aside for the listening and viewing audience.

Automatic door See Door

Automatic fire alarm

A detector that automatically sounds a signal notifying the presence of a fire.

Awning

A roof-like cover of canvas or other lightweight material, extending in front of a doorway or window, or over a deck, providing protection from the sun or rain.

Awning window See Window

Axial composition

A design with a central axis that features bilateral symmetry.

Axial plan

The placing of several buildings or rooms longitudinally, such as along a single line.

Axis

An imaginary straight line, about which parts of a building, or group of buildings, can be arranged or measured.

Axonometric perspective

A form of orthographic projection in which a rectangular object, projected on a plane, shows three faces.

Axonometric projection See Projection drawing

Aztec architecture

An architecture (1100–1520) that emerged from the austere forms of the Toltecs, characterized by strong grid plans, monumental scale, and brightly colored exteriors, often with highly stylized surface carvings of human figures, floral patterns and images of gods.

Pyramids often supported two temples with parallel stairways. Destruction by the Spanish left very few remains, as the Aztec capital of Tenochtitlan is entirely buried under modern Mexico City.

Bb

Babcock, Charles (1839–1913)
American architect who worked with Upjohn, was one of the founders of the American Institute of Architects; he later designed buildings for Cornell University, Ithaca.

Babylonian architecture
An architecture (2000–1600 B.C.) characterized by mud-brick walls articulated by pilasters and faced with glazed brick. The city of Babylon contained the famous Tower of Babel and the Ishtar Gate, decorated with enameled brick friezes of bulls and lions, and the Hanging Gardens of Semiramis.

The ruins of the Assyrian Palace of Khorsabad show evidence of monumental sculptural decoration. The Palace of Darius at Persepolis featured magnificent relief carvings.

Back arch See Arch

Back building
A detached or contiguous subsidiary structure behind the main building.

Backband molding See Molding

Backfill
Crushed stone or coarse soil placed around foundation walls to provide drainage for water collecting in the soil behind the wall.

Backing brick See Brick

Backlighting
Lighting of an object from the rear, used to provide drama and emphasis.

Backup material
A material placed at the back of a curtain wall for fire or insulation purposes, or behind a finished face of masonry.

Baffle
An opaque or translucent plate used to shield a light source from direct view at certain angles: a flat deflector designed to reduce sound transmission.

Bailey
Stockade or walled enclosure surrounding a castle; also an open court in a medieval fortification.

Baked enamel
A hard, glossy metal finish composed of synthetic resins baked in an oven; used at one time for the spandrel panel of curtain wall construction.

Balance
A harmonizing or satisfying arrangement, or proportion of various parts, as in a design or composition: the state of equipoise between different architectural elements.

formal balance
Designs that are almost always characterized by symmetrical elements.

formal balance

informal balance
Designs where the forms are mostly asymmetrical.

Balconet
A pseudo-balcony; a low ornamental railing to a window, projecting but slightly beyond the plane of the window, threshold or sill, having the appearance of a balcony when the window is fully open.

Balcony
A projecting platform usually on the exterior of a building, sometimes supported from below by brackets or corbels, or cantilevered by projecting members of wood, metal or masonry. They are most often enclosed with a railing, balustrade, or other parapet.

Balcony

Balcony beam
Horizontal beam which supports a balcony.

Bald cypress See **Wood**

Baldachino
A permanent canopy over a throne or altar, supported by four columns.

Balistraria
A loophole or similar aperture in a medieval wall, most often cruciform in shape, through which bowmen fired arrows.

Ballflower
A spherical ornament composed of three conventionalized petals enclosing a ball, usually in a hollow molding: popular in the English Decorated style.

Balloon framing
A system of framing a wooden building wherein all vertical studs in the exterior bearing walls and partitions extend the full height of the frame from sill to roof plate; the floor joists are supported by sills.

Ballroom
A large room in a dwelling, hotel, or public building such as a town hall designed for dancing, concerts, and similar entertainment.

Balsam fir See **Wood**

Balsam poplar See **Wood**

Balteus
The vertical bead between the scrolls at the side of the Ionic capital.

Baluster
One of a number of short vertical members used to support a stair railing.

Baluster column See **Column**

Baluster side
The rounded side of an Ionic capital.

Balustrade
An entire railing system, as along the edge of a balcony, including a top rail, bottom rail and balusters.

Balustrade order
One of the Neoclassical Orders of balusters and rails.

Band
A flat horizontal fascia, or a continuous member or series of moldings projecting slightly from the wall plane, encircling a building or along a wall, that makes a division in the wall.

Band molding See **Molding**

Banded architrave
A door or window architrave that is broken at regular intervals by a series of projecting blocks.

Banded column See **Column**

Banded door See **Door**

Banded rustication
Alternating smooth ashlar and roughly textured stone.

Banderole ornament See **Ornament**

Banding
Horizontal subdivisions of a column or wall using profile or material change.

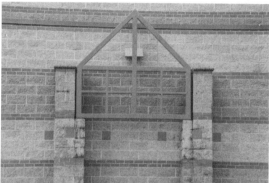

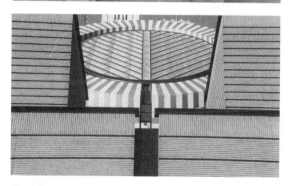

Banister
A slender pillar turned on a lathe, used to support the handrail of a stair.

Bank barn
A two-level barn built against a bank or hillside, with an upper level that can be reached directly from the hill slope.

Baptistry
A building for Christian baptismal rites containing the font; often located in a structure separate from the church.

Bar
A long, thin strip of material, especially iron, used for a variety of building purposes, particularly when inserted into an opening to prevent entry; often placed on the outside of a glazed window.

Bar joist
An open web joist with diagonal struts made of round or square steel bars with the top and bottom chords made up from pairs of steel angles.

Bar molding See **Molding**

Bar tracery See **Tracery**

Barbican
An outer defense of a castle or city, in particular a tower above a gate or drawbridge.

Barge cornice
A raked cornice at the top of a gable end.

Bargeboard
A trim board used on the edge of gables where the roof extends over the wall; it either covers the rafter or occupies the place of a rafter. Originally it was ornately carved.

Bargecourse
The coping of a wall, formed by a course of bricks set on edge.

Bargestone
One of the projecting units of masonry, which forms the sloping top of a gable wall.

Barn
A building for housing animals and storing farm equipment, hay, and other agricultural produce.

Barnes, Edward Larrabee
His most noted early work is the Crown Center, Kansas City (1968). Later works include the IBM Building, New York City (1983), and the Walker Art Center, Minneapolis (1971).

Baroque architecture
A style (1600–1760) named for the French word meaning bizarre, fantastic or irregular. It was the most lavish of all styles, both in its use of materials and the effects that it achieved. Mannerist styles were often adopted and carried to the extreme as bold, opulent and intentionally distorted. Pediments are broken and facades designed with undulating forms, while interiors are more theatrical, exhibiting a dramatic combination of architecture, sculpture, painting and the decorative arts.

36

Barracks
Temporary or permanent housing erected for soldiers or groups of workers.

Barrel and groin vaulting See **Vault**

Barrel arch See **Arch**

Barrel roof See **Roof**

Barrel vault See **Vault**

Barroco-mudejar style
An architectural style of the Mexican colonial period that employs Italian Baroque features and Moorish decorative motifs: thick adobe walls, scrolled parapet copings, elaborately carved window and door surrounds and concave shell-shaped ornamentation over the door head.

Barry, Sir Charles (1795–1860)
Versatile English architect of the early Victorian period, inspired by Renaissance models. The Houses of Parliament, London, is his most important work.

Basalt See **Stone**

Bascule
A structure that rotates about an axis, as a seesaw, with a counterbalance equal to the weight of the structure at one end, used for movable bridges.

Bascule bridge See **Bridge**

Base
The lowest and most visible part of a building, often treated with distinctive materials, such as rustication; also pertains to the lowest part of a column or pier that rests on a pedestal, plinth, or stylobate.

Baseboard
A flat projection from an interior wall or partition at the floor, covering the joint between the floor and wall, and protecting the wall: it may be plain or molded.

Base block
A block of any material, generally with little or no ornament, forming the lowest member of a base at the foot of a door or window.

Base cabinet
Kitchen cabinet that rests on the floor and supports the counter.

Base cap
Molding that rests on or overlaps the top of a baseboard.

Base coat
The first coat of plaster finish, typically composed of lime, cement, and sand; the first layer of any coating applied in a liquid or plastic state, such as paint.

Base course
The lowest course on a masonry wall or pier, may also be part of the footing.

Base map
Graphic representation of a defined area, such as a particular site or a neighborhood, town, region, or state, showing legal boundaries and physical features.

Base molding See **Molding**

Basement
Usually the lowest story of a building, either partly or entirely below grade.

Baseplate
A steel plate for transmitting and distributing a column load to the supporting foundation material.

Basic services
The services performed by an architect during the following five phases of a project: schematic design, design development, construction documentation, bidding or negotiation, and contract administration.

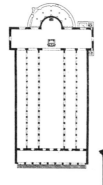

Basilica
A Roman hall of justice with a high central space lit by a clerestory with a timbered gable roof. It became the form of the early Christian church, with a semicircular apse at the end preceded by a vestibule and atrium.

Basket capital See **Capital**

Basket-handle arch See **Arch**

Basketweave bond See **Bond**

Bas-relief See **Relief**

Bastion
A projecting portion of a fortification designed to defend the adjacent curtain wall; it typically approximates a semi-hexagon, with the two outer faces meeting at an acute angle, and two flanks abutting a curtain wall on each side.

Bath

An open tub used as a fixture for bathing: the room containing the bathtub; the Roman public bathing structure consisting of hot, warm and cool pools, sweat rooms, athletics and other related facilities.

Bathhouse

A building equipped with bathing facilities: a small structure containing rooms or lockers for bathers, as at the seaside.

Bathroom

A room with bathing facilities; typically containing a bathtub, water closet, and lavatory.

Batt insulation

Loosely packed fibrous insulation more than one inch thick; types of fiber include fiberglass and wood.

Batten

A narrow strip of wood that is applied over a joint between parallel boards in the same plane. In roofing, a strip applied over boards or structural members as a base for attaching slate, wood, or clay shingles.

Batten door See **Door**

Batter

A wall that gently slopes inward toward the top.

Battered

Forms that slope from a true vertical plane from bottom to top, as in the outside surface of a wall.

Battlement

A parapet having a regular alternation of solid parts and openings, originally for defense, but later used as a decorative motif.

Bauhaus style

An architectural style developed at the school of design established by Walter Gropius in 1919 in Weimar, Germany. It moved to Dessau in 1926 and closed in 1933. The term became virtually synonymous with modern teaching methods in architecture and the applied arts and with the functional aesthetics for the industrial age. It epitomized the marriage of modern design, mass production and industrial design.

Bay

A principal compartment or division in the architectural arrangement of a building. marked either by buttresses or pilasters in the wall, by the disposition of the main arches and pillars, or by any repeated spatial units that separate it into corresponding portions.

cant bay

A bay erected on a canted outline.

The Atrium on Bay

Beam
A rigid structural member whose prime function is to carry and transfer transverse loads across a span to the supports; as a joist, girder, rafter, or purlin.

bolster beam
A timber or steel beam that supports the end of a bridge truss on an abutment or pier: it is set perpendicular to the trusses.

box beam
One or more vertical plywood webs laminated to seasoned wood flanges. Vertical spacers separate the flanges at intervals along the length of the beam to distribute the loads and to provide stiffness.

built-up beam
A beam composed of multiple parts, such as a box beam, compound beam, lattice beam, and angle girder.

camber beam
A beam curved slightly upward toward the center.

channel beam
A channel used as a beam, typically with the web in the vertical position.

collar beam
A horizontal member that ties together two opposite common rafters, usually at a point halfway up the length of the rafters below the ridge.

continuous beam
Beam that is continuous over intermediate supports and thus statically indeterminate; as opposed to a simply supported beam.

crossbeam
A beam that runs transversely through the centerline of a structure: any transverse beam in a structure such as a joist.

edge beam
A beam at the edge of a shell plate structure; providing stiffness that provides an increase in the load-bearing capacity.

encased beam
Iron and steel beams that are encased in a variety of materials for protection against fire.

grade beam
Reinforced concrete beam or slab that is normally placed directly on the ground.

hammer beam
One of a pair of short horizontal members, attached to the foot of a principal rafter, located within a roof structure in place of a tie beam.

I-beam
An iron or steel beam with a symmetrical I-shaped cross section.

laminated beam
A wood beam composed of a series of overlapping wood members that are glued together.

open web beam
A truss with parallel top and bottom chords formed by a pair of angles, employing a web of diagonal struts and used as a beam; the struts connecting the top and bottom chords are also composed of steel bars.

plate girder
A steel beam built up from vertical web plates and horizontal flange plates.

simple beam
A beam without restraint or continuity at the supports, as opposed to a fixed-end beam.

summerbeam
A large horizontal beam in the ceiling of an early American colonial timber-framed house.

T-beam
An iron or steel rolled beam with a T-shaped cross section.

tie beam
In roof framing, a horizontal timber connecting two opposite rafters at their lower ends to prevent them from spreading.

trussed beam
A beam or purlin stiffened with a tie rod.

welded beam
A large steel I-section, fabricated by welding from plates instead of hot rolling; same as a plate girder.

Beam ceiling
A ceiling formed by the underside of the floor, exposing the beams supporting it; also applies to a false ceiling imitating exposed beams.

Bearing pile
A pile that carries a vertical load, as compared with a sheet pile, which resists earth pressure.

Bearing plate
A metal plate at the end of a beam or bottom of a column to distribute the load over a larger surface.

Bearing wall See Wall

Bestiary See Ornament: animal forms

Beaux-Arts Classicism
Grandiose compositions with exuberant ornamental detail and a variety of stone finishes characterize this style (1890–1920). Classical colossal columns were grouped in pairs on projecting facades with enriched molding and freestanding statuary; pronounced cornices and enriched entablatures are topped with a tall parapet, balustrade, or attic story. It fostered an era of academic revivals, principally public buildings featuring monumental flights of steps.

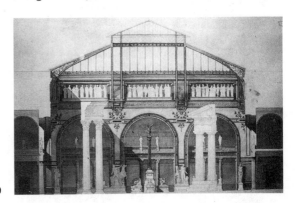

Beaux-Arts style

Historical and eclectic design on a monumental scale, as taught at the Ecole des Beaux-Arts in Paris, typified this style (1860– 1883). It was one of the most influential schools in the nineteenth century, and its teaching system was based on lectures combined with practical work in studios and in architectural offices. Its conception of architecture lies in the composition of well-proportioned elements in a symmetrical and often monumental scheme.

Becket, Welton

Head of his successful Los Angeles architectural firm. Designed the Hyatt Regency Hotel and Reunion Tower, Dallas (1978), and the Kaiser Center, Oakland (1960), and numerous office buildings.

Bed molding See Molding

Bed mortar joint See Joint

Bedroom

A room used for sleeping; a bedchamber.

Beeby, Thomas (1941–)

American architect who was a partner in the firm Hammond, Beeby and Babka, whose major project was winning the competition for the Harold Washington Library Center, Chicago (1991).

Beehive tomb

A conical-shaped subterranean tomb constructed as a corbeled vault and found on pre-Archaic Greek sites.

Behrens, Peter (1868–1940)

Noted especially for his early factory designs in the Modern style.

Belfry
A room at or near the top of a tower that contains bells and their supporting timbers.

Belgian block See **Stone**

Bell
The body of a Corinthian capital or a Composite capital without the foliage.

Bell arch See **Arch**

Bell cage
Timber framework which supports the bells in a belfry or steeple.

Bell chamber
A room containing one or more large bells hung on their bell cage.

Bell gable
A small turret placed on the ridge of a church roof to hold one or more bells.

Bell roof See **Roof**

Bell tower
A tall structure either independent or part of a building used to contain one or more bells; it is also called a campanile.

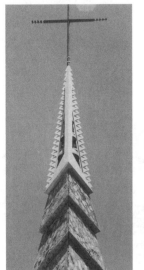

Bell turret
A small tower; usually topped with a spire or pinnacle, containing one or more bells.

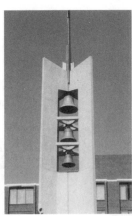

Bell-cast roof See **Roof**

Bell-shaped dome See **Dome**

Belluschi, Peter (1899–1994)
Italian-born architect and engineer; he showed an inclination to the International Modernism style. His Equitable Life Assurance Building, Portland, Oregon (1944), was one of the first examples of an aluminum and glass curtain wall enclosing a concrete frame tower. He became dean of the School of Architecture at MIT, Cambridge, Massachusetts.

Beltcourse
A projecting horizontal course of masonry. of the same or dissimilar material used to throw off water from the wall; it usually coincides with the edge of an interior floor.

Belvedere
A building, architectural feature, or rooftop pavilion from which a vista can be enjoyed.

Bench
A seat with or without a back; most often it is constructed of wood.

Benchmark
A permanent reference mark, fixed to a building or to the ground, whose height above a standard datum level has been accurately determined by survey.

Bent
A framework, which is transverse to the length of a framed structure; usually designed to carry both a lateral and a vertical load.

Bent sash
A window sash that is curved in plan.

Bent window See **Window**

Berlage, Hendrik P. (1856–1934)
Designed the Amsterdam Stock Exchange of brick, using a stone trim, which was a fresh interpretation of the Romanesque style.

Berm
The horizontal surface between a moat and the exterior slope of a fortified rampart: a continuous bank of earth piled against one or more exterior walls of a building as a protection against the elements.

Bernini, Gian Lorenzo (1598–1680)
Italian architect and sculptor whose works include the Trevi fountain, Rome (1632). He designed St. Peter's Piazza, the Vatican, and Colonnade, a huge elliptical space surrounded by a colonnade with columns four deep (1656).

Bethlehem column See **Column**

Beton brut
Concrete textured by leaving the impression of the form in which it was molded, as when wood is used to create a grained effect on the surface.

Bevel
A sloped or canted surface resembling a splay or other chamfer, where the sides are sloped for the purpose of enlarging or reducing them.

Beveled joint See **Joint**

Beveled molding See **Molding**

Beveled siding See **Wood**

Bezant
An ornament shaped like a coin or disc. sometimes used in a series in decorative molding designs.

Bibiena, Guiseppe (1657–1748)
Italian artist, and member of an important family of painters, theatrical designers, and architects.

Bidding
In construction, the process of extending invitations and receiving price proposals from contractors or sub-contractors for a defined scope of work, typically based on the construction documents and specifications.

Bi-fold door See **Door**

Bifron capital See **Capital**

Bi-lateral symmetry See **Symmetry**

Billet molding See **Molding**

Biotecture
A term (1966–1970) combining "biology" and "architecture" coined by Rudolph Doernach. It denotes architecture as an artificial "super system," live, dynamic, and mobile.

Birch See **Wood**

Birds See **Ornament: animal forms**

Birkirts, Gunnar (1925–)
Latvian-born American architect; much influenced by Eero Saarinen. He designed the Federal Reserve Bank, Minneapolis (1973), the IBM Corporate Computer Center, Sterling Forest, New York (1972), and the Museum of Glass, Corning, New York (1976).

Black-figure technique
The silhouetting of dark figures against a light background of natural reddish clay on early Greek pottery.

Blank door See **Door**

Blank window See **Window**

Blemish
A minor defect in appearance that does not affect the durability or strength of wood, marble, or other material.

Blending
A gradual merging of one element into another.

Blind
A device to obstruct vision or keep out light, consisting of a shade, screen, or an assemblage of panels or slats.

Blind arcade See **Arcade**

Blind arch See **Arch**

Blind door See **Door**

Blind hinge
A hinge for a cabinet or door designed so that it is not visible when the door is closed.

Blind joint See **Joint**

Blind pocket
A pocket in the ceiling at a window head to accommodate a venetian blind when raised.

Blind stop
The molding used to stop an outside door or window shutter in the closed position.

Blind story
A floor level without exterior windows.

Blind tracery See **Tracery**

Blind window See **Window**

Block
A masonry unit, or a solid piece of wood or other material; a large piece of stone, taken from the quarry to the mill for sawing and further working.

Block modillion See **Modillion**

Blocking
Pieces of wood used to secure, join, or reinforce framing members or to fill spaces between them.

Blueprint
A reproduction of a drawing by a contact printing process on light-sensitive paper, producing a negative image of white lines on a blue background; refers to architectural working drawings for construction.

Bluestone See **Stone**

Blunt arch See **Arch**

Board
A long thin piece of lumber cut from a log; typically with a rectangular cross section; can be hand-hewn, hand-sawn, or mill-sawn.

Board and batten
A form of sheathing for wood frame buildings consisting of wide boards, usually placed vertically, whose joints are covered by narrow strips of wood over the joints or cracks.

Boardwalk
A walkway, usually above a beach, whose surface is constructed of parallel planks; which are often set on a diagonal to the framing timbers below.

Boardwalk

Boathouse
A structure for storing boats when not in use: generally built at the water's edge or partly over water, and sometimes included provisions for social activities.

Bodhika
The capital of a column, found in Indian architecture.

Bofill Levi, Ricardo (1939–)
Barcelona-born architect, who designed a series of enormous Post-modern housing blocks, such as Les Espaces d'Abraxas, Marne-La-Vallee (1979), near Paris. It is a typical example of his monumental stripped Neo-classical style.

Boiserie
Wood paneling decorated with carvings in shallow relief.

Bolection molding See **Molding**

Bollard
A low single post, or one of a series, usually made of stone or concrete, set upright in the pavement, closely spaced to prevent motor vehicles from entering an area.

Bollman Truss See **Truss**

Bolster
A horizontal piece of timber that caps a column, pillar, or post to provide a greater bearing area to support a load from above; often has a carved profile or ornamental detail.

Bolster beam See **Beam**

Bolt
A rod or pin, with a permanent head on one end, that holds parts of a building or structure together.

Bolted connection
A connection between structural members made with plates and bolts, as opposed to a riveted or welded construction.

Bond
An arrangement of masonry units to provide strength, stability and in some cases beauty by setting a pattern of overlapping units on one another to increase the strength and to enhance the appearance, or by connecting them with metal ties. Some units may extend into adjacent courses, or extend through the wall, and vertical joints are not continuous. Adhesion exists between the mortar and the masonry units, or with the steel reinforcement.

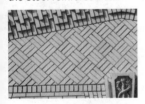

basketweave bond
A checkerboard pattern of bricks, laid either horizontally and vertically, or on the diagonal.

basketweave bond

bull header bond
A brick header unit which is laid on edge so that the end of the masonry unit is exposed vertically.

bull stretcher bond
Any stretcher which is laid on edge exposing its broad face horizontally.

Chain bond
A masonry wall bond formed by horizontal metal bars or pieces of lumber built into a wall.

common bond
A bond in which every fifth or sixth course consists of headers, the other courses by stretchers.

cross bond
A brick bond with courses of Flemish bond alternating with courses of stretchers and with the joints of every other row of stretchers centered on a vertical line of headers.

diagonal bond
A type of raking bond in masonry walls, consisting of a header course with the bricks laid at a diagonal in the face of the wall.

dogtooth course
A stringcourse of bricks laid diagonally so that one corner projects beyond the face of the wall.

46

dogtooth course

Dutch bond
Same as English cross bond or Flemish bond.

English bond
Brickwork that has alternate courses of headers and stretchers, forming a strong bond which is easy to lay.

Flemish bond
In brickwork, a bond in which each course consists of headers and stretchers laid alternately, each header is centered with respect to the stretcher above and the stretcher below it.

Flemish diagonal bond
A bond in which a course of alternate headers and stretchers is followed by a course of stretchers, resulting in a diagonal pattern.

header bond
A pattern of brickwork consisting entirely of headers; usually displaced by one-half the width of one header in the course above and below.

herringbone bond
A brick wall bond with concealed diagonal headers laid at right angles to each other in a herringbone pattern.

raking bond
A method of bricklaying in which the bricks are laid at an angle in the face of the wall; either in a diagonal bond or herringbone bond pattern.

Rowlock
A brick laid on its edge so that its end is exposed; used on a sloping window sill, or to cap a low brick wall.

running bond
Same as stretcher bond.

sailor
A brick laid vertically with the broad face exposed.

shiner
A brick laid horizontally on the longer edge with the broad face exposed.

skintled bond
Brickwork laid so as to form a wall with an irregular face, produced by the rough appearance of the skintled joints.

soldier
A brick laid vertically with the longer, narrow face exposed.

stack bond
In brickwork, a patterned bond where the facing brick is laid with all vertical joints aligned; in stone veneer masonry, a pattern in which single units are set with continuous vertical and horizontal joints.

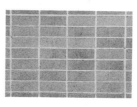

stack bond

Bond course
A horizontal row containing brick headers in a masonry structure.

Bond timber
Horizontal timbers once used as a bond for a brick wall.

Bonnet
A small, self-supporting protective hood or roof over an exterior doorway; may be constructed of any exterior material.

Book matched
Wood veneer or sliced marble installed so that the grain of pairs of pieces is installed as a mirror image aligned at the center; also known as herringbone matched.

Boom
A cantilevered or projecting structural member, such as a beam or spar, which is used to support, hoist, or move a load.

Border
A margin, rim, or edge around or along an element; a design or a decorative strip on the edge of an element.

Borromini, Francesco (1599–1677)
Highly original Italian Baroque architect who rivaled Bernini; he designed San Carlo Alle Quattro Fontane, in Rome (1638–1671), a church in which convex and concave wall surfaces are juxtaposed both on the facade and on the interior.

Boss
A projecting ornament, usually richly carved and placed at the intersection of ribs, groins, beams, or at the termination of a molding.

Bossage
In masonry work, a projecting, rough-finished stone left during construction for carving later into final decorative form.

Botanical garden
Greenhouse where a variety of plants are grown for recreational viewing.

Botta, Mario (1943–)
Swiss architect; worked with Le Corbusier and Louis Kahn. He designed a series of private houses in Lugano, Switzerland, which were set alone in the landscape, and the Botta House at Riva SanVitale (1972), which had strong geometric forms. His late work includes the Museum of Modern Art in San Francisco (1994).

Bottom chord
Chord along the lower perimeter of a truss; one of a pair with a top chord.

Boullée, Etienne-Louis (1728–1799)
His designs were extreme reactions against the Baroque style; they stressed plain shapes of enormous size without softening elements.

Bouquet ornament See **Ornament**

Bovine See **Ornament: animal forms.**

Bow girder
A girder curved horizontally in plan, i.e., an arch turned through a right angle, to serve as a spandrel on a curved facade or to support curved balconies.

Bow knot ornament See **Ornament**

Bow window See **Window**

Bower
A shelter or covered place in a pleasure ground or garden, usually made with boughs of trees bent and twined together for shade; also a crude dwelling made from sticks, bark, and natural materials.

Bowstring truss See **Truss**

Box beam See **Beam**

Box column See **Column**

Box frame
A rigid frame formed by load-bearing walls and floor slabs, most suitable for structures that are permanently divided into small repetitive units.

Box girder
A hollow beam with either a square, rectangular or circular cross section; sometimes vertical instead of horizontal, and attached firmly to the ground like a cantilever.

Box stair See **Stair**

Boxed cornice See **Cornice**

Boxed out
Rectangular or square framing around an opening or penetration, such as around a vertical pipe.

Box-head window See **Window**

Brace
A metal or wood member used to stiffen or support a structure; a strut that supports or fixes another member in position, or a tie used for the same purpose.

angle brace
Supporting member across the corner of a rectangular frame or structure.

counterbrace
A subordinate diagonal brace, crossing the main brace of a truss, which resists variable live loads and dampens any vibration.

cross bracing
A pair of diagonal braces crossing each other to stabilize a structural frame against lateral forces.

diagonal bracing
A system of inclined members for bracing the angles between the members of a structural frame against horizontal forces, such as wind.

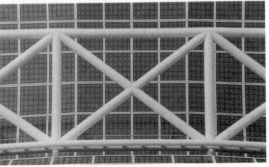

knee brace
A diagonal corner member for bracing the angle between two joined members; being joined to each other partway along its path serves to stiffen and strengthen the joint.

lateral bracing
Stabilizing a wall beam or structural system against lateral forces by means of diagonal or cross bracing, either horizontally by roof or floor construction or vertically by pilasters, columns or cross walls.

sway brace
A diagonal member designed to resist wind loads or other horizontal forces acting on a light structural frame.

x-brace
A truss panel, or similar structure, with a pair of diagonal braces from corner to corner that form a crossed shape; may be either struts in compression or tie rods in tension.

Braced frame
The frame of a building in which resistance to lateral forces is provided by diagonal bracing, knee-bracing or cross-bracing; sometimes using girts that are mortised into solid posts which are full frame height.

Bracket
A projection from a vertical surface providing structural or visual support under cornices, balconies, windows, or any other overhanging member.

Bracket

Bracket capital See **Capital**

Bracketed cornice See **Cornice**

Bracketed hood
A projecting surface that is supported on brackets above a door or window; provides shelter or serves as ornamentation.

Bracketed hood

Bramante, Donato (1444–1514)
High Renaissance architect, based in Milan, Italy. He designed the Tempietro of St. Pietro, which became a source work for designs for St. Peter's, Rome (1506).

Branch tracery See **Tracery**

Brass See **Metal**

Brattice
A tower or bay of timber construction, erected at the top of a wall on medieval fortifications during a siege.

Breast
That portion of a wall between the floor and a window above; a defensive wall built about breast high.

Breezeway
A covered passageway, open to the outdoors; connecting either two parts of a building or two buildings.

Breuer, Marcel (1902–1981)
An important Modernist, born in Hungary. He taught at the Bauhaus at Weimar, Germany, and invented a series of furniture designs using bent steel tubes finished in chrome. His last work was the Whitney Museum of Art in New York City.

Brick

A solid or hollow masonry unit of clay mixed with sand, that is molded into a small rectangular shape while in a plastic state, then baked in a kiln or dried in the sun.

adobe brick

Large, roughly molded, sun-dried clay brick of varying size and thickness.

brick bat

A broken or cut brick that has one complete end remaining and is less than half a full brick in length.

backing brick

A relatively low-quality brick used behind the face brick or behind other masonry.

bull header

A brick made with one long corner rounded or angled, used for sills and corners.

clinker brick

A very hard burnt brick whose shape is distorted by vitrification; used mainly for paving or ornamental accents.

closer

The last stretcher brick that completes a course of brickwork; types include a king closer and queen closer.

common brick

Brick for building purposes not treated for texture or color.

face brick

Brick made or selected to give an attractive appearance when used without rendering of plaster or other surface treatment of the wall: made of selected clays, or treated to produce the desired color.

firebrick

Brick made of a ceramic material which will resist high temperatures; used to line furnaces, fireplaces and chimneys.

gauged brick

Brick that has been cast, ground, or otherwise manufactured to exact and accurate dimensions.

glazed brick

Brick or tile having a ceramic glaze finish.

king closer

A three-quarter brick used as a closer; a diagonal piece is cut off one corner to keep the bond straight at corners of brick walls.

modular brick

A brick with nominal dimensions based on a 4 inch module.

pressed brick

A masonry unit without holes made by pressing a relatively dry clay mix into a mold, as opposed to one that is extruded.

queen closer

A brick cut in half along its length to keep the bond correct at the corner of a brick wall.

rustic brick

A fire-clay brick having a rough-textured surface, used for facing work: often multicolored.

tapestry brick

Face brick that is laid in a decorative pattern with a combination of vertical, horizontal, and diagonal elements, such as a basketweave bond.

veneer brick

A layer of bricks built outside a masonry backing or timber frame; the frame supports the load.

wirecut brick

Bricks shaped by extrusion and then cut to length by a set of wires.

Brick bat See **Brick**

Brick veneer See **Brick**

Bridge
A structure that spans a depression or provides a passage between two points at a height above the ground: affording passage for pedestrians and vehicles.

bascule bridge
A drawbridge with one or two balanced leaves that pivot vertically on a trunion located at one end of the span.

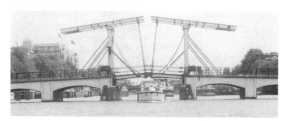

drawbridge
At the entrance to fortifications, a bridge over the moat or ditch, hinged and provided with a raising and lowering mechanism so as to hinder or permit passage.

footbridge
A narrow bridge structure that is designed to carry pedestrians only.

sidewalk bridge
A lightweight structural covering over a sidewalk to protect pedestrians from construction or cleaning of the structures overhead.

skywalk
A walkway that is located over the ground level and the street; and often connects buildings across a street.

Bridge

suspension bridge
A bridge hung from cables that are strung between two towers or a tower and abutment.

swing bridge
A bridge that opens by turning horizontally on a turntable supported on a pier.

Bridging
A continuous row of stiffeners between floor joists or other parallel structural members to prevent rotation about their vertical axes; it includes cross bracing.

Bridle joint See **Joint**

Brise-soleil
A fixed or movable device, such as a fin or louver, designed to block the direct entrance of sun into a building.

Broach
A half pyramid above the corners of a square tower to provide a transition to an octagonal spire.

Broken arch See **Arch**

Broken gable See **Gable**

Broken joint See **Joint**

Broken pediment See **Pediment**

Broken rangework masonry See **Masonry**

Bronze See **Metal**

Bronze Age
A period of human culture between the Stone Age and the Iron Age (4000–3000 B.C.), characterized by the use of bronze implements and weapons.

Brownstone See **Stone**

Bruder, Will (1946–)
American architect; whose major buildings includes the Central Library, Phoenix, Arizona (1995).

Brunelleschi, Filippo (1337–1446)
Florence-born architect who designed the dome of the Florence Cathedral (1420–1434), the Foundling Hospital, Florence (1421); St. Lorenzo, Florence (1425); and St. Spirito, Florence (1436).

Brutalism
An uncompromisingly modern style (1945–1960) which was expressed in large scale using raw and exposed materials emphasizing stark forms. It was distinguished by its weighty, textured surfaces and massiveness; created mainly by large areas of patterned concrete.

Windows consist of tiny openings, and the combination of voids and solids gave walls an egg-crate appearance. Mechanical systems are left exposed on the interior of the bare structure.

Bucranium See **Ornament: animal forms**

Bud
An Egyptian style column capital in the form of a stylized lotus bud; also, a small, foliated portion of a Corinthian capital located between the base of two acanthus leaves above the caulicoles.

Building
An enclosed and permanent structure for residential, commercial, industrial, institutional or office use, as distinguished from mobile structures or those not intended for occupancy.

Building adaptive reuse
To make suitable for a particular purpose or new requirement or condition: by means of modifications or changes to an existing building or structure.

Building addition
A floor or floors, room, wing or other expansion to an existing building: any new construction that increases the height or floor area of an existing building or adds to it in any fashion.

Building alteration
Construction in a building that changes the structure, equipment or location of openings, without increasing the overall area or dimensions: as distinct from additions to an existing structure.

Building area
The total area of a site covered by buildings, as measured on a horizontal plane at ground level; terraces and uncovered porches are usually not included in this total.

Building artifact
An element on a building demonstrating human crafting, such as a stained-glass window or an ornament of archaeological or historic interest .

Building code
A collection of regulations by local authorities having the jurisdiction to control the design and construction of buildings, alterations, repairs, quality of materials, use and occupancy; it contains minimum architectural, structural, and mechanical standards for sanitation, public health, safety, and welfare, and the provision of light and air.

Building component
An element manufactured as an independent unit, which can be joined with other elements, including electrical, fire protection, mechanical, plumbing, structural and all other systems affecting health and safety.

Building conservation
The management of a building to prevent its decay, destruction, misuse, or neglect; may Include a record of the history of the building and conservation measures applied.

Building construction
The fabrication and erection of a building by the process of assembly, or by combining building components or systems.

Building envelope
The outer bounds, in all directions, of an enclosed structure; the maximum extent of any building type may be defined by zoning laws.

Building environment
The combination of conditions that affect a person, piece of equipment or system in a building, such as lighting, noise, temperature and relative humidity.

Building grade
The ground elevation; established by a regulating authority, that determines the height of a building in a specific area.

Building height
The vertical distance measured from the grade level to a flat roof or to the average height of a pitched, gable, hip, or gambrel roof, not including bulkheads or penthouses.

Building inspector
A member of the building department who inspects construction to determine conformity to the building code and the approved plans, or one who inspects occupied buildings for violations of the building code.

Building line
A line or lines established by law or agreement, usually parallel to the property lines, beyond which a structure may not extend; it usually does not apply to uncovered entrance platforms or terraces.

Building maintenance
Actions ensuring that a building remains in working conditions by preserving it from deterioration, decline, or failure.

Building material
Any material used in the construction of buildings, such as steel, concrete, brick, masonry, glass, and wood.

Building occupancy
A general classification of the type of use of a structure, such as residential or commercial; used in building codes to determine the level of fire hazard, and consequently, the size and type of construction permitted, egress requirements, and other restrictions.

Building permit
A written document that is granted by the municipal agency having jurisdiction, authorizing an applicant to proceed with construction of a specific project after the plans have been filed and reviewed.

Building preservation
The process of applying measures to maintain and sustain all of the existing materials, integrity, and form of a building, including its structure and building artifacts.

Building reconstruction
The reproduction by new construction of the exact form and details of a building that no longer exists or artifacts as they once appeared.

Building rehabilitation
To restore a building to a useful life: by repair, alteration or modification.

Building remodeling
To replace all or a portion, to reconstruct, or renovate.

Building renovation
To restore to an earlier condition, or improve by repairing or remodeling.

Building restoration
The process of returning a building as nearly as possible to its original form and condition, usually as it appeared at a particular time: may require removal of later work or reconstruction of work that had been previously removed.

Building retrofit
The addition of new building materials or new building elements, and components not provided in the original construction to upgrade or change its functioning.

Building services
The utilities and services supplied and distributed within a building, including heating, air conditioning, lighting, water supply, drainage, gas and electric supply, fire protection and security protection.

Building stone
Any type of stone suitable for use in exterior construction; including granite, limestone, sandstone, and marble.

Building subsystem
An assembly of components that performs a specific function in a building; for example, an air-conditioning system consisting of its components, such as ductwork, a fan, air diffusers, and controls.

Building survey
Detailed record of the present condition of a structure.

Built environment
That portion of the physical surroundings created by humans, such as roads, bridges, and building structures, as opposed to the natural environment.

Built-up beam See **Beam**

Built-up roofing See **Roof**

Bulkhead
A horizontal or inclined door over a stairway giving access to a cellar; a structure on the roof of a building covering a water tank, shaft or service equipment.

Bull header See **Brick**

Bull header bond See **Bond**

Bull stretcher bond See **Bond**

Bullfinch, Charles (1763–1844)
Architect of Boston churches and the Massachusetts State House (1795), a combination of Palladian and pure Classicism styles.

Bull-nosed step See **Step**

Bungalow
A one-story frame house, or a summer cottage, often surrounded by a large covered veranda, with a widely bracketed gable roof; often built of rustic materials.

Bungalow door See **Door**

Bungalow style
This residential style (1890–1940), typified by a one-story house with gently pitched gables, had its roots in the Arts and Crafts movement. A lower gable usually covers a screen porch, which features battered piers at the corners. Rafters extend beyond the roof and are often exposed. Wood shingles are the favored exterior covering and are left natural. Windows are sash or casement with numerous lights.

Bungalow window See Window

Bunshaft, Gordon (1909–1990)
Partner of the firm Skidmore, Owings & Merrill. Designed Lever House, New York City (1952), a 21-story curtain-walled skyscraper slab set on a lower podium.

Burgee, John (1933–)
American-born architect who became a partner with Philip Johnson (1968–1991), and participated in a series of office towers that included Pennzoil Place, Houston.

Burl See Wood

Burnham, Daniel H. (1846–1912)
An American architect who partnered with John Wellborn Root. The firm was responsible for starting the Chicago School of Skyscraper Designs. He first designed the Monadnock Building (1891), then the Reliance Building (1890), both in Chicago. The latter is based on a metal steel skeleton and terra-cotta cladding. He also designed the Flatiron Building, in New York City (1902).

Bush-hammered concrete
Concrete having an exposed aggregate finish, usually obtained with a power-operated hammer which removes the sand-cement matrix around the aggregate particles to a depth of one-quarter inch.

Bush-hammered finish
A stone or concrete surface dressed with a bush-hammer; used decoratively, or to provide a roughened surface for treads, floors, and pavement requiring greater traction.

Butt joint See Joint

Butt splice See Splice

Butterfly roof See Roof

Buttress
An exterior mass of masonry projecting from the wall to absorb the lateral thrusts from roof vaults; either unbroken in their height or broken into stages, with a successive reduction in their projection and width.

angle buttress
One of the two buttresses at right angles to each other; forming the corner of a structure.

diagonal buttress
A buttress that bisects the 270-degree angle at the outside corner of a building.

flying buttress

A characteristic feature of Gothic construction in which the lateral thrusts of a roof or vault are carried by a segmental masonry arch, usually sloping, to a solid pier or support that is sufficiently massive to receive the thrust.

Byzantine architecture

When the seat of the Roman Empire moved to Byzantium, a new style (300–1450) became the official architecture of the church. Plans were based on a Greek cross, with a large cupola rising from the center and smaller ones crowning the four small arms.

The style was characterized by large domes supported on pendentives, circular or horseshoe arches, elaborate columns and richness in decorative elements. Doorways were square-headed with a semicircular arch over the flat lintel. The round arch, segmented dome, extensive use of marble veneer and rich frescoes with colored glass mosaics are also characteristic of this style. The most well-known example is the Hagia Sophia in Istanbul.

Byzantine architecture

Byzantine Revival style

A late nineteenth century style using Byzantine forms and decoration, including domes supported on high drums, arcades with plain, shafted columns, and bas-relief decorative work.

Cc

Cabin
A small, crudely constructed dwelling, which may have a living room with a fireplace, plus one or more small rooms; also a room aboard a vessel.

Cabinet
A built-in or free-standing piece of furniture fitted with drawers and/or shelves, typically behind one or a pair of doors.

Cabinet window See Window

Cabinetmaker
A craftsman specializing in fine joinery, with the skills, materials, and tools necessary to make furniture and other pieces of woodwork.

Cable molding See Molding

Cable stays
Straight cables connected directly to a roof or floor structure, and anchored to a mast, allowing greater clear spans within the structure. They transfer loads from the structure to the top of the mast, which transmits them to the foundations.

Cable-fluted column See Column

Cabled fluting molding See Molding

Calatrava, Santiago (1951–)
Spanish-born architect and engineer based in Zurich, Switzerland, who combined architecture and engineering in structures which resemble elegant, skeletal sculptures. Works include Alamillo Bridge, Seville (1992), Telecommunications Tower, Barcelona (1992), Bilbao Airport (1991), Kuwaiti Pavilion, Seville (1992).

Caldarium
The hot room in a Roman bath.

Calendar
A sculptured or painted emblematic series depicting the months of the year, often including the signs and symbols of the zodiac.

Calf's tongue molding See Molding

Callicrates (c. 5th C B.C.)
Leading Athenian architect; famous for the design of the Parthenon along with Ictinus. He also designed the Temple of Nike Apteros and part of the defensive Long Walls connecting Athens to the port at Piraeus.

Camber
A slight convex curvature intentionally built into a beam, girder, or truss to compensate for an anticipated deflection so that it will not sag under load; any curved surface to designed to facilitate the runoff of water.

Camber arch See **Arch**

Camber beam See **Beam**

Camber window See **Window**

Came
A slender rod of cast lead, with or without grooves, used in casements and stained-glass windows to hold the panes or pieces of glass together.

Campaniform capital See **Capital**

Campanile
A bell tower detached from the main body of a church.

Campen, Jacob van (1595–1657)
Dutch Classical architect, who introduced a version of the Palladian style into Holland, which became very popular. Works include the Town Hall, Amsterdam.

Canal
A channel or groove as in the recessed portions of the face of a triglyph.

Canalis
Concave area of the Ionic volute, between the two lines of the spiral and the cushion above the cymation.

Candela, Felix (1910–1981)
Designed the Church of the Miraculous Virgin, Narvarte, Mexico, an Expressionist building made of concrete in the form of a hyperbolic paraboloid.

Canephora
An ornament representing a young maiden bearing a basket of ceremonial offerings on her head, used either as a column support or freestanding garden ornament.

Canopy
A decorative hood above a niche, pulpit, or stall: a covered area that extends from the wall of a building, protecting an enclosure.

Canopy

Canopy roof See **Roof**

Cant

A salient corner: a line or surface angled in relation to another, as in a wall or surface sloped away from the perpendicular.

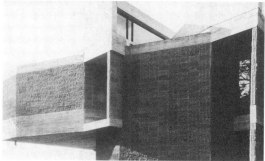

Cant molding See **Molding**

Cant strip

A filler piece cut at an angle, most often at 45 degrees, to make a transition from a horizontal roof to a vertical parapet.

Cant wall See **Wall**

Cant window See **Window**

Cantilever

A structural member or any other element projecting beyond its supporting wall or column and weighted at one end to carry a proportionate weight on the projecting end.

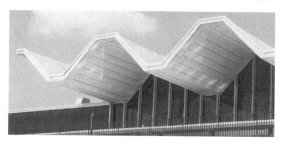

Cantilever retaining wall See **Wall**

Cantilevered

Refers to forms that have rigid structural members or surfaces that project significantly beyond their vertical support.

Cantilevered step See **Step**

Cap

The top member of any vertical architectural element; often projecting, with a drip for protection from the weather; the coping of a wall, the top of a pedestal or buttress, or the lintel of a door.

Cap molding See **Molding**

Capital

The upper member of a column, pillar, pier or pilaster, crowning the shaft; usually decorated. It may carry an architrave, arcade or impost block. The classical orders each have their own distinctive representative capitals.

aeolic capital

A primitive type of Ionic capital featuring a palm-like design; evolved by the Greeks in Asia Minor.

angle capital

A capital occurring at a corner column, especially an Ionic capital where the four volutes project equally on the diagonals, instead of along two parallel planes.

basket capital

A capital with interlaced bands resembling the weave of a basket, found in Byzantine architecture.

bifron capital

A capital with two fronts or faces looking in two directions: similar to a double herm.

bracket capital

A capital extended by brackets, lessening the clear span between posts, seen in Near Eastern, Muslim, Indian, and Spanish architecture.

campaniform capital
A bell shaped Egyptian capital representing an open papyrus profile.

composite capital
One of the five classical orders which combines acanthus leaves of the Corinthian order with volutes of the Ionic order.

cushion capital
A capital resembling a cushion that is weighted down; in medieval architecture, a cubic capital with its lower angles rounded off.

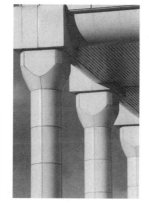

geminated capital
Coupled or dual capitals.

lotus capital
In ancient Egyptian architecture, a capital having the shape of a lotus bud.

Moorish capital
The capital in the style developed by the Moors in the late Middle Ages.

palm capital
A type of Egyptian capital resembling the spreading crown of a palm tree; a column capital resembling the leaves of a palm tree.

papyriform capital
A capital of an Egyptian column with the form of a cluster of papyrus flowers.

quadrafron capital
Having four fronts or faces looking in four directions.

quadrafron capital

scalloped capital
A medieval block or cushion capital, when each lunette is developed into several truncated cones.

Capital improvement
An improvement made to real estate that has an extended lifetime and increases the property's value, such as new construction, rehabilitation, or replacement of mechanical equipment, as opposed to routine maintenance work.

Capitol
A building where state and national legislative and judicial bodies convene.

Capstone
The top row of stones on a retaining wall; the top stone on a pier or on top of a corbeled vault.

Cardboard models
Used in the design process to show formal and spatial relationships without regard to the materials or functions of the final building.

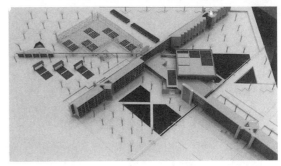

Cardinal points
North, South, East, and West: elevations facing these directions are called cardinal fronts.

Cardinal, Douglas (1934–)
A Canadian-born architect of Native American descent, whose best known work is the Canadian Museum of Civilization, Hull, Quebec (1989), which features powerful curved forms in the style of Organic Architecture.

Carolingian architecture
The early Romanesque architecture (750–980) located in France and Germany, based on an attempt by the Emperor Charlemagne to re-create Imperial Roman styles and forms.

Carpenter
A craftsman who is skilled in the transformation of timber into framing and enclosing a structure.

Carpenter Gothic style
A style (1800–1880) characterized by the application of Victorian Gothic motifs, often elaborate: by artisan woodworkers using modern machinery to produce ornamentation for building facades.

Carpenter Gothic style

Carport
A roofed automobile shelter adjoining a house and open on two or more sides.

Carriage house
A building, or part thereof, for housing carriages or automobiles when they are not in use.

Carriage porch
A roofed structure over a driveway at the door to a building, protecting those entering or leaving, or getting in or out of vehicles, from the weather.

Cartoon See **Design drawing**

Cartouche

Carved work
In stonework, any hand-cut ornamental features that cannot be applied from patterns.

Carver
A craftsman who is skilled in the ornamental engraving and cutting of wood or stone, in various forms of relief.

Caryatic order
A repeated series of
caryatids and the
entablature that they
support.

Caryatid

Caryatid
A supporting member
serving the function of a
pier, column, or pilaster,
and carved and molded
in the form of a draped,
human figure; in Greek
architecture, as in the
Erectheum at the Acropo-
lis in Athens.

Cascade
An artificial waterfall
that breaks the water
as it flows over stone
steps, usually found
in a garden setting.

Cased frame
The wood window frame of a double-hung window, including the sash pockets.

Cased opening
An interior window or doorway trimmed with casing but without a sash or door.

Casement window See **Window**

Casework
High-quality shelving and display cases such as for a store; also used to describe cabinetwork.

Casing
A trim member, molding, framing or lining around door and window openings which give a finished appearance. They may be flat or molded.

Casino
A building used for public recreation and gambling activities.

Cast iron See **Metal**

Cast stone
A mixture of fine stone chips and Portland cement in a matrix. Once cast, it may be ground, polished or otherwise treated to simulate natural stone.

Castellated
Bearing the external fortification elements of a castle, in particular, battlements, turrets, crenellated patterns.

Castellation
A notched or indented parapet, originally used for fortifications, but afterwards used on church facades and was intended to be used as ornament.

Cast-in-place concrete See **Concrete**

Cast-iron facade
A load-bearing facade composed of prefabricated parts, commonly used on buildings around 1850-1870.

Cast-iron lacework
A panel of ironwork employing an intricate ornamental design that is formed by a mass-produced casting process.

Castle
A building, or group of buildings intended primarily to serve as a fortified post; a fortified residence of a nobleman.

Castle style
A type of eighteenth century architecture employing battlements, loopholes, and turrets to create the impression of a fortified dwelling; some of these same elements were also used to create follies, picturesque cottages, and fake ruins.

Catacombs
Subterranean burial places consisting of galleries with niches for sarcophagi and small chapels for funeral feasts and commemorative services.

Catch basin
A masonry or concrete-walled pit that collects surface stormwater and directs it into a storm sewer.

Catenary
The curve assumed by a flexible uniform cable suspended freely between two points. When uniformly loaded, the curve takes the form of a parabola.

Catenary arch See **Arch**

Cathedral
The principal church of a diocese, which contains the home throne of a bishop, called the cathedra.

Cathri
A pierced screen or metal railing formed by super-imposing perpendicular and diagonal crosses.

Catwalk
A narrow walkway located at the side of a bridge or near the ceiling of a building, as in a theater.

Caudill, William
Partner in the firm Caudill, Rowlett, Scott (CRS), most well known for its method of involving the "user groups" to participate in the design "charrette" process, from 1958 to 1973.

Caulicoli
The eight stalks that support the volutes in a Corinthian capital.

Caulk
To render a joint tight against the elements by means of filling the seam with a malleable substance such as tar, lead, putty and the like.

Caulking compound
A soft material intended for sealing joints in buildings, preventing leakage, or providing a seal at expansion joints.

Cavetto molding See **Molding**

Cavity wall See **Wall**

Cavity wall masonry See **Masonry**

Cavo-relievo See **Relief**

Cedar See **Wood**

Ceiling
The under-covering of a roof or floor; generally concealing the structural members from the room or roof above, or the underside surface or vaulting. It may have a flat or curved surface, and self-supporting, suspended from the floor above, or supported from hidden or exposed beams.

suspended ceiling
A nonstructural ceiling suspended below the overhead structural slab or from the structural elements of a building and not bearing on the walls.

Ceiling diffuser
An air outlet from an air-conditioning duct, which diffuses the air over a large area to produce an even distribution and avoid drafts.

Ceiling fan
A slowly rotating overhead fan with a wide sweep, moving large volumes of air at low speed; used in hot, humid climates to improve thermal circulation.

Ceiling grid
A rectangular grid of metal supports for a suspended ceiling, especially for acoustical tile: typically, the supports are inverted T-shaped bars.

Ceiling joist See **Joist**

Ceiling medallion
A bas-relief ornament on a ceiling, especially a relatively large, circular one located in the center of a room.

Cell
A small compartment, such as a room in a dormitory, but especially a confined study-bedroom allotted to a monk or nun in a monastery.

Cella
The sanctuary of a classical temple containing the cult statue of the god.

Cellar
That part of a building, the ceiling of which is entirely below grade; or having half or more of its clear height below grade.

Cellular construction
Construction with concrete elements in which part of the interior concrete is replaced by voids.

Celtic Revival
A revival in the nineteenth century of Celtic art and ornament, mostly in Britain and Ireland, which influenced the Arts and Crafts movement as well as the development of Art Nouveau.

Cement
A material, or a mixture of materials without aggregate, which when in a plastic state, possesses adhesive and cohesive properties and hardens in place.

Cement plaster
Plaster with portland cement as the binder; sand and lime are added on the job before installation.

Cement siding
Same as stucco made with Portland cement.

Cenotaph
An empty tomb; a commemorative monument not intended for burial.

Centaur See **Ornament: animal forms**

Center of Vision See **Perspective projection**

Center to center
A linear measurement taken from the middle of one member to the middle of the next member.

Center hung door See **Door**

Centering
A temporary wooden framework placed under vaults and arches to sustain them while under construction; the form was covered with mortar so that the undersurface of the vault showed an impression of the boards used.

Centerpiece
An ornament placed in the middle of an area, such as a decoration in the center of a ceiling.

Central air-conditioning
An air-conditioning system in which the air is treated by equipment at one or more central locations and conveyed to and from these spaces by means of fans and pumps through ducts and pipes.

Central Business District (CBD)
The main commercial area with concentrated office and retail stores located in an urban area.

Central heating
A system where heat is supplied to all areas of a building from a central plant through a network of ducts or pipes.

Central Visual Axis See **Perspective projection**

Centralized organization See **Organization**

Centralized structure
Building in which all the principal axes are of the same length.

Centrally planned
A structure that radiates from a central point, as opposed to one based on an axial plan.

Ceramic mosaic tile See **Tile**

Ceramic veneer
Architectural terra-cotta with either ceramic vitreous or glazed surfaces, characterized by large face dimensions and their sections; the back is either scored or ribbed.

Ceramics
A brittle, non-corrosive and non-conductive product made of clay or similar material, fired during its manufacture to produce porcelain or a hard terra-cotta.

Certificate of Occupancy (C of O)
A permit from a local government agency granting permission to use a building or site for a particular purpose; issued after the satisfactory completion of construction.

Certified historic structure.
A structure that the U.S. National Park Service has determined is eligible to obtain a "Certificate of Significance."

Chain bond See **bond**

Chain molding See Molding

Chain-link fence
A fence composed of steel wire woven in a diamond pattern, with steel-pipe posts and top rails; typically without any decorative elements.

Chains
Vertical strips of rusticated masonry rising between the horizontal moldings and the cornice, dividing the facade into bays or panels.

Chair rail
A horizontal wood strip affixed to a plaster wall at a height that prevents the backs of chairs from damaging the wall surface.

Chaitya
A chaitya hall is a structure, or artificial cave, with an apse encircling a stupa.

Chaitya arch
A term for a recurring motif in Hindu architecture depicting miniature arches derived from a cross section of a vaulted chaitya hall.

Chalet
A timber house in the Alps, distinguished by exposed and decorative use of structural members, balconies, and stairs; the upper floors usually project beyond the story below.

Chalet

Chamber
A room used for private living, conversation, consultation or deliberation, in contrast to more public and formal activities.

Chambranle
A structural feature, enclosing the sides and top of a doorway, window, fireplace or other opening, often highly ornamental.

Chamfer
The groove or oblique surface made when an edge or corner is beveled or cut away, usually at a 45 degree angle.

Chamfer stop
Any ornamentation which terminates a chamfer.

Chamfered rustication
Rustication in which the smooth face of the stone parallel to the wall is deeply beveled at the joints so that, when the two meet, the chamfering forms a right angle.

Chancel
The part of a large church that is located beyond the transept, containing the altar and choir.

Chancery
A building or suite of rooms designed to house any of the following: a low court with special functions, archives, a secretarial, a chancellery.

Chandelier
A fixture with multiple arms hung from the ceiling to support lights; originally for candles, but later manufactured for gas, then electric lights.

Channel
A rolled iron or steel or extruded aluminum shape with a vertical flange and horizontal top and bottom webs that project on the same side as the flange.

Channel beam See Beam

Channel column See Column

Channeling
A decorative groove in carpentry or masonry: a series of grooves in an architectural member, such as the flutes in a column.

Chaos
A state of utter disorder and confusion.

Chapel
A small area within a larger church, containing an altar and intended for private prayer; a small secondary church in a parish; a room designated for religious use within the complex of a school, college, or hospital.

Chapter house
A place for business meetings of a religious or fraternal organization; usually a building that is attached to a hall for gatherings; occasionally contains living quarters for members of such groups.

Charrette See Design

Chase
A covered recess in a wall that forms a vertical shaft, in which plumbing pipes or electrical wires are inserted.

Chashitsu
A small Japanese structure, or room, for the tea ceremony.

Chateau
A castle or imposing country residence of nobility in old France: any large country estate.

Chateau style
A style (1860–1898) characterized by massive and irregular forms, steeply pitched hipped or gable roofs with dormers, towers, and tall elaborately decorated chimneys featuring corbeled caps. Windows are paired and divided by a mullion and transom bar. Renaissance elements such as semicircular arches or pilasters are mixed with Tudor arches, and Gothic finials.

Chateauesque style

A house style based on sixteenth century French chateau mixed with Gothic and Renaissance details, popular for large houses and mansions of the late nineteenth and early twentieth centuries; characteristic details include steeply pitched mansard roofs, dormers with pinnacles, and parapeted gables and turrets.

Chatri

An Indian pavilion consisting of a horizontal slab carried on four colonnettes, recurring in Hindu architecture.

Chattra

A stone umbrella on top of a stupa, symbolizing dignity, composed of a stone disk on a vertical pole.

Chaumukh

In Indian architecture, four images, each facing a cardinal point, which are placed back-to-back.

Chavin style

A Peruvian style (900–200 B.C.) based on the worship of the jaguar god and characterized by grandiose terraced platforms constructed of stone, which were grouped around large sunken plazas, excellent stone sculpture, elaborate gold work, and remarkable ceremonies. The style is named after a town in central Peru, where a complex of massive stone buildings with subterranean galleries, was surrounded by courtyards.

Chavin style

Checker

One of the squares in a checkered pattern, that is contrasted to its neighbor by color or texture: often only two of the effects are alternated, similar to a chessboard.

Checkered

Those forms that are marked off with a pattern of checks or squares that is divided into different colors, or variegated by a checked or square pattern of different materials.

Checkerwork

In a wall or pavement, a pattern formed by laying masonry units so as to produce a checkerboard effect.

Cheek

A narrow upright face, forming the end or side of an architectural or structural member or one side of an opening.

Cheneau
A gutter at the eaves of a building, especially one that is ornamental; an ornament, crest, or cornice.

Chermayeff, Serge (1900–1996)
Born in Russia, he immigrated to England in 1910 and worked as a designer before joining Eric Mendelsohn. He designed many Modern movement buildings and immigrated to America in 1940.

Chernikov, Iakov (1889–1951)
Russian-born architect and teacher; his work focused on architectural compositions in perspective, illustrating forms and structures of the imagination, following the Constructivist principles.

Cherry See Wood

Cherubs
A decorative sculpture or painting representing chubby, usually naked infants: They are also called amorini or putti.

Cherubs

Chestnut See Wood

Chevet
The rounded east end of a Gothic cathedral, including the apse and ambulatory.

Chevron
A symmetrical "V" shape that represents a triangle with its third side removed. It can be bordered, interlaced and often repeated in various patterns that point up or down, with an angle between 60 and 75 degrees.

Chiaroscuro
The effect of light and shadow within an area or composition, brought about by the use of deep variations to enhance the forms.

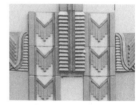

Chiattone, Mario (1891–1957)
Studied in Milan, became a member of the Futurist movement, and with fellow student Sant'Elia exhibited a collection of drawings in Milan called *Structures for a Modern Metropolis* (1914).

Chicago School
A group of active architects working in Chicago (1880–1910) known for major innovations in high-rise construction and for the development of modern commercial building design. The group included Daniel.H. Burnham, John. W. Root, William Lee Baron Jenney, W.B.Mundie, William Holabird, and Louis Sullivan.

Chicago window See **Window**

Chigi
A pair of crossed timbers that are placed at the end of the ridge of a roof of a Shinto shrine; also called forked finials.

Chimera See **Ornament: animal forms**

Chimney
A vertical noncombustible structure, containing one or more flues to carry smoke from the fireplaces to the outside, usually rising above the roof.

Chimney breast
A projection into a room of the fireplace walls that form the front portion of the chimney stack.

Chimney cap
A cornice forming a crowning termination of a chimney.

Chimney cricket
A small false roof built over the main roof behind a chimney, used to provide protection against water leakage where the chimney penetrates the roof.

Chimney hood
A covering which protects a chimney opening.

Chimney piece
An ornamental embellishment: above or around the fireplace opening.

Chimney pot
Cylindrical shape placed on top of a chimney to increase its height; often of terra-cotta and treated as an ornamental device.

Chimney stack
That part of a chimney that is carried above the roof of a building: a group of chimneys carried up together.

Chimu architecture
A style dominant in northern Peru (1150–1400) featured houses built in rows along symmetrically laid out streets inside high city walls. Buildings were constructed of adobe brick with wooden lintels. Walls were decorated with wide moldings featuring geometrical designs.

Ch'in architecture
A dynasty in China (221–206 B.C.), marked by the construction of the Great Wall of China.

Chinese architecture
A homogeneous traditional architecture (400–1600) that was repeated over the centuries in structures consisting of a wooden framework of columns and beams; stone and brick were used for permanent structures such as fortifications.

The most prominent feature was tile-covered gabled roofs, with widely overhanging and upward curving eaves resting on complex multiple brackets. In the design of pagodas, each floor was articulated in a distinctive rhythmical, horizontal effect.

Chinoiserie
A western style of architecture and decoration, utilizing Chinese design elements.

Chip carving
Hand decoration of a wooden surface by slicing away chips, resulting in incised geometric patterns.

Choir
That part of a church where the religious service is accompanied by singing, usually part of the chancel and often separated by an ornamental screen.

Chord
A principal member or pair of members of a truss extending from one end to the other, to resist bending.

Chroma
The attribute of a color that allows the observer to judge how much color it contains.

Church
An edifice or place of assemblage specifically set apart for Christian worship.

Churrigueresque style
A lavishly ornamented Spanish Baroque style (1700–1750) named after architect Jose Churriguera; the style was also adapted in South America.

CIAM (Congres Internationaux d'Architecture Moderne)
A declaration signed by 24 architects, representing France (6), Switzerland (6), Germany (3), Holland (3), Italy (2), Spain (2), Austria (1), and Belgium (1), emphasized "building" rather than architecture. Advocated the introduction of efficient production methods in the building industry, (1928–).

Cincture
A ring of moldings around the top or bottom of the shaft of a column, separating the shaft from the capital or base; a fillet around a post.

Cinquefoil See Tracery

Cinqefoil arch See Arch

Circle
The simplest and most fundamental of geometric shapes; a continuous curved line, every point of which is equidistant from a central point.

Circular arch See **Arch**

Circular barn
A barn that has a circular plan; similar to that built by Shakers in Hancock, Massachusetts, in 1826; also called a round barn.

Circular stair See **Stair**

Circular window See **Window**

Circulation space
Space within a facility that provides access between functional areas for people, goods and services.

Circus
In ancient Rome, a large oval arena surrounded by rising tiers of seats, for the performance of public spectacles.

Cistern
Artificial reservoir or a tank for storing water, such as rainwater collected from a roof.

Citadel
A fortress or castle in or near a city: a refuge in case of a siege, or a place to keep prisoners.

City Hall
Building which houses the administrative offices of a city.

City plan
Large-scale map of a city that depicts streets, buildings, and other urban features.

Cityscape
Represented by the silhouette of groups of urban structures that make up a skyline, including distinguished landmarks as well as natural elements, such as rolling hills, mountains or large bodies of water.

Civic center
An area of a city containing a grouping of municipal buildings; often includes the city hall, courthouse, public library, and other public buildings.

Cladding
The process or the resulting product produced by the bonding of one metal to another, to protect the inner metal from weathering.

Clapboard siding See **Wood products.**

Classical architecture
The architecture of Hellenic Greece and Imperial Rome on which the Italian Renaissance and subsequent styles were based. The five orders; the Doric, Ionic, Corinthian, Tuscan, and Composite are a characteristic feature.

Classic Revival
An architectural movement based on the use of pure Roman and/or Greek forms, in reaction to Rococo and Baroque design.

Clathri
A lattice of bars as gratings for windows.

Clay tile See **Tile**

Clear span
Distance between the inside faces of the supports on both sides.

Clerestory
An upper story or row of windows rising above the adjoining parts of the building, designed as a means of admitting increased light into the inner space of the building,

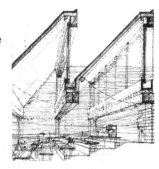

Cliff dwelling
Dwellings built by natives in the southwestern U.S. under cliff overhangs and on cliff tops, typically constructed of natural stone slabs with mud for mortar; roofs were constructed of earth-covered poles, or the underside of the natural ledge above was used as a roof.

Climax
A number of design ideas so arranged that each succeeding one makes a stronger statement than its predecessor. The final culmination or highest point is the summation of the process.

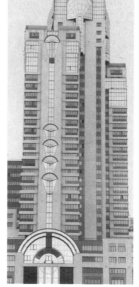

Clinic
A medical facility: independent or part of a hospital in which ambulatory patients receive diagnostic and therapeutic medical and surgical care.

Clinker brick See **Brick**.

Clock
Any instrument for measuring or indicating time, especially a mechanical device with a numbered dial and moving hands or pointers.

Clocktower
Any instrument for measuring or indicating time; such as a mechanical device with a numbered dial and moving hands or pointers positioned in a single tower, or a tower-like portion of a structure.

Cloister
A square court surrounded by an open arcade, a covered walk around a courtyard, or the whole courtyard.

Closed string stair See **Stair**

Closer See **Brick**

Cluster
Any configuration of elements that are grouped or gathered closely together.

Cluster housing
Suburban, medium-density apartment or row house complexes.

Clustered column See **Column**

Clustered organization See **Organization**

Coach house
A building or part for housing carriages or automobiles when they are not in use. See also carriage house.

Coat of arms
A tablet containing a representation of a heraldic symbol.

Cobble See **Stone**

Cobblestone See **Stone**

Coffer
A recessed box-like panel in a ceiling or vault, usually square, but often octagonal or lozenge shaped, sometimes dressed with simple moldings or elaborately ornamented.

Coffering
A ceiling with deeply recessed panels, often highly ornamental, executed in marble, brick, concrete, plaster, or stucco; a sunken panel in a vaulted ceiling.

Cogeneration
In a building, the on-site electric power generation utilizing both the electrical power and power from the steam or hot water which is developed.

Cogged joint See Joint

Coliseum
Any large Roman amphitheater; any large sports arena, open or roofed.

Collage See **Design drawing**

Collar beam See **Beam**

Collar brace
A structural member which reinforces a collar beam in medieval roof framing.

Collar joint
The joint between a roof structure and a collar beam.

Collar tie
In wood construction, a timber that prevents the roof framing from changing shape.

Collegiate Gothic style
Architecture in the style of the late-Gothic universities of England, such as Oxford and Cambridge; commonly used for domestic campuses in the late nineteenth century.

Colonial architecture
A classification pertaining to any architectural style that is transplanted from the motherland to their overseas colonies. Examples are the Portuguese Colonial in Brazil, Dutch Colonial in New York, French Colonial in New Orleans, and English Colonial in all the North American colonies.

Colonial Revival style
The reuse of Georgian and Colonial design in the United States towards the end of the nineteenth and twentieth centuries, typically In bank buildings, churches, and suburban homes.

Colonnade

A combination or grouping of columns paced at regular intervals, and arranged with regard to their structural or ornamental relationship to the building. They can be aligned either straight or arced in a circular pattern.

Colonnette

A small column, usually decorative, found at the edge of windows; a thin round shaft to give a vertical line in elevation, or as an element in a compound pier.

Colossal order

A Classical order consisting of giant columns rising from the ground through more than one story.

Colossus

A statue which is larger than life-size.

Color

The appearance of an object or surface, distinct from its form, shape, size, or position; depends on the spectral composition of incident light, spectral reflectance of the object, and spectral response of the observer.

Colored glass See **Glass**

Column

A vertical structural compression member or shaft supporting a load, which acts in the direction of its vertical axis and has both a base and a capital, designed to support both an entablature or balcony.

angle column

A free-standing or engaged column placed outside the corner of a building or portico.

baluster column

A short, thick-set column in a subordinate position, as in the windows of early Italian Renaissance facades.

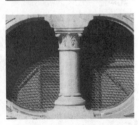

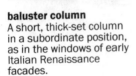

banded column

A column or pilaster with drums alternately larger and smaller, alternately plainer and richer in decoration, or alternately protruding.

Bethlehem column

Rolled steel H-section used as a column; it is manufactured by Bethlehem Steel Company as a replacement for columns built up from steel plate and angle irons.

box column

A hollow, built-up column constructed of wood, usually rectangular or square in section.

cabled column

A column in the shape of twisted strands of a large-fiber rope.

cable-fluted column

A column or pilaster with semicircular convex moldings in the center of the flutes, usually starting at the base of the column and stopping at one-third or one-half the column height; the moldings may be plain or ornamental.

channel column

A hollow steel column composed of a pair of channels that are attached with plates so that the channels are facing outward.

clustered column

A column or pillar composed of a cluster of attached or semi-attached additional shafts, grouped together to act as a single structural and design element.

diminished column

A column with a greater diameter at its base than at its capital.

composite column

A column in which a metal structural member is completely encased in concrete containing special spiral reinforcement.

coupled column

Columns set as close pairs with a much wider space between the pairs.

embedded column

Column that is partly, but not wholly, built into a wall.

engaged column

A column that is attached and appears to emerge from the wall, as decoration or as a structural buttress.

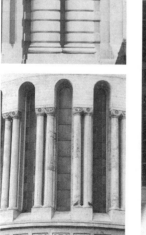

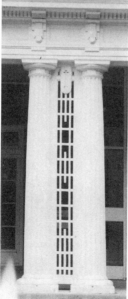

grouped columns

Three or more closely spaced columns or pilasters forming a group, often on one pedestal.

half-column
An engaged column, projecting approximately one half its diameter, usually slightly more.

insulated column
A column which is entirely detached from a main building or structure.

knotted column
A column with a shaft carved to resemble a knot or two intertwined ropes.

Lally column
A proprietary name for a cylindrical column that is filled with concrete: used as a structural column to provide support to beams or girders.

long column
Column whose slenderness ratio is high, making it liable to failure by buckling.

mid-wall column
A column that carries a portion of a wall above it that is much thicker than its own diameter.

monolithic column
One whose shaft is of one piece of stone, wood, or marble as opposed to one made up from components.

mushroom column
A column with an enlarged head supporting a flat slab.

pipe column
A column made from steel tubing, frequently filled with concrete to increase its strength and stiffness.

solomonic column
A twisted column with a helical shaft and Classical capital and base; often used in Baroque architecture.

tension column
A column subjected to tensile stresses only.

transfer column
A column in a multistory building that does not go down to the foundation but is supported by a transfer girder, which transfers its load to adjacent columns.

wall column
A column which is embedded or partially embedded in a wall.

wreathed column
A column shaft that is entwined with a raised spiraling molding.

Column baseplate
A horizontal plate beneath the bottom of a column which transmits and distributes the column load to the supporting materials below the plate.

Columniation
A system in Classical architecture of grouping columns in a colonnade based on the diameters of the columns.

Commercial style
A skeletal, rectangular style (1890–1915) of the first five- to fifteen-story skyscrapers, brought to full form in Chicago, New York, and Philadelphia. It was characterized by flat roofs, and minimal ornament; except for slight variations in the spacing of windows. Extensive use of glass was made possible by its steel-frame construction, which could bear the structural loads that masonry could not.

Common bond See **Bond**

Common brick See **Brick**

Compartment
A small space within a larger enclosed area, often separated by partitions.

Compass roof See **Roof**

Compass window See **Window**

Complexity
Consisting of various parts united or connected together, formed by a combination of different elements; intricate, interconnecting parts that are not easily disentangled.

Complementary colors
Those pairs of colors, such as red and green, that together embrace the entire spectrum. The complement of one of the three primary colors is a mixture of the other two.

Compluvian
The opening in the center of the roof of the atrium in an ancient Roman house; it slopes inward to discharge rainwater into a cistern in the center of the atrium.

Composite arch See **Arch**

Composite capital See **Capital**

Composite column See **Column**

Composite construction
A type of construction made up of different materials.

Composite order
One of the five classical orders; a Roman elaboration of the Corinthian order; the acanthus leaves of its capitals are combined with the large volutes of the Ionic order and set on the diagonal in plan view.

Composition See **Design**

Composition board
A building board fabricated of wood fibers in a binder, compressed under pressure at an elevated temperature.

Composition shingle
Any shingle made with a mixture of binder materials and fibers; types include asbestos shingle and asphalt shingle.

Compound arch See **Arch.**

Compound pier
A pier that has several engaged shafts against its surface, used often in Romanesque and Gothic structures.

Compound vault See **Vault**

Compression
Direct pushing force, in line with the axis of the member: the opposite of tension.

Computer-aided design
The analysis and/or design, modeling, simulation, or layout of building design with the aid of a computer.

Concave
Forms that are curved like the inner surface of a hollow sphere or circular arc.

Concave mortar joint See **Mortar joint**

Concentrated load
A load acting on a very small area of the structure's surface: the opposite of a distributed load.

Concentric
Having a common center.

Concentric

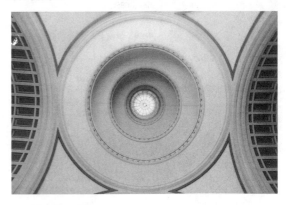

Concentric walls
Fortification consisting of one complete system of defense inside another.

Conception See **Design**

Conceptual architecture
A form of architecture (1960–1993) representing plans and drawings for buildings and cities never constructed. It can also be regarded as architecture arrested at the conceptual stage of development.

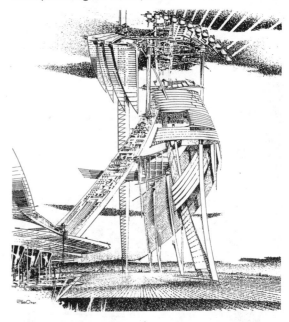

Conch
Semidome vaulting of an apse or eastern end of a church.

Concourse
An open space where several roads or paths meet; an open space for accommodating large crowds in a building, such as in a railway terminal or airport.

Concourse

Concrete

A composite artificial building material consisting of an aggregate of broken stone mixed with sand, water and cement to bind the entire mass; fluid and plastic when wet and hard and strong when dry.

cast-in-place concrete
Concrete which is deposited in the place where it will harden as an integral part of the structure, as opposed to pre-cast concrete.

precast concrete
Material that reduces the need for on-site formwork with a process known as "tilt-up" construction, in which precast panels are lifted into a vertical position and then attached to the structural frame.

prestressed concrete
A process of anchoring steel rods into the ends of forms, then stretching them before the concrete is poured, putting them under tension. When the concrete hardens, they spring back to their original shape, providing additional strength.

Concrete block
A hollow concrete masonry unit, rectangular in shape, made from Portland cement and other aggregates.

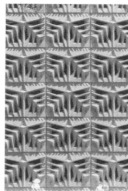
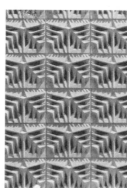

decorative concrete block
A concrete masonry unit having special treatment of its exposed face for architectural effect: which may consist of exposed aggregates or beveled recesses for a patterned appearance, especially when Illuminated obliquely.

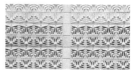

Concrete frame
A structure consisting of concrete beams, girders, and columns, which are rigidly joined.

Concrete grille
An openwork barrier used to conceal, decorate, or protect an opening.

85

Concrete masonry See **Masonry**

Concrete panel
A panel that is pre-cast and prefabricated elsewhere and placed in the structure, rather than cast in place.

Concrete shell
A curved thin membrane which is usually poured or sprayed over forms with a network of steel rods and wire mesh; most often a lightweight aggregate is used to decrease the weight= to=strength ratio.

Condominium
An apartment house, office building or other multiple-unit complex; the units are individually owned, and there is joint ownership of common elements such as hallways, elevators, and all mechanical systems.

Conduit
A hollow pipe used for installing electric wiring, telephone cable, or similar wiring.

Cone of vision See **Perspective projection**

Configuration
The form of a figure as determined by the arrangement of its parts, outline, or contour.

Conic sections
Circle, ellipse, parabola, and hyperbola; all produced by cutting a plane through a cone at different angles.

Conical
Pertaining to a cone shape, generated by rotating a right triangle around one of its legs.

Conical roof See **Roof**

Conical vault See **Vault.**

Conifer See **Wood**

Conservation
The repair and maintenance of cultural artifacts, including buildings and historic materials, extending their longevity and esthetic qualities.

Conservatory
A glass-enclosed room in a house, originally for the cultivation of plants, now including rooms as solariums.

Console
A vertical decorative bracket in the form of a scroll, projecting from a wall to support a cornice, window, or a piece of sculpture.

Console table
A table attached to a wall and supported on consoles.

Construction

The on-site work done in building or altering structures, from land clearance through completion, including excavation, erection and the assembly and installation of components and equipment.

Construction administration

The special management services performed by the architect or others during the construction phase of the project: under either a separate or special agreement with the owner.

Construction documents

The third phase of architectural basic services wherein the approved design development documents are used to prepare the working drawings, specifications and the bidding information for approval by the owner.

Construction joint See Joint

Construction loads

The loads imposed on the building during construction due to the erection, assembly, and installation of the building components and equipment.

Construction observation

An on-site visit by the design architect or engineer to determine if the construction materials and installations are in accordance with the construction documents and specifications, including review of testing reports.

Constructivism

A movement (1920–1935) originating in Moscow based on order, logic, structure, abstraction and geometry, primarily in sculpture but with broad applications to architecture. An expression of construction was the base for all building design with emphasis on functional machine parts. Vladimir Tatlin's monument is the most notable example of this style.

The industrial fantasies of Jacob Tchernikhov, published in 1933, show buildings perched on cantilevered structures, suggesting construction for construction's sake. The movement can be regarded as part of the broader movement of functionalism, with an accent on constructional expression. All traditional accessories, such as ornamental details were discarded in favor of mass and space in relation to the new sculptural forms.

Consulate

A building where a consul conducts official business.

Contemporary style

A term loosely applied to any of a number of styles from the 1940s to the 1980s, often referring to the term "modern architecture."

Contextual

Any doctrine emphasizing the importance of the context in establishing the meaning of terms, such as the setting into which a building is placed, its site, its natural environment, or its neighborhood.

Contextualism

An approach to urban planning (1960–1970) that considers the city in its totality, the view that the experience of a city is greater than the sum of its parts. All architecture must fit into, respond to, and mediate its surroundings.

Continuous beam See Beam

Continuous footing See Footing

Contour map

A topographic map which portrays relief by the use of con- tour lines which connect points of equal elevation; the closer the spacing of lines, the greater relative slope in that area.

Contract administration
Architectural services that are commonly provided during construction of a project; these typically include construction observation, review of shop drawings and materials samples, processing change orders, and approving certificates of payment for the contractor.

Contract documents
Those documents that comprise a contract: including plans and/or drawings, specifications, all addenda, modifications and changes, together with any other items stipulated as being specifically included.

Contractor
One who undertakes the performance of construction, and who provides labor and materials in accordance with plans and specifications, and contracts for a specific cost and schedule for completion of the work.

Contrapposto
The disposition of the human figure in which one part is turned in opposition to another, creating a counterpositioning of the body about its central axis.

Contrast
A juxtaposition of dissimilar elements to show the differences of form or color, or to set in opposition in order to emphasize the differences.

Control joint See **Joint.**

Convex
Forms that have a surface or boundary that curves outward: as in the exterior or outer surface of a sphere.

Cook, Peter (1936–   )
Founder of Archigram in 1960, consisting of a group of designers, who disbanded in 1975. They promoted the High-Tech style through seductive futuristic graphics. His Plug-in City was a matrix of changeable parts inserted into gridlike structures.

Cool color
Blue, green, and violet; they generally appear to recede.

Cooling tower
A structure; usually located on the roof of a building, over which water is circulated so as to cool it by evaporation.

Cooperative apartment
A unit in a building owned and managed by a nonprofit corporation that sells shares in the building, entitling the shareholders to occupy apartments in the building.

Coped
Cut to conform to the irregular outline of an abutting piece, such as where two moldings meet at an inside corner.

Coping
A protective covering over the top course of a wall or parapet, either flat or sloping on the upper surface to throw off water.

raking coping
A coping set on an inclined surface, as at a gable end.

Coping course
The row of roofing tiles at the edge of a roof that forms the coping of the wall below.

Coping stone
Stone block that forms a coping to a wall.

Copper See **Metal**

Coquillage
A representation of the forms of seashells used as a decorative carving over doors and windows, and in friezes and architraves.

Corbel
In masonry construction, a series of projections: each one stepped progressively outward from the vertical face of the wall as it rises up to support a cornice or overhanging member above.

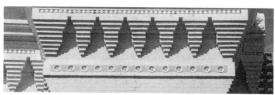

Corbel

Corbel arch See **Arch.**

Corbel table
A raised band composed of small arches resting on corbels; a projecting course of masonry supported on corbels near the top of a wall, such as a parapet or cornice.

Corbel vault See **Vault**

Corbeled chimney cap
The termination of a chimney using a series of successive courses of bricks that step out with the increasing height.

Corbeling
Masonry courses wherein each is extended out farther from the one below to form a rough arch-shaped lintel, vault, or dome.

Corbiestep
The stepped edge of an incline that terminates a masonry gable end-wall, masking the surface of a pitched roof beyond; used in northern European masonry construction.

Corinthian Order
The most ornamental of the three orders of architecture used by the Greeks, characterized by a high base, pedestal, slender fluted shaft with fillets, ornate capitals using stylized acanthus leaves, and an elaborate cornice.

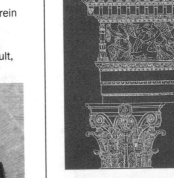

Corner
The position at which two lines or surfaces meet; the immediate exterior of the angle formed by the two lines or surfaces, as in the corner of a building or structure. The corner is one of the most important zones expressing the junction of two facades. Corners can take many forms such as, recessed, rounded, stepped, retracted, or framed. They can be angular, curved, or articulated in many different ways.

90

Corner

Corner bead molding See **Molding**

Corner board
A board which is used as trim on the external corner of a wood frame structure and against which the ends of the siding are fitted.

Corner drop ornament See **Ornament**

Cornerstone
A stone that is situated at a corner of a building uniting two intersecting walls, usually located near the base, and often carrying information about the structure.

Cornice
The uppermost division of an entablature: a projecting shelf along the top of a wall supported by a series of brackets; the exterior trim at the meeting of a roof and wall, consisting of soffit, fascia and crown molding.

boxed cornice
A hollow cornice, built up of boards and moldings, resulting in a soffit under the eaves.

bracketed cornice
A deep cornice having large, widely spaced ornamental brackets supporting an overhanging eave; it is common in the Italianate style.

horizontal cornice
The level cornice of the pediment under the two inclined cornices.

modillion cornice
A cornice supported by a series of modillions, often found In Composite and Corinthian orders.

open cornice
Overhanging eaves where the rafters are exposed at the eaves and can be seen from below.

raking cornice
A cornice following the slope of a gable, pediment, or roof.

Cornice return
The extension of a cornice in a new direction, particularly where the raked cornice of a gable end returns a short distance in a horizontal direction.

Cornucopia ornament See **Ornament**

Corona
The overhanging vertical member of a classical cornice supported by the bed moldings, crowned by the cymateum; usually incorporating a drip.

Corridor
A narrow passageway or gallery connecting several rooms or apartments within a residence, school, hospital, office building or other structure.

Corrosion
The deterioration of marble or concrete by a chemical reaction resulting from exposure to weathering, moisture, chemicals, or other agents in the environment in which it is placed.

Corrugated
Forms that are shaped into folds of parallel and alternating ridges and valleys; either to provide additional strength or to vary the surface pattern.

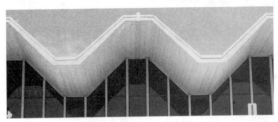

Corrugated glass See **Glass**

Corrugated metal.
Sheet metal that has been drawn or rolled into parallel ridges and furrows to provide additional mechanical strength; aluminum and galvanized sheet metal are the most widely used.

Cortile
An interior courtyard enclosed by the walls of a palace or other large building.

Cottage
A small rustic country house of the late eighteenth century.

Counter
A horizontal work surface, display, or serving surface, such as in a store, in a restaurant, or on top of a kitchen cabinet.

Counter arch See **Arch**

Counter brace See **Brace**

Counterflashing
Waterproof material, such as sheet metal, installed on the face of a wall that overlaps and seals the top of the vertical flashing below.

Counterpoint
A contrasting but parallel element or theme.

interweaving counterpoint
The forms or elements are integrated, with each one being a part of the other.

overlapping counterpoint
The forms are in contact but are not connected to each other.

parallel counterpoint
The ideas run together, but do not cross or interweave, as in bands running in the same direction.

Counterpoise
The disposition of the parts of the body so that the weight-bearing leg, or engaged leg, is distinguished from the raised leg, or free leg, resulting in a shift in the axis between the hips and shoulders.

Counterweight
A heavy component used to counterbalance the weight of a movable element; connected either with a cable over a pulley as in elevators or at one end of a lever as in a bascule bridge.

Coupled column See **Column**

Coupled window See **Window**

Course
A layer of masonry units running horizontally in a wall or over an arch that is bonded with mortar. The horizontal joints run the entire length; the vertical joints are broken so that no two form a continuous line.

Coursed masonry See Masonry

Coursed rubble See Masonry

Court
An open space about which a building or several buildings are grouped, completely or partially enclosing the space. They may be roofed over with glass or open to the air.

Courthouse
A building designed to contain one or more courtrooms and related facilities, such as judge's chambers, jury rooms, and administrative offices.

Courtyard
An open area within the confines of other structures, sometimes as a semipublic space.

Coussinet
The stone placed on the impost of a pier to receive the first stone of an arch.

Cove
Concave surface that connects a wall and ceiling.

Cove ceiling
A ceiling having a cove at the wall line or elsewhere.

Cove molding See **Molding**

Coved eave
Eaves of a building that are enclosed with a concave curved surface, so that the rafters are not exposed.

Cover molding See **Molding**

Craftsman style
A style of house most popular in the early 1900s, influenced by the Arts and Crafts movement, and published by Gustav Stickley in his magazine, *The craftsman,* published from 1901 to 1916.

Cram, Ralph Adams (1863–1942)
Leading Gothic revivalist in the United States, he was influenced by William Morris and John Ruskin.

Crane
A piece of construction machinery containing a mechanical device for lifting or lowering a load and moving it horizontally; the hoisting mechanism is an integral part of the boom.

Crawl space
The space under a suspended floor needed for access to services.

Crenel
The open space between the solid members of a battlement producing a pattern of repeated and identical indentations.

Crenelet
A small crenel, used as a decorative design.

Crenelated molding See **Molding**

Crenellation
A pattern of repeated depressed openings in a fortification parapet wall.

Crescent
Shape similar to the visible part of the moon in its first or last quarter; also the shape of a row of townhouse fronts constructed in the approximate shape of a circular or elliptical arc.

Crescent arch See **Arch**

Crespidoma
The solid mass of masonry at the base: forming the stepped platform upon which a classical temple is constructed.

Crest
An ornament on a roof, a roof screen or wall, which is frequently perforated, and consists of rhythmic and identical patterns that are highly decorative.

Crest

Crest tile See **Tile**

Cricket
A small element with two slopes, in the form of a miniature gable roof, placed behind a chimney that penetrates a sloping roof, to shed water.

Cripple
Any member shorter than most of the others in a structure, such as a stud beneath a window.

Cripple window See **Window**

Critical Path Method (CPM)
A construction scheduling device that diagrams the interrelationships between activities and identifies the critical path that optimizes the sequence of operations to minimize the construction period.

Crocket capital See **Capital**

Crocket ornament See **Ornament**

Cross
Two lines intersecting each other at right angles so that the four arms are of equal length.

Cross bond See **Bond**

Cross bracing See **Brace**

Cross vault See **Vault**

Crossbeam See **Beam**

Crossette
A lateral projection of the architrave moldings of classical doors and windows at the extremities of the lintel or head.

Crossing
The square space of a cruciform church, created by the intersection of the nave and chancel with the transept. Intersection of two elements in the form of a cross, such as the ridges of a cross gable.

Crossing square
The area in a church formed by the intersection of a nave and a transept of equal width.

Crown
Any uppermost or terminal features in architecture; the top of an arch including the keystone; the corona of a cornice, often including the elements above it .

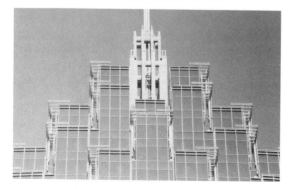

Crown glass See **Glass**

Crown molding See **Molding.**

Crowstep gable See **Gable**

Crowstone
The top stone of the stepped edge of a gable.

Cruciform
The characteristic cross-shaped plan for Gothic and other large churches that is formed by the intersection of nave, chancel, and apse with the transepts.

Cruck
One of a pair of large curved structural timbers, forming the wall posts and roof rafters of timber-framed houses; they are joined at the top of the frame where they support a ridge beam.

Crypt
A story in a church, below or partly below ground level, and under the main floor, often containing chapels and sometimes tombs; a hidden subterranean chamber or complex of chambers and passages,

Crypta
In ancient Roman architecture, a long, narrow vault sometimes below ground level, for the storage of grain.

Crystalline
A three-dimensional structure consisting of periodically repeated, identically constituted, congruent unit cells; found abundantly in natural objects.

Cube
A solid figure, bounded by six squares, and hence also called a hexahedron.

Cubit
The principal measure of length used in Ancient Egypt, Babylon, Israel and Greece. It was based on the length of the forearm, and varied from 525 to 445 mm. The forearm measure was called "braccia" in medieval and Renaissance Italy, and varied from city to city.

Cunieform
Designs having a wedge-shaped form; especially applied to characters, or to the inscriptions in such characters, of the ancient Mesopotamians and Persians.

Cupola
A tower-like device rising from the roof, usually terminating in a miniature dome or turret with a lantern or windows to let the light in.

Curb roof See **Roof**

Curtail
A spiral scroll-like termination of any architectural member, as at the end of a stair rail.

Curtail step See **Step**

Curtain wall See **Wall.**

Curvilinear
Forms that are bounded by or characterized by curved lines, whether geometric or free-flowing.

Curvilinear

Curvilinear tracery See **Tracery**

Curvilles, Francois (1695–1768)
Belgian-born architect who became the principal exponent of the Rococo style in Southern Germany; the style combined fantastic exuberance with delicacy and elegance.

Cushion capital See **Capital**

Cusp
The intersection of two arcs or foliations in a tracery; the figure formed by the intersection of tracery arcs or foliations.

Cusped arch See **Arch**

Cuspidation
Any system of ornamentation that consists of, or contains cusps.

96

Cut stone
Any stone cut or machined to a specified size and shape to conform to drawings, for installation in a designated place; it can also be carved by the intaglio method.

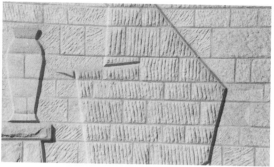

Cutaway See **Projection drawing**

Cyberspace
A conceptual space consisting of information elements as opposed to physical elements.

Cyclopean masonry See **Masonry**

Cylindrical
Having the shape of a cylinder, generated by rotating a rectangle around one of its sides.

Cylindrical

Cylindrical shell
A roof structure which forms part of a cylinder; its cross-section is generally a circular arc, though elliptical and catenary cylindrical shells have been built.

Cyma molding See **Molding**

Cyma recta molding See **Molding**

Cyma reversa molding See **Molding**

Cymatium molding See **Molding**

Cypress See **Wood**

Dd

Dado
A rectangular groove cut across the full width of a piece of wood to receive the end of another piece.

Date stone
A stone that is carved with the date of completion of the structure and embedded in the walls; found in many colonial buildings.

Daubing See **Plaster**

Davis, Alexander (1803–1892)
American architect who produced mostly Greek Revival style buildings.

Daylight factor
A factor describing the efficiency of a window in a particular room; defined as the ratio of the illuminance at a point in a room compared to the same point exposed to the unobstructed sky.

Daylighting
Lighting of a space with daylight, either from a skylight or with direct or indirect sunlight.

De Stijl
Term meaning "The Style," derived from the name of a group of Dutch artists and the journal founded by painter Theo van Doesberg in 1917; other members of the group included Piet Mondrian, Reitveld, and Oud.

It was influenced by Cubism, and proposed an abstracted expression, wholly divorced from nature, advocating straight lines, pure planes, right angles, and primary colors. It had a profound influence on the Bauhaus movement.

Decastyle
A structure comprising ten columns on the portico side.

Deck
The flooring of a building or other structure; a flat open platform, as on a roof.

Deconstructivism
An architectural style (1984–) known as "Neo-modernism," or "Post-structuralism," It takes many of its forms from the work of the Constructivists of the 1920s, such as work by Tchernikhov and Leonidou. It takes modernist abstraction to an extreme and exaggerates already known motifs. It is an antisocial architecture, based on intellectual abstraction. Some examples are Bernard Tschumi's designs for the Parc de la Villette, Paris; Peter Eisenman's Wexner Center for the Visual Arts, Ohio; and work by Frank Gehry, Architectonica, SITE, and Morphosis.

Decor
The combination of materials, furnishings, and objects used in interior decoration to create an atmosphere or style.

Decorated style
The second of three phases of English Gothic (1280–1350) was characterized by rich decoration and geometric tracery and by the use of multiple ribs in the vaulting. The earliest development was geometric, while the later forms were curvilinear, with complicated rib vaulting and naturalistic carved foliage that displayed a refinement of stonecutting techniques.

Decoration
A treatment applied to the surface of a structure with the intent of enhancing its beauty; includes gilding, stenciling, painting and marbleizing.

Decorative glass See **Glass**

Decorator
Person who performs the interior decoration of residences or commercial offices.

Dedication
Ceremony that officially begins the occupation and use of a building; also applies to the donation of land to the public for development of a tract of land, such as a road or easement.

Deflection
The deformation or displacement of a structural member as a result of loads acting on it.

Demolition
The intentional destruction of all or a part of a structure; may include removal of structural elements, partitions, mechanical equipment, and electrical equipment and wiring.

Dentil
A series of closely spaced ornamental rectangular blocks resembling teeth, used as moldings; most often found in continuous bands just below the cornice.

Dentil band
A plain, uncarved band; occupying the position in a cornice where dentils would normally occur.

Depressed arch See Arch.

Depression Modern style
Designs from the decade of economic depression (1935–1945) are represented in this style, which marked a reaction against the Art Deco style. It was characterized by simplicity, smoothness of forms, clarity of line, horizontality, streamlining and functional expressiveness.

Depth
The extent, measurement or distance from top to bottom (downward) or from front to back (inward), or an element consisting of several layers.

Design
To compose a plan for a building; the architectural concept of a building as represented by plans, elevations, renderings, and other drawings; any visual concept of a constructed object, as of a work of art.

charrette
The intense effort to complete an academic architectural problem within a specified time; from the French word meaning the "cart" that was used to carry the student work at the École des Beaux-Arts to be judged.

composition
The combining of various elements into proper position; to form an entity in terms of structure or organization.

conception
A drawing of something that does not yet exist.

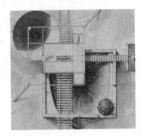

image
Any representation of form or features, especially one of the entire figure of a person; a statue, effigy, bust, relief, intaglio.

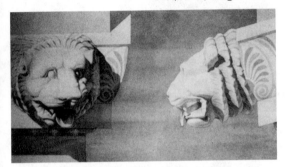

isometric drawing
A three-dimensional projection in which all planes are drawn parallel to the corresponding axes at true dimensions; all the horizontals are at 30 degrees from the normal horizontal axis; verticals are still parallel to the vertical axis.

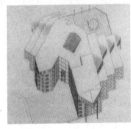

mock-up
A model of an object in the course of design, as in a cross section of a window or its parts; built to scale or full size, for studying construction details, judging its appearance, and/or testing performance.

model
A representation or reproduction, usually at a small scale: for studying or to illustrate construction.

parti
Any scheme or concept for the design of a building that is represented by a diagram.

perspective drawing
A graphic representation of a project or portion thereof, as it would appear in three dimensions.

preliminary drawing
Drawings prepared during the early stages of the design stages of a project.

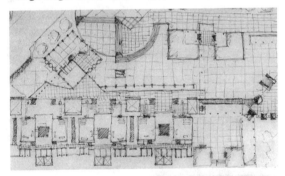

presentation drawing
Any of a set of design drawings made to articulate and communicate a design concept or proposal; such as for an exhibition, review, or publication.

Design controls
Regulations by local governments regarding alterations to existing structures in historic towns or districts; usually restricted to the exterior use of materials and overall design style.

Design development
The second phase of the architect's basic services: drawings that describe the character of the project as to structural, mechanical, and electrical systems; materials and all other essentials, and probable construction costs.

Design drawing
Any of the drawings made to aid in the visualization, exploration, and evaluation of a concept in the design process.

cartoon
A drawing or painting made as a detailed model of an architectural embellishment, often full-scale, to be transferred in preparation for a fresco, mosaic or tapestry.

collage
An artistic composition of diverse materials and objects, in unlikely or unexpected juxtaposition: which are pasted over a surface, often with unifying lines or color.

detail
A small or secondary part of a painting, statue, building, or other work of art, especially when considered or represented in isolation.

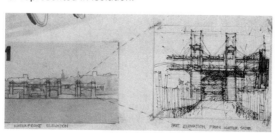

diagram
A plan, sketch, drawing, chart or graph, not necessarily representational, that explains, demonstrates or clarifies the arrangement and relationship of the parts to a whole.

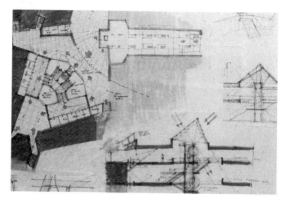

draft
A preliminary sketch of a design or plan, especially one executed with the idea of potential revision or refinement .

esquisse
A first sketch or very rough design drawing showing the general features of a proposed project.

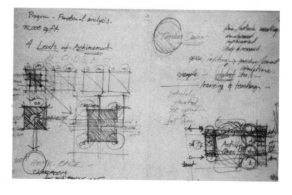

rendering
A drawing, especially a perspective of a building or interior space, artistically delineating materials, shades and shadows, done for the purpose of presentation and persuasion

scheme
The basic arrangement of an architectural composition; a preliminary sketch for a design.

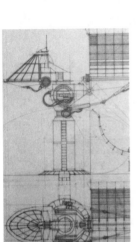

study
A drawing executed as an educational exercise produced as a preliminary to a final work or made to record observations.

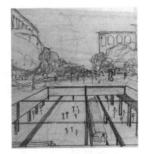

vignette
A drawing that is shaded off gradually into the surrounding background so as to leave no definite line at the border.

Design guidelines
Recommendations typically adopted and published by local regulating agencies, which control new construction, additions, and alterations, in historic towns or districts.

Detail See **Design drawing.**

Developer
A person or organization that controls and manages the process of construction of buildings or other facilities by arranging financing for the project, hiring the architect or contractor, obtaining zoning, regulatory approvals, and building permits, and that leases, sells, or manages the completed property.

Diaglyph See **Relief**

Diagonal
Joins two nonadjacent sides of a polygon with a slanted or oblique direction from one corner to the other; their use in a square or rectangle produces two triangular shapes.

Diagonal bond See **Bond**

Diagonal brace See **Brace**

Diagonal buttress See **Buttress**

Diagonal chimney stack
A group of chimney stacks that are square in cross section and set on a diagonal alignment: they are often corbeled and joined at the top.

Diagonal compressive stress
One of the stresses resulting from the combination of horizontal and vertical shear stresses in a beam.

Diagonal rib
A projecting rib that crosses a square or rectangular rib vault from corner to corner.

Diagonal sheathing
A covering of wood boards placed over exterior studding at a diagonal with respect to the vertical; provides a base for the application of wall cladding.

Diagonal tensile stress
One of the stresses resulting from the combination of horizontal and vertical shear stresses in a beam or slab.

Diagram See **Design drawing**

Diamond fret
A molding that is usually continuous, consisting of fillets that intersect to form a diamond shape, or rhombus.

Diamondwork masonry See **Masonry**

Diaper patterns
Flat patterns based on grids, containing either straight or curved lines; the grid may overlap or produce figures by connecting the diagonals and by combining them with circles, arcs and segments.

Diaphragm
A relatively thin element in a structural member, which is capable of withstanding shear in its plane; it stiffens the structural member.

Diffuser
A device used to alter the distribution of the light from a luminaire; some are designed to reduce the brightness of the lamp.

Dimension
The measured distance between two points; which when shown on a drawing is to become the precise distance between two points in a building.

Dimensional coordination
The design of building components to conform to a dimensional standard, such as a module.

Dimensional stability
Applies to material that has little moisture movement and creep, since thermal and elastic deformation are unavoidable.

Dimensional timber See **Wood**

Dimetric projection See **Projection drawing**

Diminished arch See **Arch**

Diminished column See **Column**

Diminution
The decrease in size of a column toward the top; typically employed as a device to overcome or correct an optical appearance of the top being larger than the bottom.

Dining hall
A large room in a school or other institution for group dining.

Dining room
A room in a residence for eating while seated at a table.

Dinkeloo, John (1918–1981)
An American architect who began work in Eero Saarinen's office, and established a partnership with Kevin Roche (1922–) after Saarinen's death. Their first work was the Oakland Art Museum, California (1961), a vast building with terraces and gardens throughout the four-city-block site. Later work includes the Ford Foundation Headquarters, New York (1963), which contains an indoor garden atrium, and extensions to the Metropolitan Museum of Art, New York (1967–1985), which includes the Pavilion for the Ancient Egyptian temple of Dendur.

Diorama
A large painting, or series of paintings, intended for exhibition in a darkened room in a manner that produces an appearance of reality created by optical illusions; a building in which such paintings are exhibited.

Dipteros
Temple surrounded by a double row of columns.

Direct lighting
Lighting using luminaires that direct most of the flux toward the surface being lit, as opposed to indirect lighting.

Direct solar gain
Solar energy obtained directly through a window.

Discharging arch See **Arch**

Discontinuous construction
Construction where there is no solid connection between the rooms of a building and the structure or between one section and another; used to prevent the transmission of sound along a solid path.

Disk
A flat, circular, raised ornament, carved as a series of disks adjacent to each other.

Distributed load
A load distributed over the surface; unless otherwise described it is usually considered uniformly distributed.

District
A geographically definable urban or rural area with a concentration of sites, structures, or uses connected historically or esthetically by plan or development.

Distyle
Having two columns.

Divided light
Window in which the glass is divided into several smaller panes.

Dodecagon
A 12-sided regular polygon, the angle included between the 12 equal sides is 115 degrees.

Doesburg, Theo van (1883–1931)
He began his career as a painter and established the De Stijl movement with J. J. P. Oud. He later taught at the Bauhaus.

Dog's tooth course See **Bond**

Dogleg stair See **Stair**

Dogtooth bond See **Bond**

Dogtooth ornament See **Ornament**

Dollman, George von (1830–1895)
A German Gothic Revival and Romantic architect, who designed Schloss Neuschwanstein (1886) and Schloss Linderhoff (1881), two palaces for Ludwig II of Bavaria, in an extravagant Neo-rococo style.

Dolmen
Several large stones capped with a covering slab, erected in prehistoric times.

Dolomite See **Stone**

Dome
A curved roof structure that spans an area on a circular base, producing an equal thrust in all directions. A cross section of the dome can be semicircular, pointed or segmented.

bell-shaped dome
A dome in which the cross section is shaped in the form of a bell.

double dome
An outer dome built over an inner dome, with a space between them; used to provide a supporting structure for the outer dome, or a different shape or architectural treatment to each one individually.

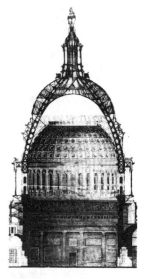

elliptical dome
A dome with a cross section in the shape of an arc of an ellipse; may have a circular base or an elliptical-shaped base.

geodesic dome
Consisting of a multiplicity of similar straight linear elements, arranged in triangles or pentagons, the members in tension having a minimal cross section, and making up a spherical surface usually in the shape of a dome.

geodesic dome

hemispherical dome
A dome with a constant radius of curvature that comes vertically from its springing; the horizontal component of the thrust is absorbed by a continuous ring or chain at the base of the dome.

imperial dome
A round roof in the shape of an onion with a flared skirt at the base; it is commonly found in Greek Orthodox churches; also known as an onion dome.

interdome
The space between the inner and outer shells of a dome.

lattice dome
A steel dome structure having members which follow the circles of latitude and two sets of diagonals replacing the lines of longitude, forming a series of isosceles triangles.

melon dome
A melon-like ribbed dome, either on the interior or on the exterior.

onion dome
In Russian Orthodox church architecture, a bulbous dome which terminates in a point and serves as a roof structure over a cupola or tower.

radial dome
A dome built with steel or timber trusses arranged in a radial manner and connected by polygonal rings at various heights.

saucerdome
A dome whose rise is much smaller than its radius.

semicircular dome
A dome in the shape of a half sphere.

semidome
A dome equivalent to one-quarter of a hollow sphere, covering a semicircular area, such as an apse.

Turkish dome
An onion-shaped dome with a pointed top and a cylinder base; named for its use in Byzantine architecture.

Turkish dome

Dome light
Any window or opening in a dome.

Domenig, Gunther (1934–)
Austrian-born architect; a proponent of Organic Architecture, his Z-Bank in Vienna (1979) is his best-known work, and features an undulating metal facade, and exposed mechanical and electrical systems in flexible pipe ducts on the interior.

Domical vault See **Vault**

Dominance
Occupying a preeminent or influential position; forms that exercise the most influence or governing control.

Door
A hinged, sliding, tilting, or folding panel for closing openings in a wall or at entrances to buildings. Doors must relate to the facade or wall in which they are placed. They are an important element in setting the style of the exterior and are an important transitional element to the interior space.

Door buck
A metal or wood surface set in a wall, to which the finished frame is attached.

Door casing
The finished frame surrounding a door; the visible frame.

Doorframe
An assembly built into a wall consisting of two upright members (jambs) and a head (lintel) over the doorway; encloses the doorway and provides support on which to hang the door.

Door head
The uppermost member of a door frame; a horizontal projection above a door.

Doorjamb
The vertical member located on each side of a door.

Doorknocker
A knob, bar, or ring of metal, attached to the outside of an exterior door to enable a person to announce his or her presence, usually held by a hinge so that it can be lifted to strike a metal plate.

107

Doorknocker

Door light
Glass area in a door.

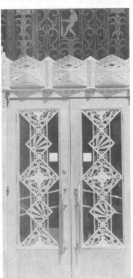

Door louvers
Blades or slats, which may or may not be adjustable, in a door to permit ventilation while the door is closed.

Door mullion
The center vertical member of a double-door opening set between two single active leaves, usually the strike side of each leaf.

Door muntin
An intermediate vertical member used to divide the panels of a paneled door.

Door panel
A distinct section or division of a door, recessed below or raised above the general level, or one enclosed by a frame.

Door rail
A horizontal cross member connecting the hinge stile to the lock stile, both at the top and bottom of the door and at intermediate locations, may be exposed as in panel doors, or concealed, as in flush doors

Door sill
The horizontal member: usually consisting of a board covering the floor joint on the threshold of a door.

Door stile
One of the upright structural members of the frame that is located at the outer edge of a door.

Doorstop
A strip against which a door shuts in its frame; a device placed on a wall behind a door or mounted on the floor to prevent the door from opening too wide.

Door surround
An ornamental border encircling the sides and top of a door frame.

Door threshold
A strip fastened to the floor beneath a door, usually required to cover the joint where two types of floor material meet; may provide weather protection at exterior doors.

Door transom
A crossbar separating a door from a light or window that is located above it.

Door types

accordion door
A hinged door consisting of a system of panels hung from an overhead track, folding back like the bellows of an accordion; when open the panels close flat; when closed, the panels interlock with each other.

acoustical door
A door having a sound-deadening core, stops along the top and sides sealed by gaskets, and an automatic drop seal along the bottom; especially constructed to reduce noise transmission through it.

aluminum door
Used for storefront entrances, due to its capacity for high corrosion resistance.

automatic door
A power-operated door, which opens automatically at the approach of a person or vehicle and closes automatically.

banded door
A wood door with a thin molded band applied to the outside edge of the face of each stile and the top and bottom rail.

batten door
A door formed by full height boards glued edge to edge with horizontal and vertical battens applied to give the appearance of paneling; a single batten door has battens on one side, and a double batten door has them on both sides.

bi-fold door
A folding door that divides into two parts, the inner leaf of each part being hung from an overhead track, and the outer leaf hinged at the jamb.

blank door
A recess in a wall, having the appearance of a door, usually used for symmetry of design: any door that has been sealed off but is still visible on the surface.

blind door
The representation of a door, inserted to complete a series of doors, or to give the appearance of symmetry.

bungalow door
Any of various front door designs featuring lights in the top portion of the door.

center-hung door
A door that is supported by and swings on a pivot that is recessed in the floor at a point located on the center line of the door's thickness; may be either single-swing or double-acting.

double door
A pair of swinging doors with hinges on each jamb, meeting in the middle.

double-framed door
A door with stiles, rails, and panels set within a frame of stiles and rails.

Dutch door
A door consisting of two separate leaves one above the other: the leaves may operate independently or together.

fire door
A sheet-metal-clad door that automatically closes in the event of a fire; typically designed to slide across a doorway.

flush door
A smooth-surfaced door having faces in the same plane as the surface and which conceal its rails and stiles or other structural features.

flush paneled door
A paneled door in which, on one or both faces, the panels are finished flush with the rails and stiles.

folding door
One of two or more doors which are hinged together so that they can open and fold in a confined space.

French door
A door having a top rail, bottom rail, and stiles, which has glass panes throughout Its entire length; often used in pairs.

glass door
A door consisting of heat-strengthened or tempered glass, with or without rails or stiles; used primarily as an entrance door for retail stores.

half door
A short door installed in the frame with space left above and below the door.

hollow-core door
A wood flush door having a framework of stiles and rails encasing a honeycombed core of corrugated fiberboard or a grid of interlocking horizontal and vertical wood strips.

interior door
A hollow-core or solid-core door made to be soundproof.

jib door
A concealed door flush with the wall and usually decorated to match it.

louvered door
A door having a louvered opening, usually with horizontal blades, that allows for the passage or circulation of air while the door Is closed

metal-clad door
A flush door having face sheets of light-gauge steel bonded to a steel channel frame: or a door having a structural wood core clad with galvanized sheet metal.

overhead door
A door of either the swing-up or the roll-up type constructed of one or several leaves: when open, it assumes a horizontal position above the door opening.

paneled door
A door having a framework of stiles, rails, and muntins which form one or more frames around thinner recessed panels.

pivoted door
A door hung on center or offset pivots as distinguished from one hung on hinges or a sliding mechanism.

pocket door
A door that slides in and out of a recess in a doorway wall requiring no room for the door swing.

revolving door
An exterior entrance door consisting of four leaves at right angles to each other, set in the form of a cross, which pivot about a vertical axis within a cylindrical-shaped vestibule.

rolling door
A large door consisting of horizontal, interlocking metal slats guided by a track on either side, opening by coiling about an overhead drum at the head of the door opening.

roll-up door
A door made of small horizontal interlocking metal slats that are guided in a track; the configuration coils around an overhead drum which is housed at the head; may be manually or electrically operated.

self-closing door
A door for the control of fire or smoke, which closes by itself by the action of a spring which is held open by a fusible link which melts in a fire, causing the door to close.

sliding door
A door that is mounted on a track, which slides in a horizontal direction parallel to the wall on which it is mounted.

solid-core door
A wood flush door having a solid core of lumber or particle- board, or one consisting of mineral composition.

storm door
Auxiliary door installed in the same frame, as an entrance door to a house.

swinging door
A door that turns on hinges or pivots about a vertical edge when opened.

tempered glass door
Common application for commercial use.

venetian door
A door having a long narrow window at each side similar in form to that of a venetian window, or a Palladian door.

wood door
Either solid core or hollow core with veneer; exterior doors are coated with waterproof adhesives.

Doorway
The framework in which the door hangs, or the entrance to a building: the key area of interest in a façade as a natural focal point and design element giving human scale.

Doorway

Doric capital See **Capital**

Doric order
The first and simplest of the orders, developed by the Dorian Greeks, consisting of relatively short shafts with flutes meeting with a sharp arris, simple undecorated capital, a square abacus, and no base. The entablature consists of a plain architrave, a frieze of triglyphs and metopes, and a cornice. The corona contained mutules in the soffit.

Dormer
A structure projecting from a sloping roof, usually housing a vertical window that is placed in a small gable, or containing a ventilating louver.

arched dormer
A dormer that has a semi-cylindrical-shaped roof; the head of the window in the dormer may be either rounded or flat.

eyebrow dormer
A low dormer on the slope of a roof. It has no sides; the roof is carried over it in a continuous wavy line.

hipped dormer
A dormer whose roof has a miniature hipped appearance in front, dying into the main roof surface at the back.

recessed dormer
A dormer with all or part of the window set back into the roof surface, resulting in the sill being lower than the roof.

shed dormer
A dormer whose eave line is parallel to the main eave line of the roof, and whose flat roof plane slopes downward in a direction away from the ridge line of the main roof.

wall dormer
Dormer whose face is integral with the face of the wall below.

Dormer cheek
The vertical sides of a dormer.

Dormer window See **Window**

Dormitory
A multiple-occupancy building which contains a series of sleeping rooms, bathrooms, and common areas.

Dosseret
A deep block sometimes placed above a Byzantine capital to support the wide voissoirs of an arch above; also, an isolated section of an entablature above a column.

Dot
A small square tile at the intersection of four larger tiles; usually placed at a 45-degree angle to the grid of the larger tiles.

Double dome See **Dome**

Double door See **Door**

Double glazing See **Glass**

Double lancet window See **Window**

Double vault See **Vault**

Double window See **Window**

Double-framed door See **Door**

Double-gable roof See **Roof**

Double-hipped roof See **Roof**

Double-hung window See **Window**

Double-pitched roof See **Roof**

Double-sunk
Recessed or lowered in two steps, as when a panel is sunk below the surface of a larger panel.

Douglas fir See **Wood.**

Dougong
Chinese term for a cluster of brackets cantilevered out from the top of a column to carry the rafters and overhanging eaves of a roof.

Dovetail joint See **Joint**

Dovetail molding See **Molding**

Dow, Alden (1904–1983)
An American architect; he worked with Frank Lloyd Wright in 1933, before setting up his own practice in 1935. His later work represented his own style.

Dowel
A small pin inserted into two abutting pieces of wood; in stone or masonry construction, a wooden or metal pin placed between the different courses to prevent shifting.

Downlight
Luminaire that directs the majority of its flux downward, usually within a restricted cone.

Downspout
A vertical pipe that carries water from the roof gutters to the ground or cistern.

Draft See **Design drawing**

Drafted margin
A narrow dressed border around the face of a stone, usually about the width of a chisel edge.

Drain
A channel, conduit, or pipe used to remove rain, wastewater, or sewage.

Drainage
An assembly of pipes and fittings, in the ground, used for the removal of wastewater or rainwater from a building or site.

Drainage hole
A hole in a retaining wall; an open joint in masonry, to drain unwanted water.

Drainpipe
Any pipe used to convey drainage liquids; includes soil pipes and waste pipes.

Drawbridge See **Bridge**

Drawing
A sketch, design, or representation by lines.

Drawing room
A large formal space for entertaining.

Dress
To prepare or finish a wood member by planing or cutting a stone piece by chipping away the irregularities.

Dressed lumber
Lumber having one or more of its faces planed smooth.

Dressed stone
Stone that has been worked to a desired shape; the faces to be exposed are smooth, usually ready for installation.

Dressing
Masonry and moldings of better quality than the facing materials, used around openings or at corners of buildings.

Drip cap
A horizontal molding fixed to a door or window frame to divert the water from the top rail, causing it to drip beyond the outside of the frame.

Drip molding See **Molding**

Dripstone
A hoodmold on the outside of a wall, often used in Gothic architecture.

Dripstone cap
A continuous horizontal cap containing a drip molding on a masonry wall.

Dripstone course
A continuous horizontal drip molding in a masonry wall.

Drop
Any one of the guttae attached to the underside of the mutules or triglyphs of a Doric entablature.

Drop arch See **Arch**

Drop molding See **Molding**

Drop panel
The portion of a flat slab or flat plate that is thickened throughout the area surrounding the top of the column, to reduce the magnitude of shear stress.

Drum
One of the cylinders of stone that form a column: a cylindrical or polygonal wall below a dome; often pierced with windows.

Drum

Dry masonry
Masonry wall laid up without mortar.

Drywall
An interior wall constructed with a material such as gypsum board or plywood; usually supplied in large sheets or panels, which do not require water to apply.

Duct
A nonmetallic or metallic tube for housing wires or cables, may be underground or embedded in concrete floor slabs: a duct usually fabricated of metal, used to transfer air from one location to another.

Ductwork
An assembly of ducts and duct fittings, usually of sheet metal, arranged for the distribution of air in an air-conditioning and mechanical ventilation system.

Dudok, Willem (1884–1974)
A Dutch architect based in Hilversum who designed the Snellius School in Hilversum, Holland (1922), as a compositions of asymmetrical rectangular blocks, predating the International Style; and the Town Hall, Hilversum (1931), in a distinctive version of the International style.

Dumbbell tenement
A five-to-seven-story multiple dwelling unit in urban areas, characterized by a long, narrow plan with an indentation on each side, forming a shaft for light and air; hence its resemblance in plan to a dumbbell.

Duplex
A house having a separate apartment for two families, especially a two-story house having two separate entrances and a complete apartment on each floor; an apartment with rooms on two connected floors.

Dutch bond See Bond

Dutch Colonial style
A style adopted by the Dutch settlers in New York and New Jersey (1650–1700), characterized by the use of brick and stone walls with gambrel or double-pitched roofs and flared lower eaves which extend beyond the front and rear walls, forming a deep overhang.

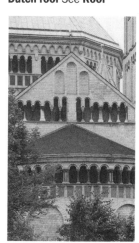

Dutch door See Door

Dutch gable See Gable

Dutch gambrel roof See Roof

Dutch roof See Roof

Dwarf order
A miniature range of columns or pilasters; for instance, those found on an attic story.

Dwarf order

Dymaxion house
A unique circular house proposal, it was conceived by R. Buckminster Fuller in 1928, to be mass produced at the Beech Aircraft Company: a full-sized prototype featured a central shaft containing all the building's services, such as electrical wiring and waste disposal facilities within it.

Ee

Eagle See **Ornament: animal forms**

Eames, Charles (1907–1973)
An architect and designer in partnership with his wife Ray Eames (1941–1978). Best known for the Eames House and for the design of modern furniture, mostly for the Knoll Furniture Company. The design of his own house in Santa Monica was influential because of its construction from prefabricated standard components in a totally Modern style.

Early Christian architecture
The final phase of Roman architecture (200–1025) was influenced by the adoption of Christianity as the state religion and the rise of the Byzantine style. The Roman basilican form was adopted as the ground plan for most early Christian churches. These simple rectangular plans consisted of a nave with two side aisles and a longitudinal and horizontal emphasis.

Early English architecture
The first English Gothic style (1200–1250) to follow the Norman style featured moldings, consisting of rounds and deep hollows, which produced a strong effect of light and shadow. Arches were lancet-shaped; doorways were deeply recessed with numerous moldings in the arch and jambs. Windows were long, narrow, and almost always pointed. Pillars consisted of small shafts arranged around a larger central pier.

Ears
Projections on the sides of the upper part of door and window surrounds. Also called shoulders.

Earth colors
Pigments such as yellow ochre and umber.

Earthwork
Any construction that involves moving, forming, cutting or filling earth.

Easement
A deed restriction on a piece of property granting rights to others to use the property; may include restrictions for use or development on the property.

Eastern Stick style
An American residential style (1855–1900) characterized by exposed framing overlaid on clapboard in horizontal, vertical or diagonal patterns to suggest the frame structure underneath. Steeply pitched gable roofs, cross gables, towers and pointed dormers, and porches and verandas are also characteristic. Oversized corner posts, purlins, brackets, and railings complement decorative woodwork produced by the stickwork.

Eastern Stick style

Eastlake style
A style (1870–1880) characterized by a massive quality, in which posts, railings and balusters were turned on a mechanical lathe. Large curved brackets, scrolls and other stylized elements are placed at every corner or projection along the facade. Perforated gables, carved panels and a profusion of spindles and latticework along porch eaves are typical. Lighter elements are combined with oversized members to exaggerate the three-dimensional facade.

Eave
The projecting overhang at the lower edge of a roof that sheds rain water.

Eaves channel
A channel or small gutter along the top of a wall; it conveys the roof rainwater to downspouts.

Ebony See **Wood**

Eccentric
Not having the same center or center line: departing or deviating from the conventional or established norm.

Echinus
The convex projecting molding of eccentric curve supporting the abacus of a Doric capital.

Eclectic style
The selection of elements from diverse styles for architectural decorative designs: particularly during the late nineteenth century in Europe and America.

Eclecticism
The practice of selecting from various sources, sometimes to form a new style.

Ecole des Beaux-Arts
A school founded in 1648 in Paris to teach painting and sculpture, literally the "School of Fine Arts"; architecture was added to the studies in 1819, emphasizing the study of classical Greek and Roman buildings; students were grouped in ateliers supervised by a master. Richard Morris Hunt was the first American to study at the school, followed by many other late nineteenth century and early twentieth century architects.

Ecological architecture
A style of architecture (1970–) developed in response to the problems of expensive fuels and other environmental factors. Various projects were undertaken to construct self-sufficient, or self-serving buildings, independent of public utilities, by exploiting ambient energy sources, such as wind power, solar radiation, and a variety of recycling techniques.

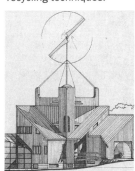
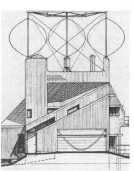

Edge beam See **Beam**

Edge to edge
Two surfaces that butt together but do not overlap each other.

Efflorescence
A deposit, usually white, formed on the surface of a brick, block, or concrete wall; it consists of salts leached from the surface of the wall.

Egg-and-dart molding See **Molding**

Egyptian architecture
An ancient architecture along the Nile River from Neolithic times (3000 B.C.–200 A.D.), built of reed huts with inward sloping walls and thick bases to resist the annual inundation. The decorative "bundling" of reeds later influenced stone construction of fluted columns and capitals.

Massive funerary monuments and temples were built of stone using post-and-lintel construction, with closely spaced columns carrying the stone lintels supporting a flat roof. A hypostyle hall, which was crowded with columns, received light from clerestories above. Walls were carved in ornamental hieroglyphs in low relief.

There were many varieties of columns, often used side by side, their capitals were distinctly ornate, based on the lotus, papyrus, or palm.

Egyptian cornice

The characteristic cornice of most Egyptian buildings, consisting of a large cavetto decorated with vertical leaves and a roll molding below.

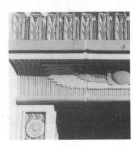

Egyptian Revival style

A revival style (1830–1850) distinguished by distinctive columns and capitals and a smooth monolithic exterior finish. Characteristic battered walls are edged with roll moldings, tall straight-headed windows with splayed jambs, and a deep cavetto or gorge-and-roll cornice.

Roofs are flat, and the smooth wall surface lends a monumental appearance reminiscent of pylons or gateways to Egyptian temples.

Ehrankrantz, Ezra (1932–)

An American architect, who invented a system for low-cost school buildings, using standardized prefabricated components.

Eiffel, Gustave (1832–1923)

Designed the Eiffel Tower, Paris, which was built of exposed steel for the 1887 Paris Exhibition and for 40 years was the tallest structure in the world.

Eisenman, John (1851–1924)

Best known for his design of the Cleveland Arcade, Cleveland (1882), with its two 9-story round arched blocks flanking a galleried iron-and-glass facade.

Eisenman, Peter (1932–)

Founded the Institute of Architecture and Urban Studies in New York City, and was associated with the New York Five from 1972. He is associated with Deconstructivism. His well-known Wexner Center for the Visual Arts, Columbus, Ohio (1989), is set on an angle to the existing campus buildings, as is the Convention Center, Columbus, Ohio (1993).

El Tajin style

A style of Mesoamerican architecture (200–900 A.D.) as seen at the Pyramid of Niches, El Tajin, the Totonac capital in Veracruz, Mexico, characterized by elaborately carved recessed niches with geometric ornamentation.

Elastic deformation
Deformation that occurs instantly when a load is applied and is instantly and fully recovered when the load is removed.

Elastic limit
Limit of stress beyond which the strain cannot fully recover.

Elasticity
The ability of a material to deform instantly under load and to recover its original shape instantly when the load is removed.

Elastomeric
Any material having the properties of being able to return to its original shape after being stressed; such as a roofing material which can expand and contract without rupture.

Elbow
Sharp corner in a pipe or conduit, as opposed to a bend, which has a larger radius of curvature.

Electrical system
The entire apparatus for supplying and distributing electricity; including transformers, meters, cables, circuit breakers, wires, switches, fixtures and outlets.

Elevation
A drawing showing the vertical elements of a building, either interior or exterior, as a direct projection to a vertical plane.

Elevator
A platform or enclosure that can be raised or lowered in a vertical shaft that transports people or freight. The hoisting or lowering mechanism which serves two or more floors, is equipped with a cab or platform which moves in vertical guide-rails for stability.

Elgin Marbles
A collection of sculptures, taken from the Parthenon in Athens by Lord Elgin; preserved in the British Museum since 1816. The finest surviving work of Greek sculptural decoration of the Classical age; the collection includes a number of metopes, fragments of pediment statues, and an extended series of blocks carved in low relief of the cella frieze.

Elizabethan style
A transitional style between the Gothic and Renaissance in England (1558-1603), named after the queen, consisting mostly of designs for country houses, characterized by large windows and by strap iron ornamentation.

Ellipse
A closed loop obtained by cutting a right circular cone by a plane.

Elliptical
A plane figure resembling an ellipse, whose radius of curvature is continually changing: a three-centered arch is an example of one constructed to an elliptical curve.

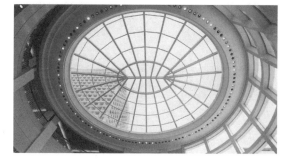

Elliptical arch See **Arch**

Elliptical Dome See **Dome**

Elliptical stair See **Stair**

Ellwood, Craig (1921–1992)
Designed mainly private residences and apartments of elegant proportions and detailing with standardized components of Mies Van der Rohe such as the Carson Roberts Building, Los Angeles (1961). Later he used exposed trusses at the Art Center College of Design, Pasadena (1970).

Elm See **wood**

Elmslie, George (1871–1952)
Partnered with William Greg Purcell (1880–1965), they were best known for their houses of the Prairie School style. Elmslie worked briefly with Louis Sullivan on the Carson Pirie Scott store in Chicago.

Embattlements
Having battlements: a crenelated molding.

Embedded column See **Column**

Embedded organization See **Organization**

Embellishment
Ornamentation; adornment with decorative elements.

Emboss
To raise or indent a pattern on the surface of a material; sometimes produced by the use of patterned rollers.

Embrasure
The crenels or spaces between the merlons of a battlement; an enlargement of a door or window opening at the inside face of a wall by means of splayed sides.

Emphasis
A special importance or significance placed upon or imparted to an element or form by means of contrast or counterpoint; a sharpness or vividness of outline.

Empire style
The elaborate Neo-classic style (1800–1830) of the French Empire in the wake of Napoleon, characterized by the use of delicate but elaborate ornamentation, imitated from Greek and Roman examples, and by the use of military and Egyptian motifs.

Encarpus
A sculptural festoon of fruit and flowers.

Encased beam See **Beam**

Encaustic tile See **Tile**

End grain
The face of a piece of timber exposed when the fibers are cut transversely; exposure of this surface to the elements causes deterioration.

End-lap joint See **Joint**

Engaged
Applied or partially buried in a wall, such as a column with half or more of its shaft visible.

Engaged column See **Column**

Engineer
A person trained and experienced in the profession of engineering; one licensed to practice the profession by the authority in the area.

Engineering
The design of the civil, structural, and electrical portions of a construction project.

English bond See **Bond**

English cross bond See **Bond**

Engraving
A design is incised in reverse on a copper plate; this is coated with printer's ink, which remains in the incised lines when the plate is wiped off. Damp paper is put on the plate and the two are put into a press; the paper soaks up the ink and produces a print of the original.

Enriched
Having embellishments.

Entablature
The superstructure composed of an architrave immediately above the columns, central frieze, and upper projecting cornice, consisting of a series of moldings. The proportions and detailing are different for each order, and they are strictly prescribed.

Entasis
Intentional slight curvature given to the vertical profile of a tapered column to correct the optical illusion that it appears thinner in the middle if the sides are left straight.

Entrance
Any passage that affords entry into a building; an exterior door, vestibule or lobby.

Envelope
The imaginary shape of a building indicating its maximum volume; used primarily to check the plan, setback, and other restrictions regarding zoning regulations.

Envelope forms
With curtain-wall systems, the actual construction and arrangement of the surfaces enclosing the building are totally independent of the bearing system.

Environment
The combination of all external conditions which may influence, modify, or affect the actions of a person, piece of equipment, or any system.

Environmental design
The professions collectively responsible for the design of man's physical environment, including architecture, engineering, landscape architecture, urban planning and similar environment-related professions.

Environmental impact
Includes all the social and physical effects of a development or government policy on the natural and built environment.

Environmental impact statement
A detailed analysis of the probable environmental consequences of proposed federal legislation, or large-scale construction making use of federal funds, likely to have significant effects on environmental quality .

Equilateral arch See Arch

Equilateral triangle
A triangle where all three sides are of equal length, with three equal inside angles.

Equilibrium
The state of a body in which the forces acting on it are equally balanced.

Erection
The hoisting and installing in place of the structural components of a building, using a crane, hoist, or any other power system.

Erection bracing
Bracing which is installed during erection to hold the framework in a safe condition until sufficient permanent construction is in place to provide full stability.

Erection stresses
Those stresses caused by construction loads and by the weight of components while they are being lifted into position.

Erickson, Arthur (1924–)
Canadian architect influenced by Le Corbusier, Kahn, and Rudolph, who gained international recognition with his plan for the Central Covered Mall, Vancouver, Canada (1963).

Ersatz style
A German word meaning "substitute" or "replacement ," used by architectural critic Charles Jencks to describe architecture (1973–1975) with forms that are borrowed indiscriminately from various sources. This is partly the result of modern technology, which is capable of producing architecture in any style. It can also be considered as any "pastiche" which captures the essence of the original design.

Erskine, Ralph (1914–)
British architect, whose work includes "The Ark," Hammersmith, London (1991).

Escalator
A moving stairway consisting of steps attached to an inclined continuously moving belt for transporting passengers up or down between the floors in a structure.

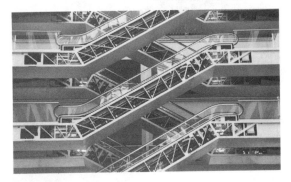

Escutcheon
A protective plate that surrounds the keyhole of a door or door handle.

Escutcheon pin
A small nail, usually brass, for fixing an escutcheon, often ornamental.

Esherick, Joseph (1914–)
San Francisco architect most noted for the renovation and redevelopment of the Cannery (1968), a retail complex on Fisherman's Wharf, San Francisco, and the Monterey Bay Aquarium, Monterey, California (1984).

Esplanade
A flat open space used as a walkway.

Esquisse See **Design drawing**

Esthetic
The distinctive vocabulary of a given style.

Etruscan architecture
A style (700–280 B.C.) which flourished in western central Italy until the Roman conquest; it is largely lost, except for underground tombs and city walls, but the characteristic true stone arch influenced later Roman construction methods. Examples that have survived show forms that were rich in ornamentation.

Eurhythmy
Harmony, orderliness, and elegance of proportions.

Evolutionary architecture
This style is defined by its major proponent, Eugene Tsui, as design that grows and develops based on climatic and ecological elements, as well as advances in science and technology. The design is approached as a living organism as if natural forces had shaped the structure.

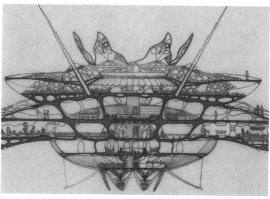

Excavation
The removal of earth from its natural position; the cavity that results from the removal of earth.

Exedra
A large niche or recess, either roofed or unroofed. semicircular or rectangular in plan, usually including a bench or seats.

Exhaust fan
A fan that withdraws air that is not to be returned to the central air-treatment center and is exhausted to the outside.

Exoskeleton
The system of supports in a French Gothic church, including the ribbed vaults, flying buttresses, and pier buttresses.

Expanded metal
Metal network formed from sheet metal by cutting a pattern of slits, followed by pulling the metal into a diamond pattern; used as metal lath for plaster, as reinforcing in concrete, and for making screens.

Expansion anchor
Bolt that is inserted into a hole drilled into masonry or other material, with a device on the end that expands, prohibiting the bolt from being withdrawn.

Expansion joint See **Joint**

Experimental architecture
Architecture that is committed to experimentation with form, materials, technology, and construction methodologies. It was the title of a book by Peter Cook (1971), and identified architects who were involved in experimental architecture, such as Friedman, Goff, Soleri, Otto, Tange, and groups like Archigram and the Metabolists.

Exploded view See **Projection drawing**

Exposed aggregate
A decorative finish for concrete; formed by removing the outer surface of cement mortar before it has hardened or by sprinkling aggregate on the wet concrete after placing.

Expressionism

A northern European style (1903-1925) that did not treat buildings only as purely functional structures, but as sculptural objects in their own right. Works typical of this style were by Antonio Gaudi in Spain, P.W. Jensen Klint in Denmark, and Eric Mendelsohn and Hans Poelzig in Germany.

Exterior wall See **Wall**

Extrados

The exterior curve or boundary on the visible face of the arch.

Extradosed arch See **Arch.**

Eye

The convex disk at the vortex of an Ionic volute spiral.

Eye of the dome

An aperture or skylight at the top of a dome; also known as an oculus.

Eyebar

A metal tension member having an enlarged end, and containing a hole used to make a pinned connection to another part of the structure.

Eyebrow

A curved molding over the top of a window or door, often referred to as a hood.

Eyebrow dormer See **Dormer**

Eyebrow eave

Eave that is carried over a door entry in a wavy line.

Eyebrow lintel

A lintel above a window and carried in a wavy line.

Eyebrow window See **Window**

Ff

Fabric
An underlying framework or structure consisting of similar connected parts.

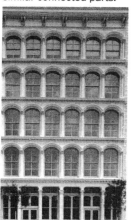

Facade
The main exterior face of a building, particularly one of its main sides, almost always containing an entrance and characterized by an elaboration of stylistic details.

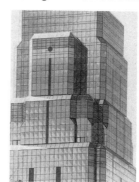

Facadism
Preserving the facade of a building while demolishing or altering the rest of the building.

Faceted
Shapes that resemble any of the flat, angular surfaces that are similar to those cut on a gemstone.

Face
The front facade of a building or the finished surface of an exposed member.

Face brick See **Brick.**

Face string See **String**

Facility
A physical environment containing open space, such as parks and gardens; infrastructure, such as roads and utilities; and built structures, such as homes, schools, hospitals, and factories.

Facing
A veneer of nonstructural material forming part of a wall and used as a finishing surface of a rougher or less attractive material, such as stone, terra-cotta, metal, stucco, plaster, and wood.

Factor of safety
A factor used in structural design to provide a margin of safety against collapse or serious structural damage. It allows for inaccurate assumptions in the loading conditions, inadequate control over the quality of workmanship, imperfections in materials, but not mathematical errors.

Factory
A building or group of buildings containing machinery and other facilities for the manufacture of goods.

Failure
A condition when a structure or material ceases to fulfill its required purpose. The failure of a structural member may be caused by elastic deformation, fracture, or by excessive deflection. The nonstructural failure of a material may be due to weathering, abrasion, or chemical action.

False
Nonfunctional architectural element; such as a false arch, false attic, false front, false window.

False arch See **Arch**

False attic
An architectural construction concealing a roof, built without windows or enclosing rooms, and located above the main cornice.

False ceiling
A ceiling suspended or hung from the floor above, which hides the underneath and provides a space for cables and ducts.

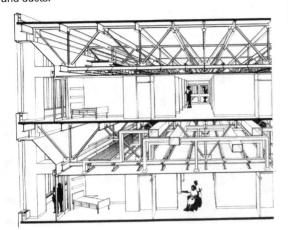

False front
A front wall which extends beyond the side walls and above the roof of a building to create a more imposing facade.

False window See **Window**

Fan Tracery See **Tracery**

Fan vault See **Vault**

Fanlight
A semicircular window, usually over a door with radiating bars suggesting an open fan.

Fantastic architecture
Imaginative architecture, such as the later work of Antonio Gaudi, Bruno Taut, and Hans Poelzig; and futuristic, high-tech megastructures, or those defying traditional logic or considerations of use.

Farrell, Terry (1938–)
British Postmodern architect, whose most well known work includes Kowloon Station (1997), and the Victoria Peak Building (1998), both in Hong Kong.

Fascia
A broad horizontal member or molding with nominal thickness, projecting from the wall.

Fashionable
Stylish; conforming to the latest mode of fashion.

Fastener
A mechanical device, weld, bolt, pin or rivet for holding two or more parts, pieces, or members together.

Feasibility study
An analysis of the possibilities for a project or structure; typically includes factors regarding zoning, alternative uses, building codes, financial, environmental, design and historic significance.

Federal style
Low-pitched roofs, a smooth facade and large glass areas characterize this style (1780–1820). Geometric forms accentuate the rhythm of the exterior wall, which is elegant and intentionally austere. Although it rejected Georgian decoration, it retained its symmetry, pilaster-framed entrance, fanlight and sidelights. Windows were simply framed, and quoins were abandoned.

Feline See **Ornament: animal forms**

Femur
The vertical surfaces of the triglyph left between the glyphs.

Fence
A structural barrier of wood or iron used to define, separate or enclose areas such as fields, yards, and gardens.

Fenestra

A loophole in the walls of a fortress or castle, from which missiles were discharged: the ancient equivalent of a window.

Fenestration

The design and placement of windows, and other exterior openings in a building.

Fenwick, James (1818–1895)

Designed St. Patrick's Cathedral, New York City, a vast Gothic church.

Ferriss, Hugh (1889–1962)

Distinguished American architectural delineator and visionary. His images of futuristic buildings were published in the _Metropolis of Tomorrow_ (1929), which impacted architecture in the 1930s.

Ferrous metal See Metal

Festoon

Hanging clusters of fruit, tied in a bunch with leaves and flowers; used as decoration on pilasters and panels, usually hung between rosettes and skulls of animals.

Fiberglass See **Plastics**

Fiber stress
A term used to denote the direct longitudinal stresses in a beam, such as tension and compression.

Fieldstone See **Stone**

Figure
Sculptural representation of a person or animal.

Filigree
Ornamental openwork of delicate or intricate design.

Finger joint See **Joint**

Finial
A small, sometimes foliated ornament at the top of a spire, pinnacle or gable which acts as a terminal.

Finish
The texture, color, and other properties of a surface that may affect its appearance.

Fink truss See **Truss**

Finsterlin, Hermann (1887–1973)
German designer of visionary buildings, many of which were published in books by Bruno Taut, but he did not construct any permanent structures.

Fir See **Wood.**

Fire barrier
Any element of a building, such as a wall, floor, or ceiling, constructed to delay the spread of fire from one part of a building to another.

Firebrick See **Brick**

Fire detector
An automatic device that signals the presence of heat or flame in a structure.

Fire door See **Door**

Fire escape
A continuous, unobstructed path of egress from a building in case of a fire.

Fire indicator panel
A control panel that indicates a signal from an alarm and the zone where the signal was initiated.

Fire resistance
The capacity of a material or construction to withstand fire or give protection from it; characterized by its ability to confine fire or to continue to perform a structural function.

Fire resistance grading
The grading of building components according to the minutes or hours of resistance in a standard fire test.

Fire wall
An interior or exterior wall having sufficiently high fire resistance and structural stability under conditions of fire to restrict its spread to adjoining areas or adjacent buildings.

Fireback
The back wall of a fireplace, constructed of heat-resistant masonry or ornamental cast or wrought metal, which radiates heat into the room.

Firehouse
A building used for sheltering firefighting equipment; often including quarters for firefighters.

Fireplace
An opening at the base of a chimney, usually an open recess in a wall, in which a fire may be built .

Fireplace cheeks
The splayed sides of a fireplace.

Fireproof construction
A method of building that employs non-combustible materials, such as a steel frame covered with a fire-resistant material.

Fireproofing
Any material that increases the resistance to fire; such as brick, stone, drywall, and sprayed asbestos.

Fire wall See **Wall**

Fish scale
An overlapping semicircular pattern in woodwork that resembles the scales of fish.

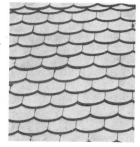

Flagpole
A pole on which a flag, banner, or emblem may be raised and displayed; may be self-supporting or attached to a building.

Flagstone See **Stone**

Flamboyant style
The last phase of French Gothic architecture (1450–1500), characterized by flame-like tracery and the profuse use of ornamentation.

Flange
A projecting collar, edge, rib, rim, or ring on a pipe, shaft, or beam.

Flank
The side of a building.

Flared eaves
An eave that projects beyond the surface of the wall and curves upward toward its outer edge.

Flashing
A thin impervious material placed in construction to prevent water penetration or provide water drainage between a roof and vertical walls and over exterior doors and windows.

Flat arch See **Arch**

Flat arris
The flat edge on a column where a fillet joins the concave surface of a flute.

Flat keystone arch See **Arch**

Flat plate slab
A reinforced-concrete floor slab of uniform thickness and without a dropped beam.

Flat roof See **Roof**

Flat slab
A concrete slab reinforced in two or more directions and supported directly on column capitals; also called mushroom slab because of the shape of the enlarged capitals.

Fleche
A comparatively small and slender spire, usually located above the ridge of a roof, especially one rising from the intersection of the nave and transept roofs of Gothic churches.

Flemish bond See **Bond**

Flemish diagonal bond See **Bond**

Flemish gable See **Gable**

Flemish Mannerism
North European mutation of Flamboyant Gothic and Mannerist styles, exploited cartouches, caryatids, grotesque ornaments, hermes, banded pilasters, obelisks, and other elaborate details; many examples are found in the Guild houses in the Grand Place, Brussels.

Fleur-de-lis ornament See **Ornament**

Fleuron
The small flower-like shape at the center of each side of the Corinthian capital abacus.

Flight See **Stair**

Float finish
A rather rough concrete finish, obtained by finishing with a wooden float.

Float glass See **Glass**

Floating floor See **Floor**

Floating house
A flat-bottomed boat with walls and a roof, outfitted to function as a floating dwelling.

Floor

The lowest surface of a room or structure, which can be a division between one story and another made up of other elements, or a homogeneous material. It is the base plane of any room or structure, and is usually characterized by a flat surface or a series of flat surfaces at different levels.

floating floor

The floor is separated from the rest of the building by supporting it on sleepers or a built-up structural system, to provide sound insulation or space for high-tech flexible electrical service, independent of wall locations.

hollow-tile floor

A reinforced concrete floor that is cast over a formwork of hollow clay tile blocks, the concrete filling the voids between the tiles.

laminated floor

A structural floor constructed of a continuous series of lumber set on edge and nailed together.

raised floor

A false floor, which provides a space for cables or ducts above the structural floor, floor sections are usually supported on short, adjustable peg columns.

Floor joist See **Joist**

Floor Plan

A drawing representing a horizontal section taken above a floor to show, diagrammatically, the enclosing walls of a building, its doors and windows, and the arrangement of its interior spaces.

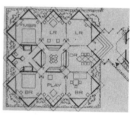

Floor tile See **Tile**

Flooring

Any material used for the surface of a floor, such as boards, bricks, planks, tile, or marble.

Florentine arch See **Arch**

Florentine mosaic See **Mosaic**

Floriated
Decorated with floral
patterns.

Florid
Highly ornate: extremely
rich to the point of being
overly decorated.

Flue
An incombustible and heat-resistant enclosed passage in
a chimney to control and carry away products of
combustion from a fireplace to the outside air.

Fluorescent lamp
An electric lamp, consisting of a tube with an inside
coating of fluorescent powder, which converts a low-
voltage electric charge through mercury vapor into visible
light.

Flush
Signifying that the adjoining
surfaces in a building or in
a wall are even, level, or
arranged so that their
edges are close together
and on the same plane.

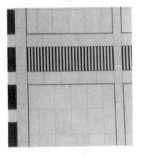

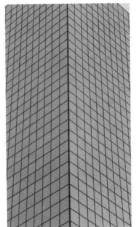

Flush bead molding See **Molding**

Flush door See **Door**

Flush joint See **Joint**

Flush molding See **Molding**

Flush mortar joint See **Joint.**

Flush paneled door See **Door**

Flute
A groove or channel that is
usually semicircular or semi-
elliptical in section; especially one of many such
parallel grooves that is used
decoratively, as along the
shaft of a column.

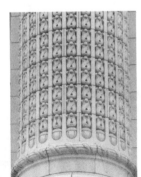

Fluting
The hollows or parallel
channels cut vertically
on the shaft of columns,
pilasters and piers,
separated by a sharp
edge or arris, or by a
small fillet.

Flying buttress See **Buttress.**

Flying facade
The continuation of the facade wall above the roofline of a building.

Focus
A center of interest or activity drawing attention to the most important aspect of a design scheme, such as the main space, materials, scale, lighting, or orientation.

Foiled arch See **Arch**

Foils
The foliation consists of the cusps, which are the projecting portions, and the spaces between the cusps.

cinquefoil
A five-lobed pattern divided by cusps.

multifoil
Having more than five foils, lobes, or arcuate divisions.

quatrefoil
Having four foils, lobes, or acute divisions.

trefoil
A three-lobed cloverleaf pattern.

Folding casement window See **Window**

Folding door See **Door**

Folding partition
A floor-to-ceiling folding door used to subdivide a room into smaller spaces.

Foliated
Adorned with foils, as on tracery; decorated with a conventionalized representation of leafage, applied to capitals, friezes, panels, or other ornamental moldings.

Folk architecture
Simple structures usually intended to provide only basic shelter suitable for the surrounding terrain, without concern for following any architectural style; built of local materials and available tools by the people who would inhabit them.

Folly
A functionally useless, whimsical or extravagant structure; often a fake ruin; sometimes built in a landscaped park to highlight a specific view, serve as a conversation piece, or to commemorate a person or event.

Foot
The lowest part of an object, such as the end of a rafter where it meets the top plate.

Footbridge See **Bridge**

Footing
That portion of the foundation of a structure that transmits loads directly to the soil; may be enlarged to distribute the load over a greater area to prevent or to reduce settling.

continuous footing See **Footing**
Combined footing, which acts like a continuous beam on the foundation.

spread footing
A footing in a foundation that is wider than the wall or column it supports in order to distribute the vertical load over a wider area.

Footprint
The projected area of a building or piece of equipment on a horizontal surface.

Forecourt
A court forming an entrance plaza for a single building or a group of several buildings.

Form
The contour and structure of an object as distinguished from the matter composing it; a distinctive appearance as determined by its visible lines, figure, outline, shape, contour, configuration and profile.

Formal balance See **Balance**

Formal garden
A garden whose plantings, walks, pools and fountains follow a definite recognizable plan; it is frequently symmetrical and emphasizes geometrical forms.

134

Formal garden

Formalism

Formalism

A term representing a new classicism in American architecture (1950–1965), manifested in buildings designed by Mies van der Rohe, Phillip Johnson, Paul Rudolph and Minuro Yamasaki.

Formwork

A temporary framework of wood to contain concrete in the desired shape until it sets.

Fort

A fortified place of exclusively military nature.

Fort-Brescia, Bernado (1951–)
Peruvian-born American architect who with his wife, the U.S. born Laurinda Hope-Spear (1950-) established the architectural firm Arquitectonica (1977). Their best-known early work includes the Atlantis Condominium, Miami (1985), while the latest is the multipurpose hotel and entertainment development in the Times Square area of New York City (2001).

Fortress
A fortification of massive scale, generally of monumental character; sometimes including an urban core, as a protected place of refuge.

Forum
A Roman public square surrounded by monumental buildings, usually including a basilica and a temple; the center of civic life was often purely commercial.

Foster, Sir Norman Robert (1935–)
English architect; and one of the most distinguished practitioners of the High-Tech style. His largest commissions were the Hong Kong and Shanghai Bank, Hong Kong (1979), Willis Faber U. Dumas Building, Ipswich (1974), Century Tower, Tokyo (1987), and the Chek Lap Kok International Airport, Hong Kong (1998), the largest enclosed space in the world (1998), and the Millennium Tower project, London (1997).

Fouilhoux, Jacques-Andre (1879–1945)
Paris-born American architect who as partner with Raymond Hood designed the McGraw-Hill Building (1932); the partners were partly responsible for the design of Rockefeller Center. When Hood died, he joined Wallace K. Harrison to complete it. He also contributed to the design of the New York World's Fair (1939).

Found space
Space within an existing building that was not utilized prior to rehabilitation; such as converting an attic, basement, or constructing new mezzanine levels.

Foundation
The lowest division of a building that serves to transmit and anchor the loads from the superstructure directly to the earth or rock, usually below ground level.

Foundation wall See Wall.

Fountain
An architectural setting that incorporates a continuous or artificial water supply, fed by a system of pipes and nozzles through which water is forced under pressure to produce a stream of ornamental jets.

Foyer
An entranceway or transitional space from the exterior of a building to the interior spaces.

Fractable
A coping on the gable end of a building when carried above the roof, often it is broken up into steps or curves, thereby forming an ornamental outline.

Frame
The timber work which encloses and supports the structural components of a building.

Frame building
A building built with a wood frame rather than masonry; includes balloon frame, half-timbered, and timber frame.

Framework
Composed of individual parts that are fitted and joined together as skeletal structures designed to produce a specific shape, or to provide temporary or permanent support.

Framing
A system of rough timber structural woodwork that is joined together in order to support or enclose, such as partitions, flooring and roofing. Any framed work, as around an opening in an exterior wall.

Francois I (Premier) style
The culmination of the early phase of French Renaissance architecture (1515–1547), named after Francis I, merged Gothic elements with the full use of Italian decoration. Fontainbleau and the chateaux of the Loire, among them Chambord, are outstanding examples.

Franzen, Ulrich (1921–)
Designed the Alley Theater, Houston (1968) and the Multi-categorical Animal Lab at Cornell University, Ithaca, New York (1974).

Fraternity house
A building used for social and residential purposes by an association of male students called a fraternity.

Freeform
Shapes that are characterized by a free-flowing rather than a geometric structure, resembling forms found in nature.

Free-form style
A style (1965–1973) relating to organic and biomorphic forms, such as kidney and boomerang shapes as opposed to rectangular or circular shapes produced by the compass. These forms were also popular in applied arts and the design of furniture.

Freestanding
A structural element that is fixed by its foundation at its lower end but not otherwise constrained throughout its vertical height.

French arch See **Arch**

French Colonial architecture
A style developed by the French colonists in America, particularly in New Orleans from 1700 onward; featured a symmetrical facade with a porch reached by steps and a projecting roof across the entire front and sometimes around the sides; wrought-iron balconies extended over the sidewalk. They typically had high steeply pitched roofs, decorated with ornamental finials at each end of the roof ridge.

Fresco
A mural painted into freshly spread moist lime plaster; in such work, ground water-based pigments unite with the plaster base; retouching is done after it has dried.

Fret See **Ornament**

Fretting
Decoration produced by cutting away the background of a pattern in stone or wood leaving the rest as grating.

Fretwork
A rectangular motif used in early Greek border ornament or pattern, rarely as an isolated ornamental device: an angular counterpart of the spiral or wave.

Frieze
An elevated horizontal continuous band or panel that is usually located below the cornice, and often decorated with sculpture in low relief.

Frieze-band window See **Window**

Frigidarium
The cold water swimming bath in a Roman bath.

Front-gabled See **Gable**

Frontispiece
The decorated front wall or bay of a building; a part or feature of a facade, often treated as a separate element, and ornamented highly; an ornamental porch or main pediment.

Frontispiece

Frosted
Rusticated, with formalized stalactites or icicles; given an even, granular surface to avoid shine; closely reticulated or matted to avoid transparency.

Full round
Sculpture in full and completely rounded form.

Fuller, R. Buckminster (1895–1983)
Developed the geodesic dome, protecting an interior space, suitable for any arrangement, by using a vast "space frame." The most well known of these are the American Pavilion, Expo 67, Montreal (1967), and Epcot Center, Disneyworld, Florida (1982).

Functionalism

A design movement (1920–1940) evolved from several previous movements in Europe, advocating the design of buildings and furnishings as a direct fulfillment of functional requirements. The construction, materials, and purpose was clearly expressed, with the aesthetic effect derived chiefly from proportions and finish, to the exclusion or subordination of purely decorative effects.

Funk architecture

An alternative form of architecture (1969–1979), using makeshift structures erected from waste materials, developed by members of rural communes.

Furness, Frank (1839–1912)

American architect who designed the Provident Life and Trust Company, Philadelphia (1876), in the high Victorian Gothic style, and the Academy of Fine Arts, also in Philadelphia (1876). Louis Sullivan worked in his office before moving to Chicago.

Furring

A series of parallel wood strips used to support and level plaster lathing, drywall, or sheathing, and to form an air space; typically used on walls, beams, columns, and ceilings.

Futurist style

A movement (1914–1916) that began with a publication by two young architects, Antonio Sant'Elia and Mario Chiattone. They presented a series of designs for a city of the future. Their manifesto proclaimed that architecture was breaking free from tradition, starting from scratch. It had a preference for what is light and practical. None of these designs were ever constructed.

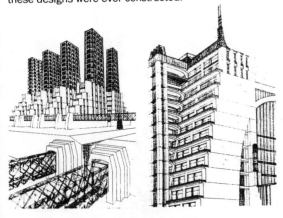

Gg

Gable
The entire triangular end of a wall, above the level of the eaves, the top of which conforms to the slope of the roof which abuts against it; sometimes stepped and sometimes curved in a scroll shape.

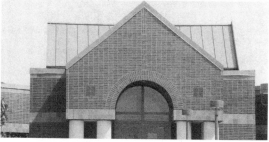

bell gable
A gable-end parapet with an opening that supports a bell: it is found in Spanish Colonial architecture.

broken gable
A vertical surface at the end of a building having a broken-pitch roof; extending from the level of the cornice to the ridge of the roof.

crowstep gable
A masonry gable extended above the roof with a series of setbacks; often found in European medieval architecture, especially Dutch architecture.

Dutch gable
A gable, each side of which is multicurved and surmounted by a pediment.

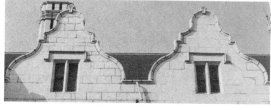

Flemish gable
A masonry gable extended above the roof with setback stages that may be stepped or curved profiles in any of a wide variety of combinations.

front-gabled
A term describing a building having a gable on its main facade.

hanging gable
A small extension of the roof structure at the gable end of a barn or house.

hipped gable
The end of a roof formed into a shape intermediate between a gable and a hip; the gable rises about halfway to the ridge, resulting in a truncated shape, the roof being inclined backward from this level.

mouse-tooth gable
Dutch term referring to the infilling in the steps of a crowstep gable. Brick is laid at an angle that is perpendicular to the slope of the gable within the steps, and the gable is finished off with a smooth stone coping.

multicurved gable
A gable having an outline containing two or more curves on each side of a central ridge, as in a Flemish gable.

paired gables
A facade having two gables.

parapeted gable
A gable end wall that projects above a roof; typical shapes include boltel, fractable, and square.

side gable
Gable whose face is on one side of a house: perpendicular to the main facade.

straight-line gable
Gable that rises above the roof line; with a straight incline following the roof below it.

stepped gable
A gable with a stepped profile; usually constructed of brick; also called a corbiestep gable or a crowfoot gable.

wall gable
A portion of a wall that projects above the roof line in the form of a gable.

Gable front
Building with a gable roof where the main entrance is located in one of the gable ends; also known as front-gabled.

Gable ornamentation
Any type of decorative element, such as spindlework or scrollwork at the apex of a gable.

Gable post
A post directly under the ridge of one end of a gable roof; supports the intersection of the bargeboard at the roof edge.

142

Gable roof See **Roof**

Gable wall See **Wall**

Gable window See **Window**

Gabled tower
A tower that is finished with a gable on two or all sides, instead of terminating in a spire.

Gabriel, Jaques (1698–1782)
One of the greatest eighteenth-century Neo-classical architects in France; architect to King Louis XV, with additions to the Royal Palace at Fontainbleau (1748) and the Place de la Concorde, Paris (1753).

Gaine
A decorative pedestal, taking the place of a column, tapered downward and rectangular in cross section, forming the lower part of a herm, on which a human bust is mounted; often with a capital above.

Galleria
A long interior passageway lit by a continuous skylight and lined with retail stores; also called an arcade.

Gallery
A long covered area acting as a corridor inside or on the exterior of a building or between buildings. A room; often top-lit, used for the display of artwork.

Garage
A building or portion of a residence where motor vehicles are kept: a place for repairing and maintaining vehicles.

Garden
A piece of ground, open or enclosed, appropriated to plants, trees, shrubs, or other landscape features.

143

Garden apartment
A ground-floor apartment with access to a garden or other adjacent outdoor space: two-or three-story apartment buildings with communal gardens.

Garden house
A summer house in a garden or garden-like situation.

Gargoyle
A spout carrying water from the roofs above, frequently carved with grotesque figures or animals with open mouths, from which water is discharged away from the building's walls.

Garland
An ornament in the form of a bank, wreath, or festoon of leaves, fruits, or flowers.

bay leaf garland
A stylized laurel leaf used in the form of a garland to decorate torus moldings.

Garnier, Charles (1825–1898)
A French architect who developed the luxury flat style in the rebuilding of Paris. He also designed the grandiose Neo-baroque Opera House in Paris (1861), a triumph of rich color, ornate decoration, and highly disciplined control of mass and space. Other work includes the casino at Monte Carlo, France (1878).

Garnier, Tony (1869–1948)
While a student in Rome, published *Cite Industrial Designs* in 1918, which constituted a revolutionary plan for a model town of 35,000. This publication influenced Le Corbusier and other Modernists.

Garret
A room or space located just beneath the roof of a house usually with sloping ceilings; sometimes called an attic.

Gate
A passageway in a fence, wall, or other barrier which slides, lowers, or swings shut, and is sometime of open construction.

gopuram
In Indian architecture, a monumental gateway tower to a Hindu temple, usually highly decorative.

moon gate
A circular opening in a wall, in traditional Chinese architecture.

pai-lou
A monumental Chinese arch or gateway with one, three or five openings, erected at the entrance to a palace, tomb, or processional way; they are usually built of stone in imitation of earlier wood construction.

torana
An elaborately carved ceremonial gateway in Indian Buddhist and Hindu architecture, with two or three lintels between two posts.

tori
A monumental, freestanding gateway to a Shinto shrine, consisting of two pillars with a straight crosspiece at the top and a lintel above It, usually curving upward.

Gatehouse
A building enclosing or accompanying a gateway for a castle, manor house, or similar building of importance.

Gate tower
A tower containing a gate to a fortress.

Gateway

A passageway through a fence or wall; the structures at an entrance or gate designed for ornament or defense.

Gaudi, Antonio (1852–1926)

One of the most original architectural talents, inspired by Islamic and Gothic sources, whose work is mainly found in Barcelona, Spain. Casa Vicens (1878) was his first work, a suburban house decorated with polychrome tiles and sinuous ironwork. The commission for La Sagrada Familia church (1884) with completed transept facades, with its extraordinary ceramic-covered spires, is his most fantastic work. The Palacio Guell (1885) is dominated by a pair of parabolic arches at the entrance and topped by chimneys encrusted with colored tiles. Casa Batlo (1906) has a unique tile roof and tile facade, and Casa Mila (1910) has an undulating facade and huge ceramic-covered chimney pots on the roof. Park Guell (1914) is a playful open space surrounded by undulating and tile-encrusted benches along with fanciful gatehouses with imaginative use of rock and tile.

Antonio Gaudi

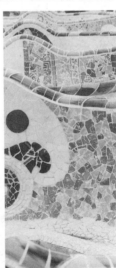

146

Antonio Gaudi

Gauge
To shape a brick by rubbing or molding it into a particular size.

Gauged arch See **Arch**

Gauged brick See **Brick**

Gazebo
A fanciful small structure, used as a summer house that is usually octagonal in plan with a steeply pitched roof that is topped by a finial. The sides are usually left open, or latticed between the supports.

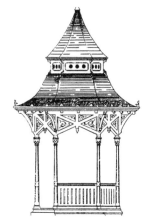

Geddes, Norman Bel (1893–1958)
American designer identified with the Streamlined style. Designed the General Motors Pavilion at the New York World's Fair (1939). He produced many interiors and developed a scheme for prefabricated housing.

Gehry, Frank O. (1929–)
Canadian-born American architect; who settled in Santa Monica, where he built several houses, specialized in using materials in an unusual way. Major early works include the California Aerospace Museum, Santa Monica (1982), and the Watt Disney Concert Hall, Los Angeles (1989).
    The recent work includes the Chait Day Headquarters, Venice, California (1989); the "Fred and Ginger" building, Prague (1995); and the Guggenheim Museum, Bilbao, Spain (1997).

Frank Gehry

Geminated
Coupled, as with columns and capitals.

Geminated capital See **Capital.**

General contractor
The building contractor who has legal responsibility for the entire construction project and who coordinates the work of all the subcontractors.

Geodesic dome See **Dome.**

Geometric style
The early development of the decorative age of English architecture (1200–1250), characterized by the geometrical forms of its window tracery.

Geometric tracery See **Tracery.**

Geometrical
Refers to forms that can be generated into three-dimensional plane figures and divided into three groups; continuous, such as those used in bands, enclosed panels, or flat patterns on walls.

Geometrical stair See **Stair**

Georgian architecture
A formal arrangement of parts within a symmetrical composition and enriched Classical detail characterize this style (1714–1776). The simple facade is often emphasized by a projecting pediment, with colossal pilasters and a Palladian window. It often includes dormers, and the entrances ornately decorated with transoms or fanlights over the doors. The style was transmitted through architectural pattern books.

Geothermal energy
Energy derived from the heat of the earth's interior, by tapping into reservoirs of steam in geothermal locations to drive steam turbines.

Gesso
A mixture of gypsum plaster, glue, and whiting; applied as a base coat for decorative painting.

Ghost mark
An outline that shows earlier construction that was removed; includes outlines created by missing plaster and patched holes showing the parts of the building that were demolished.

Gibbs surround
The surrounding trim of a doorway or window, consisting of alternating large and small blocks of stone, similar to quoins. These are often connected with a narrow raised band along the face of the door, window, or arch.

Gibbs, James (1682–1754)
English Neo-classical architect who created a restrained version of the Baroque style in Britain.

Giedion, Sigried (1888–1968)
Swiss art historian who became a powerful advocate of the Modern movement and with Le Corbusier, was a founder in CIAM. His book, *Space, Time, and Architecture* (1941), was de rigueur in schools of architecture. He also wrote several other books on architecture.

Gilbert, Cass (1859–1934)
Designed the Woolworth Building, New York City, which was the tallest building in America for 17 years. It was ornamented with Gothic details.

Gilding
Gold leaf, gold flakes, or brass, applied as a surface finish.

Gill, Irving (1870 - 1936)
Designed the Dodge House, Los Angeles, a composition of white-painted blocks reminiscent of contemporary European houses, similar to the cubistic style of Adolf Loos.

Gingerbread
The highly decorative and often superfluous wood-work applied to a Victorian style house or commercial structure.

Gingerbread style
A rich and highly decorated style (1830–1880) featuring the ornate woodworking of American buildings, particularly in vogue during the Victorian era.

Gingerbread style

Giotto, di Bondone (c. 1266–1337)
Italian architect; designed the Florence Cathedral campanile (1334), which combines Romanesque, Classical, and Gothic elements.

Girder
A large or principal beam used to support concentrated loads at isolated points along its length.

Girdle
A horizontal band ringing the shaft of a column.

Girt
In a braced frame, a horizontal member at an intermediate level between the columns, studs, or posts; a heavy beam, framed into the studs, which supports the floor joists

Glass
A hard, brittle, usually transparent or translucent substance, produced by melting a mixture of silica oxides; while molten, it may be easily blown, drawn, rolled, pressed, or cast to a variety of shapes. It can be transparent, translucent, or mirrored; and made non-glare, pigmented, or tinted. It can be shaped by casting, rolling, pressing, or baking. It can also be bonded to metal for use as an exterior cladding.

art glass
A type of decorative leaded glass window in which scenes or patterns are produced by using colored rather than stained glass; it is common in works of the Art Nouveau style.

colored glass
Originated over two thousand years ago when pieces of colored glass were embedded in heavy matrices of stone or plaster.

corrugated glass
A glass sheet manufactured by pressing molten glass in a mold, with a cross section in the form of a wave, having parallel ridges and valleys.

crown glass
An early form of window glass, cut from blown disks.

decorative glass
Embossing and sandblasting techniques create a subtle form of ornamentation. Etching and beveling are also used to create ornamentation in glass.

double glazing
Insulating glass composed of an inner and outer pane, with a sealed air space between them.

float glass
Sheets of glass made by floating the molten glass on a surface of molten metal, which produces a smooth, polished surface.

heat-absorbing glass
Glass whose solar transmittance is reduced by adding various coloring agents to the molten glass.

insulating glass
Glass that has insulating qualities, made by sandwiching two layers of glass separated by a vacuum sealed edge.

laminated glass
Two or more plies of flat glass bonded under heat and pressure to inner layers of plastic to form a shatter-resisting assembly that retains the fragments if the glass is broken; it is called safety glass.

leaded glass
Dates from the Middle Ages, where glass was set into malleable lead frames.

low-emissivity glass
Glass that transmits visible light while selectively reflecting the longer wavelengths of radiant heat; made by a coating either the glass itself or the transparent plastic film in the sealed air space of insulating glass.

luster glass
An iridescent glass, of the type made by Tiffany.

obscure glass
Glass that has one or both faces acid-etched or sandblasted to obscure vision.

opal glass
Glass that contains calcium phosphate, which is derived from bone ash, and which renders the glass white and opaque.

opalescent glass
A type of iridescent glass showing many colors; first used by Louis Comfort Tiffany in the late nineteenth century, and now called Tiffany glass.

painted glass
A type of stained glass formed by painting a plain piece of glass with enamel, then baking or firing it in a kiln at a high temperature.

patterned glass
Glass that has an irregular surface pattern formed in the rolling process to obscure vision or to diffuse light; usually on one side only, the other side is left smooth.

plate glass
A high-quality float glass sheet, formed by rolling molten glass into a plate that is subsequently ground and polished on both sides after cooling.

prismatic glass
Rolled glass that has parallel prisms on one face. These refract the transmitted light and thus change its direction.

reflective glass
Window glass having a thin, translucent metallic coating bonded to the exterior or interior surface to reflect a portion of the light and radiant heat and light that strikes it.

rolled glass
Molten glass from a furnace is passed through rollers to produce a pattern on one or both surfaces of the glass.

safety glass
Glass containing thin wire mesh reinforcement; glass laminated with transparent plastic; glass toughened by heat treatment, causing it to break into small fragments without splintering.

sheet glass
A float glass fabricated by drawing the molten glass from a furnace; the surfaces are not perfectly parallel, resulting in some distortion of vision. Used for ordinary window glass.

sound-insulating glass
Glass consisting of two lights in resilient mountings, separated by spacers, and sealed so as to leave an air space between them; the air space contains a dessicant to assure dehydration of the trapped air.

spandrel glass
An opaque glass used in curtain walls to conceal spandrel beams, columns, or other internal structural construction.

stained glass
Glass given a desired color in its molten state or by firing a stain into the surface of the glass after forming; used for decorative windows or transparent mosaics.

structural glass
Glass which is cast in the form of cubes, rectangular blocks, tile, or large rectangular plates: used widely for the surfacing of walls.

tempered glass
Annealed glass reheated to just below the softening point and then rapidly cooled with water. When fractured, it breaks into relatively harmless pieces.

tinted glass
Glass that has a chemical admixture to absorb a portion of the radiant heat and visible light that strikes it to filter out infrared solar energy, thereby reducing the solar heat gain.

vision-proof glass
Glass that has been given a pattern during its manufacture, so that it is not transparent.

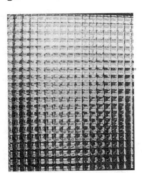

Glass block

Composed of two sheets of plate glass with an air space between them, formed into a sealed modular hollow block; laid up with mortar, similar to masonry blocks as a modular material, comes in several distinct styles, patterns and degrees of transparency and translucency.

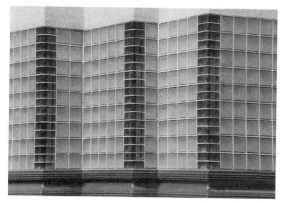

wire glass

Flat or patterned glass having a square or a diamond wire mesh embedded within the two faces to prevent shattering in the event of breakage or excessive heat. Wire glass is considered a safety glazing material.

Glass door See Door

Glass mullion system

A glazing system in which sheets of tempered glass are suspended from special clamps, stabilized by perpendicular stiffeners of tempered glass, and joined by a structural silicone sealant or by metal patch plates.

Glass mullion system

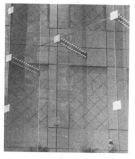

Glaze

A ceramic coating, usually thin, glossy, and glass-like, formed on the surface of pottery earthenware; the material from which the ceramic coating is made.

Glazed brick See Brick

Glazed tile See Tile

Glazed work

Brickwork built with enameled brick or glazed brick.

Glazing

The clear or translucent material through which light is transmitted into a building; usually glass, but also includes acrylic and other materials.

Glazing bars

Bars of wood or metal that hold panes of glass in place; also called astragals.

Globe

A spherical ornament, fabricated out of solid wood or a metal shell, usually found on the top of steeples and cupolas.

Glue-laminated arch See **Arch**

Gneiss See **Stone**

Goff, Bruce (1904–1982)

One of the most creative and idiosyncratic architects in America, who used found materials such as coal, rope, and glass cullets. His best-known works are the Ford House in Aurora, Illinois (1948), the Bavinger house in Norman, Oklahoma (1950), and the Price House in Bartlesville, Oklahoma (1956), all of which were treated with great individuality.

Bruce Goff

154

Gold leaf

Very thin sheets of beaten or rolled gold, used for gilding and inscribing on glass; usually contains a very small percentage of copper and silver. Heavy gold leaf can be classified as gold foil.

Goldberg, Bertrand (1913–)

Chicago architect most noted for the Hilliard Center Apartments (1966) and Marina City Apartments (1967), both in Chicago.

Golden mean

A proportional relationship devised by the Greeks that expresses the ideal relationship of unequal parts. It is obtained by dividing a line so that the shorter part is to the longer part as the longer part is to the whole line. It can be stated thus: _a is to b as b is to a + b_. If we assign the value of 1 to a, and solve as a quadratic equation, b = 1.618034. Therefore, the golden mean is 1:1.618.

Goodue, Bertram (1869–1924)

American architect; in partnership with Ralph Cram from 1892 to 1913. On his own, he designed St. Bartholomew's Church, New York City, the last in a Byzantine Roman-esque style. His most well known work is the Nebraska State Capitol, Lincoln (1920).

Bertram Goodue

Gopuram See Gate

Gorgoneion

In Classical decoration the mask of a gorgon, a woman with snakes for hair believed to avert evil influences.

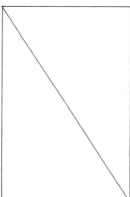 

Gothic arch See Arch

Gothic architecture

A revolutionary style of construction of the High Middle Ages in western Europe (1050–1530), which emerged from Romanesque and Byzantine forms. The term "Gothic" was originally applied as one of reproach and contempt.

The style was characterized by a delicate balance between the lateral thrust from loads and the force of gravity. It was most often found in cathedrals employing the rib vault, pointed arches, flying buttresses and the gradual reduction of the walls to a system of richly decorated fenestration.

The style's features were height and light, achieved through a mixture of skeletal structures and increasing use of windows. Walls were no longer necessary to support the roof and could be replaced with large, tall windows of stained glass. One of the finest and oldest French Gothic example is Notre Dame in Paris.

Gothic architecture

Gothic Revival style
A romantic style (1830–1860) distinguished by vertically pointed arches, steeply pitched complex gable roofs, finials, and medieval decorative motifs. Country houses featured wide verandas and octagonal towers or turrets. Windows in dormers had hood molds with gingerbread trim running along the eaves and gable ends. Variety was the standard of the style.

Gouache
A method of painting using opaque pigments pulverized in water and mixed with gum.

Grade beam See Beam

Graffiti
The designs resulting from painting words or symbols on a building, wall or other object.

Graffito
A decorative pattern produced by scratching the top layer of a two-color stucco finish.

Graham, Bruce (1925–)
Design partner in the Chicago office of SOM. He designed the John Hancock Building and the Sears Tower.

Graham, John
Designed the Space Needle at the Science Center, Seattle (1962).

Grain
The pattern of fibers found on the cut surface of wood.

Grandstand
The viewing platform with seats at a racecourse, parade, or sports event, typically covered with a roof.

Granite See Stone

Grapevine ornament See Ornament

Grate
A frame that consists of parallel metal bars, attached by cross bars at regular intervals; used as a grille or security device.

Gravel stop
A continuous band of bent sheet metal with a vertical or sloped projection that prevents gravel on a built-up roof from falling off.

Graves, Michael (1934–)
One of the most controversial American architects, he was identified as one of the New York Five, and first became known for a series of private houses based on reworked themes of Le Corbusier. His work was Postmodern. The Public Services Building, Portland, Oregon (1980), and the Humana Tower, Louisville, Kentucky (1982), the Whitney Museum of Art addition (1985), and the Walt Disney world, Dolphin and Swan Hotels (1988), are celebrated examples of his work.

Michael Graves

157 **Gravity retaining wall** See **Wall**

Greek architecture

The first manifestation of this style (800–300 B.C.) was a wooden structure of upright posts supporting beams and sloping rafters. The style was later translated into stone elements with a wood roof. It was a "kit of parts" characterized by austerity and free of ornate carvings.

The decorative column orders were an integral part of this style: the Doric, which is the simplest and sturdiest, the Ionic, which was more slender, and the Corinthian, which had a very elaborate capital.

Greek ornament is refined in character. The materials were limestone and marble, and were prepared with the highest standards of masonry, including sophisticated optical corrections for perspective (entasis).

Greek cross plan

A cruciform plan with four arms of equal length.

Greek Revival style

The Greek contribution to Neo-classical architecture (1750–1860) stood for a purity and simplicity of structure and form. The buildings are square or rectangular, proportions are broad, details are simple, facades are symmetrical and silhouettes are bold. Freestanding columns support a pedimented gable. Many government and civic buildings are designed in this style, which is more suited to these building types than to smaller domestic buildings.

Greene, Charles Sumner (1868–1957)

American-born architect, studied at MIT and set up practice with his brother Henry in Pasadena, California. They used projecting roofs, flat gables, and timber construction. The most well known is the Gambel House in Pasadena (1908).

Greene, Henry Mather (1870–1954)

Partner with Charles Sumner Greene, his brother. They both studied at MIT before setting up practice in California.

Greenhouse
A glass-enclosed, heated structure for growing plants and out-of-season fruits and vegetables under regulated, protected conditions.

Grid
Consists of a framework of parallel, crisscrossed lines or bars forming a pattern of uniform size; sets of intersecting members on a square or triangular matrix, which make up a three-dimensional structural system.

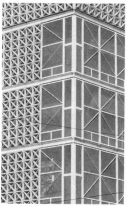

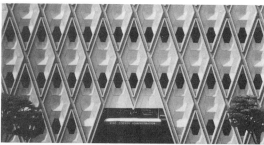

Grid-based organization See **Organization**

Gridiron plan
Town or city street layout based on a geometrical grid pattern.

Griffin See **Ornament: animal forms**

Griffin, Marion Mahony (1871–1961)
Worked for Frank Lloyd Wright in Oak Park, Illinois, and was responsible for many of the drawings of Wright's work published in the _Wasmuth Portfolio_ of 1910. She was married to architect Walter Burley Griffen.

Griffin, Walter Burley (1876–1937)
He worked in Chicago with Frank Lloyd Wright before being appointed director for the design and construction of the Federal Capitol at Canberra, Australia in 1913. Here he also designed many major works with his wife, Marion Lucy Mahoney (1871–1961).

Grille
An ornamental arrangement of bars to form a screen or partition, usually of metal, wood, stone, or concrete, used to cover, conceal, decorate, or protect an opening.

Grille

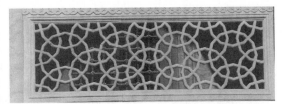

Grillwork
Materials arranged with voids to function as, or with the appearance of, a grille.

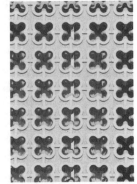

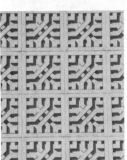

Grimshaw, Nicholas (1939–)
British architect; designed the British Pavilion, Seville Expo (1992), and the Waterloo international Terminal, London (1993).

Gris, Pierre Jeanneret (1896–1967)
Swiss architect, a relative of Le Corbusier, who joined the office of Perret and worked with Le Corbusier on designs and town planning schemes. He was a protagonist of the International Modern Movement, but was obscured by the fame of Le Corbusier.

Groin
The curved area formed by the intersection of two vaults.

Groin arch See Arch

Groined rib
A rib under the curve of a groin, used as a device to either mask or support it.

Groined vault See Vault

Gropius, Walter (1883–1969)
His design for the Bauhaus, Dessau, Germany (1925), was the first example of the new International-style architecture to be built. He left Germany in 1928. He designed the Graduate Center, Harvard University, Cambridge (1949), while professor of Architecture at Harvard.

Grotesque
Sculptured or painted ornament involving fanciful distortions of human and animal forms, sometimes combined with plant motifs, especially those without a counterpart in nature.

Grotesque

Grotto

A natural or artificial cave, often decorated with shells or stones and often incorporating waterfalls or fountains.

Ground floor

The floor or story of a building at or slightly above grade level; excluding the basement but including all the construction up to the floor above.

Ground joint See **Joint**

Ground line See **Perspective projection**

Ground plane See **Perspective projection**

Groundsill

In a framed structure, the sill which is nearest the ground or on the ground; used to distribute the concentrated loads to the foundation.

Grouped columns See **Columns**

Grouped pilasters See **Pilasters**

Grouping

Arrangement of the major architectural forms of a building; such as a main structure plus its wings, or the arrangement of elements on the facade.

Grout

Mortar containing a considerable amount of water so that it has the consistency of a viscous liquid, permitting it to be poured or pumped into joints, spaces, and cracks within masonry walls and floors.

Grouted masonry

Concrete masonry construction composed of hollow units when the hollow cells are filled with grout.

Gruen, Victor (1903–1980)

Viennese architect, who settled in the United States in 1938, starting his own firm in Los Angeles, specializing in shopping centers, such as Northland Center in Detroit (1954) and Southdale Center, Minneapolis.

Guarini, Guarino (1624–1683)

Trained as a mathematiciann he used this knowledge to create highly intricate compositions. Most were built in Turin, Italy.

Guest house

A separate residence for guests, or a small secondary house on a private estate.

Guilloche molding See **Molding**

Guimard, Hector (1867–1942)

Designed the metro stations of Paris using an Art Nouveau motif.

Guirgola, Romaldo (1920–)

Rome-born American architect; influenced primarily by the work of Louis Kahn. He designed the Volvo Headquarters, Stockholm, Sweden (1984), and the Parliament House of Australia, Canberra (1988). Partnered with American-born Ehrman Burkman Mitchell (1924–).

Gum See **Wood**

Gusset

A plate, usually triangular in shape, used to connect two or more members, or add strength to a framework at its Joints.

Gutta

A small, truncated cone-shaped ornament resembling a droplet used under the triglyph or the cornice in Classical architecture.

Gutter
A shallow channel of metal or wood at the edge of a roof eave to catch and drain water into a downspout.

Gwathmey, Charles (1938–)
Identified as one of the New York Five. He formed a partnership in 1971 with Robert Siegal. Most of their early work was private houses. Major other works include the Disney World Convention Center, Orlando (1990), and the Guggenheim Museum expansion, New York City (1992).

Gymnasium
In Greek and Roman architecture, a large open court for exercise, surrounded by colonnades and rooms for massages and lectures.

Gypsum board
A wallboard having a noncombustible gypsum core; covered on each side with a paper surface.

Gypsum plaster
A hard, fire-resistant, quick-setting plaster with ground gypsum mixed with a retardant as the main ingredient.

Hh

Hacienda
A large estate or ranch in areas once under Spanish influence; now the main house on such an estate.

Hadid, Zaha (1950–)
Iraqi architect; trained under Rem Koolhaas and associated with Deconstructivism. Her work is fragmented and jagged, as in the Monsoon Bar, Sapparo, Japan. Other work includes the extensions to the Dutch Parliament Building, the Hague (1978), the Peak Club, Hong Kong (1982), and the Cardiff Opera House (1994). Most of her designs have remained on paper.

Half arch See **Arch**

Half baluster
A baluster that projects from the surface to which it is attached, by about one-half its diameter.

Half column See **Column**

Half door See **Door**

Half landing See **Stair**

Half-round molding See **Molding**

Half-space landing See **Landing**

Half-timbered
Descriptive of buildings of the sixteenth and seventeenth centuries, which were built with strong timber foundations, supports, knees, and studs, and whose walls were filled in between with plaster or masonry materials.

Half-timbered

Half-timbered wall See **Wall**

Hall
A large room or building used for the transaction of public business and the holding of courts of justice; used also for public meetings and assemblies and other entertainment.

Hall chamber
A room directly above the hall on the upper floor or one opening directly off the hall on the ground floor.

Hall church
A church with side aisles as high, or nearly as high, as the central nave.

Hallway
A corridor or a passageway in a house, hotel, office, institutional or commercial building.

Halprin, Lawrence (1916–)
San Francisco-based landscape architect noted for his park designs employing cascading vegetation and waterfalls, as in the Seattle Freeway Park (1976).

Hammer brace
A bracket under a hammer beam to support it.

Hammer-beam roof See **Roof**

Handrail
A rail providing a handhold and serving as a support at the side of a stair or elevated platform.

Hanger
A strap or rod attached to an overhead structure to support a pipe, conduit, or the framework of a suspended ceiling; a stirrup bracket used to support the end of a beam or joist at a masonry wall or girder.

Hanging gable See **Gable**

Hanging stair See **Stair**

Hankar, Paul (1859–1901)
Belgian architect who became one of the protagonists of Art Nouveau, as in his designs for the Hotel Hankar (1893) and the Hotel Ciamberlani, both in Brussels. He was influenced by Japanese art, and his work in turn influenced Otto Wagner, who saw Hankar's lavish interiors in 1897.

Hardboard See **Wood**

Hardouin-Mansart, Jules (1646–1708)
French architect who designed the Church of the Invalides, Paris (1680), the most Baroque of Parisian churches, with a dome derived from St. Peter's, Rome.

Hardpan
An extremely hard soil containing gravel and boulders.

Hardwood See **Wood**

Hardy, Hugh (1932–)
American architect; formed a partnership with Malcolm Holzman and Norman Pfeiffer in New York City. The firm designed many theaters and became known for its use of disparate parts, seemingly thrown together, giving an impression of incompleteness.

Hugh Hardy,

Harmika
A square enclosure on top of the dome of a stupa.

Harmonic proportions
Relates the consonances of the musical harmonic scale to those of architectural design, particularly to those theories of proportion.

Harmony
The pleasing interaction or appropriate orderly combination of the elements in a composition.

Harrison, Peter (1716–1775)
Designed Kings Chapel, Boston, adapted from Gibb's style.

Harrison, Wallace K. (1895–1981)
Formed one of the most successful practices in America with Raymond Hood. He worked on Rockefeller Center, New York City; he designed the United Nations Head-quarters, with Le Corbusier; Phoenix Mutual Life Insurance building, Hartford; Lincoln Center, New York City, and the gigantic South Mall Government Complex in Albany.

Hatch
Opening in a floor or roof with a removable cover.

Haunch
The middle part of an arch, between the spring-ing point and the crown.

Haunch arch See **Arch.**

Haviland, John (1792–1852)
English-born American architect who designed in a severe Greek Revival style and later incorporated Egyptian Revivalist elements. He became know as the greatest Egyptian Revivalist.

Head
In general, the uppermost member of any structure. The upper horizontal cross-member between jambs, which forms the top of a door or window frame; may provide structural support for construction above.

Head mortar joint See **Mortar joint.**

Header
A masonry unit laid so that its short end is parallel to the face, overlapping two adjacent widths of masonry; a framing member supporting the ends of joists, transferring the weight of the latter to parallel joists and rafters.

Header bond See **Bond**

Headroom
The clear vertical distance between the ground or floor and the lowest point overhead.

Hearthstone
A single large stone forming the floor of a fireplace; materials such as firebrick and fireclay products, used to form a hearth.

Heartwood See **Wood**

Heat gain
Migration of heat into a space: by conduction, radiation, or exchange of air.

Heat loss
Migration of heat from a space: by conduction, radiation, or exchange of air.

Heat-absorbing glass See **Glass**

Heavy-timber construction
Fire-resistant construction obtained by using wood structural members of specified minimum size; wood floors and roofs of specified minimum thickness, and exterior walls of non- combustible construction.

Hejduk, John (1929–2000)
American architect and member of the New York Five, who studied and later became dean of the Cooper Union School of Art and Architecture, and designed the renovation of the school in 1975.

Helical reinforcement
Small-diameter reinforcement wrapped around the main or longitudinal reinforcement of columns; restraining the lateral expansion of the concrete under compression, and thus strengthening the column.

Helical stair See **Stair**

Helices
Figures like the tendrils of a vine.

Helix
Any spiral form, particularly a small volute or twist under the abacus of the Corinthian capital.

Hellenic architecture
Architecture (480–323 B.C.) of the Classical Greek period up to death of Alexander the great.

Hellenistic architecture
The style of Greek architecture (323–30 B.C.) after the death of Alexander the Great.

Hellmuth, George (1907–)
Design partner in the firm of Hellmuth Obata and Kassabaum, most noted for the Lambert–St. Louis Municipal Airport Terminal Building, St. Louis, Missouri (1955), (with Minuro Yamasaki).

Helm
A bulbous termination to the top of a tower, found in central and eastern Europe.

Helm roof See **Roof**

Hemispherical
A rounded form resembling half of a sphere bounded by a circle.

Hemispherical dome See **Dome**

Hemispherical vault See **Vault**

Hemlock See **Wood.**

Henry II (Deux) style
The second phase of the early French Renaissance, named after Henry II (1547–1559), who succeeded Francis I. It was characterized by Italian classic motifs which supplanted Gothic elements. The west side of the Louvre in Paris is the most characteristic example.

Henry IV (Quatre Style)
The early phase of the Classical period of French architecture (1586–1610), preceding the architecture of Louis XIII and Louis LXIV; the style was particularly strong in domestic architecture and town planning.

Heptagon
A seven-sided regular polygon; the angle included between the seven sides is 128.6 degrees.

Herm
A rectangular post, usually of stone, tapering downward, surmounted by a bust of Hermes or other divinity or by a human head.

Herrera, Juan de (1530–1597)
Spanish architect who developed a Renaissance style of great purity and simplicity that reflected the severe taste of his patron, King Phillip II. From 1572 he was in charge of completing the Escoral palace, Toledo.

Herringbone
A way of assembling, in a diagonal zigzag fashion, brick or similar rectangular blocks for paving; also strips of wood or other materials having rectangular shapes for facing walls

Herringbone blocking
Solid blocking between joists or studs with alternate blocks offset to allow for end nailing.

Herringbone bond See **Bond**

Herron, Ronald (1930–1998)
London-born architect associated with Archigram in the 1960s. His vision for "Walking Cities" was published widely and is exhibited internationally.

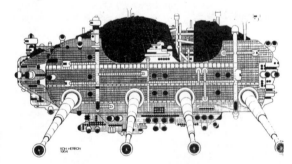

Hexagonal
Refers to a plane geometric figure containing six equal sides and six equal angles; occurring in nature as minerals, snow crystals, and honeycombs.

Hexastyle
A building having a row of six columns across a facade or portico.

Hickory See **Wood**

Hierarchy
An arrangement or system of ranking one above the other or arranged in a graded series or sequence such as size (large to small), shape (similar or dissimilar), and placement (emphasis or location).

Hieroglyph
A figure representing an idea and intended message; a word or root of a word; a sound that is part of a word, especially applied to the engraved marks and symbols found on the monuments of ancient Egypt .

High Renaissance
Refers to the culmination of the Italian Renaissance style in the late sixteenth century, characterized by the imitative use of the orders and classical compositional arrangements.

High-rise
Describing a building having a comparatively large number of stories, usually above 10-12 stories, and equipped with elevators.

High style
The more ornately detailed version of an architectural style; used in contrast to simpler examples, both from different periods or of the same period.

High-tech architecture
A style of architecture where mechanical and electrical building services and structural elements are not only exposed but emphasized by using different colors to indicate their respective functions, which accentuates the machinelike aspects of the building.

High Victorian
The more ornate architecture and interior design work of the Victorian period, which combines a variety of stylistic sources with great freedom.

High Victorian Gothic
A style characterized by complex exteriors, often with bays, towers and turrets, typically with contrasting colors and textures of brick or stone, especially as horizontal bands and voussoirs in alternating colors.

High-light window See **Window**

Hildebrandt, Johann Lucas von (1668–1745)
Leading Austrian architect, pupil of Fontana and admirer of Guarini. His Baroque facades are plain, while the interiors are dramatic and richly decorated. Works include the Residenz, Wurzburg, Germany and the Belvedere, Vienna (1724).

Hinge
A movable joint used to attach, support, and turn a door about a pivot, consisting of two plates joined by a pin which supports the door and connects it to its frame, enabling it to swing open or closed.

Hip
The external angle at the junction of two sloping roofs or sides of a roof: the rafter at the angle where two sloping roofs or sides of a roof meet.

Hip knob See **Ornament**

Hip rafter See **Rafter**

Hip roof See **Roof**

Hip and valley roof See **Roof**

Hipped dormer See **Dormer**

Hipped end
The sloping triangularly shaped end of a hipped roof.

Hipped gable See **Gable**

Hippodrome
In ancient Greece, a stadium for horse and chariot racing.

Historiated
Ornament incorporating human or animal figures or plants that have a narrative as distinct from a purely decorative function.

Historic district
Definable geographical area containing a number of related historic sites, buildings, structures, features, or objects that are united by past events. It also includes those linked esthetically by plan or physical development; that has been designated on a local, state, or on a national register of historic places; may encompass a neighbor-hood or all of a small town; some districts may comprise individual elements separated geographically but linked by association or history.

Historic preservation
Encompasses a broad range of activities related to preservation and conservation of the built environment by physical and intellectual methods.

Historic structure
Structure famous because of its association with a historic event, or the history of the locality.

Historical frieze
A frieze decorated with bas-relief scenes illustrating a historical event.

Historical marker
A permanent, descriptive sign or plaque affixed or adjacent to a historic building or other historic site.

Historical monument
Building or site having architectural or historical, municipal, state, or national significance.

Historical research
The study of documents: photographs, publications, and other data concerning a historic site, building, structure, or object.

Historic significance
The importance of an element, building, or site owing to its involvement with a significant event, person, or time period because it is an example of a past architectural style.

Hittite architecture
An architecture (2000–1200 B.C.) found in northern Syria and Asia Minor, characterized by fortifications constructed with stone masonry and gateways ornamented with sculpture.

Hoffman, Josef (1870–1956)
Designed the Stocklet House, Brussels, Belgium (1905). The exterior was enhanced with marble and bronze, while the interior featured mosaics by Gustav Klimt.

Hoist
A projecting beam with block and tackle, used for lifting goods; often seen above openings in the upper stories of medieval houses. Also, a platform for lifting people and/or materials. The platform is lifted by cables and is contained within an open frame that is supported by the building

Holabird, William (1854–1923)
Designed the Tacoma Building, Chicago, Illinois, a 12-story building that established the Chicago School of Architects as leaders in skyscraper design.

Holl, Elias (1573–1646)
Leading Renaissance architect in Germany, influenced by Palladio and Mannerism, but modified them by using typically German features such as high gables.

Holl, Steven (1947–)
American architect; designed the Chapel of St. Ignatius, Seattle (1997).

Hollien, Hans (1934–)
Austrian-born architect, who established his reputation with small well-crafted shops, detailed with meticulous care, and in sharp contrast to the surrounding facades. He also designed museums, among them the Museum of Modern Art, Frankfurt (1987), and the Haas House, Vienna (1987).

Hollow block masonry See **Masonry**

Hollow-core door See **Door**

Hollow masonry unit See **Masonry**

Hollow molding See **Molding**

Hollow square molding See **Molding**

Hollow tile See **Tile**

Hollow-tile floor See **Floor**

Hollyhock ornament See **Ornament.**

Homestead
A piece of land, limited to 160 acres, deemed adequate for the support of one family.

Homesteading
The process of acquiring land by occupying and using it; may be done through the Homestead Act or without official sanction.

Homogeneous
Likeness in nature or kind: similar, congruous and uniform in composition or structure throughout.

Honeycomb
Any hexagonal structure or pattern, or one resembling such a structure or pattern.

Honeysuckle ornament See **Ornament**

Honnecourt, Villard de (c. 1175–1235)
French architect whose notebook is an invaluable source
Of information on thirteenth-century building materials.

Hood
A projection above an
opening, such as a door or
window serving as a
screen or as protection
against the weather.

Hood mold See **Molding**

Hood, Raymond (1881–1934)
Won the competition with John Mead Howells to design
the Chicago Tribune Tower in 1922, a high point in
Beaux-Arts eclecticism with a Gothic superstructure. He
designed both the Daily News Building (1929) and the
McGraw-Hill building (1930) in New York City, in the Art
Deco Style.

Hopper window See **Window.**

Horizon line See **Perspective projection**

Horizontal cornice See **Cornice**

Horn
The diagonally projecting points of the Corinthian and
Composite orders; they are usually chamfered to protect
the sharp edges.

Horse See **Ornament: animal forms**

Horseshoe arch See **Arch**

Horta, Victor (1861–1947)
The leading architect in the Art Nouveau style (c. 1900).
The Tassel House, Brussels, Belgium (1892) was his first
work in the Art Nouveau style. Both the L'Innovation
department store (1901) and the Maison de Peuple
(1899), Brussels, Belgium (1901), had large metal and
glass Art Nouveau facades (both now demolished).

Hospital
A building or part thereof used for the medical,
obstetrical, or surgical care of patients on a 24-hour
basis.

Hotel
A building with rooms or suites for rent by the day;
typically includes public facilities for dining.

Hot-rolled sections
Structural steel sections produced by passing a red-hot
billet through a series of rollers, gradually forming it
closer to the desired shape.

House
A building in which people live.

Housing code
Regulations that define the livability of a housing unit;
usually requires minimum physical requirements for
light, ventilation, security, room size, and fire egress.

Hovel
A shed open at the sides and covered overhead for
the shelter of livestock, produce, or people; a poorly
constructed and ill-kept house.

Howe truss See **Truss**

Howe, George (1886–1973)
American architect, trained at the Ecole des Beaux Arts
in Paris, but abandoned the style in favor of modernism.
With William Lescaze, he designed the Philadelphia
Saving Fund Society office building, the paradigm of an
International Modernist skyscraper. He later joined Louis
Kahn, and in 1950 became chairman of the Department
of Architecture at Yale University.

H-section
A rolled-steel member with
an H-shaped cross section
with parallel flanges and
faces; used for structural
columns and piles, due to
its ability to withstand
rotation; usually square
in its outer dimensions.

Human scale See **Scale**

Hunt, Richard Morris (1827–1895)
Trained in France, he produced buildings in the United
States in a variety of styles, mainly grandiose pastiche,
for millionaire clients.

Hut
A small, simple shelter or dwelling.

Hydraulic elevator
An elevator powered by the energy of a liquid under pressure in a cylinder which acts on a piston or plunger to move the elevator car up and down on guide rails.

Hyperbola
The section of a right circular cone by a plane that intersects the cone on both sides of the apex.

Hyperbolic paraboloid
A shell in the form of a hyperbolic paraboloid. Generated by two systems of straight lines, its formwork is more readily constructed from straight pieces of timber than that of a dome.

Hyperthrum
A latticed window constructed over the door of an ancient building.

Hyperthyrum
A frieze and cornice that is arranged and decorated in various ways for the lintel over a door.

Hypostyle hall
A structure whose roofing was supported within the perimeter by groups of columns or piers of more than one height; clerestory lights were sometimes introduced; prevalent in ancient Egyptian architecture.

Ii

I-beam See **Beam**

Icon
An image of sacred personages that are objects of veneration; found on buildings.

Icosahedron
A regular polygon bounded by 20 equilateral triangles, with 12 vertices and 20 edges.

Ictinus (c. 5th C B.C.)
Designed the Parthenon, with Callicrates, and the Temple of Apollo Epicurius, Bassae, which had a Doric Order outside, an Ionic Order inside, and a Corinthian Order at the end.

Igloo
An Eskimo house constructed of snow blocks or various other materials such as wood, sod, poles and skins; when of snow, a domed structure is employed.

Image See **Design drawing.**

Imbrex
A curved tile, typically a half-cylinder shape; used to cover joints between roofing tiles.

Imbrication
Overlapping rows of shaped tiles or shingles that resemble overlapping fish scales; it is also called fishscale pattern.

Imhotep (c. 2600 B.C.)
History's first named architect, counselor to King Zoser of Egypt. He created the huge funerary complex at Saqqara; its stepped pyramid design, sophisticated stonework, and use of columns set the pattern for Egyptian monuments for 2,500 years.

Imitation
The representation of one material with another, generally copying the color and surface appearance of another material; the most common form is wood graining and marbleizing.

Impact resistance
Capacity of a material to resist loads that are suddenly applied.

Imperial dome See **Dome**

Impermeable
Resistance to penetration by fluids or vapor through the material.

Impervious
Resistant to water.

Impluvium
A pool for receiving water draining from the roof in an Ancient Roman atrium.

Impost
The horizontal molding or capital on top of a pilaster, pier, or corbel which receives and distributes the thrust at the end of an arch.

Impost

In cavetto See **Relief**

In the clear
The uninterrupted linear measurement of a space; not including the structural parts themselves.

Inca architecture
The last of the Pre-Columbian cultures (1200–1400), buildings were characterized by megalithic masonry, as exemplified in the ceremonial buildings of the mountain city Machu Picchu, the last fortress to resist the Spanish invaders.

Incident
Subordinate to the whole scheme, but used to give points of reference along the way, and temporarily create interest.

Incise
To cut a shallow mark into a material.

Inclinator
A platform, open or enclosed, running on an inclined rail for moving passengers to a higher level at an inclined angle, rather than as a vertical-lift elevator.

Incombustible
Material that does not burn in a standard test in a furnace.

Incrustation
The covering of wall surfaces with some precious material, such as tile or jewels.

Indented
A gap left by the omission of stone, brick, or block units in a course of masonry, used for bonding future masonry.

Indented joint See **Joint**

Indented molding See **Molding.**

Indian (Buddhist) architecture
The earliest surviving buildings (300 B.C.–320 A.D.) are of timber and mud-brick construction, of which the stupa is the most characteristic; it is a hemispherical mound with a processional path around the perimeter and elaborately carved gateways. The most typical is the stupa at Sanchi.

Indian (Buddhist) architecture

In rock-cut Buddhist temples, the main forms and details follow early wooden prototypes, with elaborately carved stone shrines in which the exterior is more important than the interior.

Indian (Hindu) architecture

All types of temples in this style (600–1750) consist of a small unlit shrine crowned by a spire and preceded by one or more porch-like halls, used for religious dancing and music. The stone was laid up rough-cut and carved in place by Hindu sculptors who treated every element on every surface as unique, using a repetition of the sculptural forms to achieve a unifying context. There was no attempt to evolve a style or to perfect any particular pillar or column.

Indian (Hindu) architecture

Indian (Hindu-Buddhist) architecture

The Hindu and Buddhist religions had a strong influence on Far East temple architecture (1113–1150). One of the most well known and representative sites is Angkor Wat located in Cambodia, a temple complex of shrines that was intended as a funerary monument.

It is perhaps one of the world's largest religious structures and was conceived as a "temple mountain" within an enormous enclosure and surrounded by a wide moat. A monumental causeway, framed by giant mythical serpents leads to the entrance gate. The temple is built on a series of stepped terraces, surrounded by towers at each corner.

Vaulted galleries receive light from an open colonnade illuminating the continuous relief friezes which adorn the inner walls. The central sanctuary is a large pagoda-like tower on top of a stepped pyramid. It is joined by passageways to towers at each of the four corners at the base.

Indian (Jain) architecture
An architecture (1000–1300) in which temples are enclosed shrines preceded by an open porch, which is often elaborately carved. They have a lighter appearance and are more elegant than Hindu temples.

Indigenous American architecture
The native styles (500 B.C.–1500 A.D.) range from the wigwams and long houses of forested areas, teepees of the Plains Indians, igloos of the Eskimos to the sophisticated communal pueblo cities carved out of mountainsides or built out of adobe in the Southwest.

Indirect lighting
Lighting reflected from the ceiling or other surface, not received directly from a luminaire.

Indus Valley architecture
Cities that flourished in the Indus Valley (1500–1200 B.C.) were carefully planned on a grid system, with main boulevards forming rectangular blocks; they were mostly of mud-brick construction.

Industrial design
Utilizing the resources of technology to create and improve products and systems which serve humans, taking into account factors such as safety, economy, and efficiency in production, distribution, and use.

Industrial Revolution style
The evolution of this style (1750–1890) was based on the production of iron and steel in quantities that could be used as a primary building material. The first iron frame structures were industrial buildings, which evolved into the steel frame skyscrapers of modern times. The few pioneers of this new style were engineers and were not architects. Walls were still made of masonry over a steel skeleton, and the use of large glass skylights was widespread.

Informal balance See Balance

Infrastructure
Any off-site utilities, services, and structures that serve a real estate development; may include gas, water, and electric service, water and sanitary sewer systems, roads, railroads; sometimes used to refer to facilities within a site or building.

Inlay
A shaped piece of one material embedded in another, usually in the same plane, as part of a surface ornamentation.

Inn
A place which provides eating and drinking, but not lodging, for the public; a tavern.

Inscription
Lettering that is carved or engraved in stone or wood, or on the surface of other materials, often of monumental scale, used primarily on exterior surfaces.

In situ pile
A concrete pile cast in its final location, with or without a casing, as distinct from a pile that is precast and subsequently driven.

Inspection
An on-site examination of construction to determine whether it is being performed according to the drawings, specifications, and building codes; may include the examination of concrete reinforcement, repointing, steel connections, and waterproofing installations.

Insulated column See column

Insulating glass See Glass.

Insulation
A material used to reduce transmission of sound or heat; types include batt insulation, loose fill insulation, and sprayed urathane foam.

Intaglio
Incised carving in which the forms are hollowed out of the surface; the relief in reverse, often used as a mold.

Intaglio

Intarsia
Italian term for the flat decorations made from pieces of variously colored woods, inlaid to form ornamental patterns, architectural perspectives, or figurative scenes.

Integral porch
A porch whose floor is set within the main structure of the house, rather than being attached to the house.

Integrated ceiling
A suspended ceiling system in which acoustical, illumination, and air-handling components are combined as an integral part of a grid.

Intelligent building
A building designed with extensive automated systems to detect, diagnose and control the response to varying environmental requirements.

Interaxial span
The distance from axis to axis of columns, which includes the width of one column; one module greater than the intercolumniation.

Intercolumniation
The spacing of the columns according to a system of proportions used in Classical architecture, based on the diameter of the column as the governing module.

Interdome See **Dome**

Interfenestration
The space between the windows in a facade.

Interior door See **Door**

Interior wall See **Wall**

Interlace
An ornament of bands or stalks elaborately intertwined, sometimes includeing fantastic images.

Interlaced
Intermixed forms that cross over each other with alternation as if woven together.

Interlaced arcade See **arcade**

Interlaced Arches
Arches, usually circular, so constructed that their forms intersect each other.

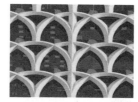

Interlaced Ornament
A band of ornamental figures that are overlapped or intertwined to create resultant forms.

Interlocked
Two or more components, members, or items of equipment which are arranged mechanically or electrically to operate in some specific relationship with each other.

Interlocking
Forms that are united firmly or joined closely by hooking or dovetailing.

Interlocking joint See **Joint**

Intermediate rib
A subordinate vault rib between primary ribs.

International style

A style of architecture (1920–1945) in both Europe and America pioneered by Le Corbusier, which spread to the Bauhaus, where it was the most influential. It was characterized by an emphasis on function combined with a rejection of traditional decorative motifs and regional characteristics.

It was further characterized by flat roofs, smooth and uniform surfaces, large expanses of windows and projecting or cantilevered upper floors. The complete absence of ornamentation is typical, and cubistic shapes were fashionable. White was the preferred color.

Horizontality was emphasized with windows that continued around corners. Roofs without eaves terminated flush with the plane of the wall. Wood and metal casement windows were set flush to the wall as well. Sliding windows were popular, and clerestory windows were also used extensively.

There were fixed panes of glass from floor to ceiling; and curtain-like walls of glass were common. Popular building materials were reinforced concrete, steel frames, and an unprecedented use of prefabricated parts, since the style had its roots in industrial architecture. The resultant forms were much akin to cubist and abstract art.

Interpenetrate

A decorative feature, such as a molding, that enters another element, such as a column, and reappears on the other side; it was commonly found in the Gothic Revival style.

Interrupted arch

A segmental pediment whose center has been omitted, often to accommodate an ornament

Intersecting tracery See **Tracery**

Intersecting vault See **Vault**

Interstices

Spaces or intervals between parts of a structure or between components.

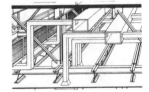

Interstitial

Forming a narrow or small space between parts of other elements, or between floors in a structure.

Interstitial condensation

Condensation that occurs within spaces inside the construction, as opposed to surface condensation.

Interweaving counterpoint See **Counterpoint**

Intonaco See **Plaster**

Intrados

The inner curve or face of an arch or vault forming the concave underside.

Inverted arch See **Arch**

Ionic order
An order of architecture invented by the Greeks, distinguished by an elegantly molded base; tall, slender shafts with flutes separated by fillets; and capitals, using a spiral volute that supports an architrave with three fascias; an ornamental frieze, and a cornice corbeled out on egg-and-dart and dentil moldings.

Iranian architecture
Decorative patterned brickwork, colored tile and molded stucco characterize this style (500–1000). Other attributes are the use of stalactite vaults. The essential elements are richly decorated surfaces with brightly colored tiles and molded stucco. The minaret evolved into a standard form that had an influence on Indian architecture.

Iron See **Metal**

Iron Age
The period (700 B.C.) characterized by the introduction of iron metallurgy for tools and weapons.

Iron framing
A system of structural ironwork for buildings.

Ironwork
Objects made of cast iron or wrought iron; most often with utilitarian form in colonial America, but thereafter elaborate and ornamental.

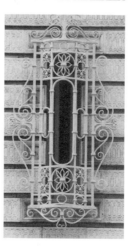 

I-section See **Beam**

Islamic architecture

Mesopotamian and Graeco-Roman forms are the two main sources for this style (600–1500), which makes use of symbolic geometry, using pure forms such as the circle and square. The major sources of decorative design are floral motifs, geometric shapes and Arabic calligraphy.

The major building types are the mosque and the palace. Mosque plans are based on strongly symmetrical layouts featuring a rectangular courtyard with a prayer hall.

Forms are repetitive and geometrical; the surfaces are richly decorated with glazed tiles, carved stucco and patterned brickwork, or bands of colored stonework. Plaster made from gypsum was carved and highly polished to give it a marble-like finish.

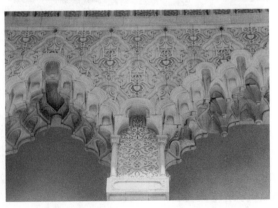

Isolation

Reduction of vibration or sound; usually involving resilient surfaces or mountings or discontinuous construction.

Isolation joint See **Joint.**

Isometric projection See **Projection drawing**

Isozaki, Arata (1931–)

Japanese architect who synthesized western and Japanese themes, concentrating on the clarity of geometry and pure forms as in the Gumma Prefectural Museum of Fine Arts, Takasaki (1974). His recent works include the Museum of Contemporary Art, Los Angeles (1981), and Team Disney Headquarters, Buena Vista, Florida (1990).

Italian Villa style

The main feature of this style (1830–1880) is the combination of a tall tower with a two-story L- or T-shaped floor plan. Gently pitched roofs resembling the pediment of Classical temples had wide projecting eaves. Windows are grouped into threes or placed within arcades. A smooth stucco finish highlighted Classic simplicity, while exuberant ornamentation recalls the Baroque. The overall massing is asymmetrical, intending to produce a picturesque quality.

Italianate style

A style (1840–1880) typified by a rectangular two or three-story house with wide eaves supported by large brackets, tall, thin first-floor windows, and a low pitched roof that is topped with a cupola. There are pronounced moldings, details and rusticated quoins. Earmarks of the style are arched windows with decorative "eyebrows" and recessed entryways. The style appeared in cast-iron facades, whose mass produced sections featured many stylized classical ornaments.

Italianate style

Iwan
In Near Eastern architecture, a large porch or shallow hall with a pointed barrel vault, as in the Sassanian palace at Ctesiphon and many later Islamic structures where it served as an entrance, or faces a courtyard.

Jj

Jack rafter See **Rafter**

Jacobean style
An English architectural and decorative style (1600–1625) adapting an Elizabethan style to continental Renaissance influence, named after James I.

Jahn, Helmut (1940–)
German-born American architect; joined the firm of C.F. Murphy in Chicago, in 1967. Studied with Mies van der Rohe, but his later work moved to a new richness of expression drawing on aspects of Art Deco for a unique expression. In Chicago, he designed O'Hare International Airport (1965); the Exhibition Building at McCormick Place (1971); Xerox Center (1980), and the State of Illinois Center (1985). He began incorporating High-Tech and Art Deco inspired elements in his later high-rise office structures, such as 750 Lexington Avenue, New York (1989), and Messe Tower, Frankfurt, Germany (1991).

Jamb

The side of a window, door, chimney, or any other vertical opening.

Jamb shaft

A small shaft having a capital and a base, placed against the jamb of a door or window.

Japanese architecture

An architecture (500–1700) based exclusively on timber construction, strongly influenced by Chinese design. Simple pavilion structures consist of a wooden framework of uprights and tie beams supported by a wooden platform.

Nonbearing walls are constructed of plaster and wood, and sliding partitions of light translucent screens divide interior spaces, with doors and windows of lightweight material.

Tiled hipped roofs project wide overhangs with upturned eaves as the result of elaborate bracket systems. Stone is used only for bases, platforms, and fortification walls.

Great emphasis is placed on the integration of buildings with their surroundings, with open verandas providing the transition. There is a strictly modular approach to the layout, based on the tatami mat, which governs the entire design of the house. Carpenters became skilled in designing individual types of wooden joints.

Japanese architecture

Jefferson, Thomas (1743–1826)

American statesman and third president of the United States, and a gifted amateur architect. Inspired by Palladio, he designed Monticello, Virginia, his own house, in 1769, and the University of Virginia, Charlottesville (1817–1826).

Jenney, William Le Baron (1832–1907)

Studied in Paris, and set up an office in Chicago. He was the first to use structural steel in a building for columns and girders. They were prototype skyscrapers. He taught Sullivan, Holabird, Roche, and Burnham in the practice of constructing tall buildings.

Jensen-Klint, P.V. (1853–1930)
A Danish architect whose design for the Grundtvig Church in Copenhagen (1926) is one of the most imaginative of Scandinavian designs. With a Gothic flavor, and built entirely of brick, it features a steep stepped-gabled facade resembling organ pipes.

Jerde, Jan (1940–)
American-born architect whose high-tech projects include the Fremont Street Experience redevelopment, Las Vegas (1995), and Canal City, Fukuoka, Japan (1996).

Jerkinhead
Gable end that slopes back at the top to form a small hipped roof end; also called a hipped gable.

Jerkinhead roof See Roof

Jettied house
A building having a second story which overhangs the lower one.

Jetty
The upper story that juts out over the lower story of a timber-framed house.

Jib door See Door

Joggle joint See Joint

Joggle post
A post made of two or more pieces joggled together.

Jogglework
A stone keyed by joggles.

Johansen, John (1916–)
American architect; he worked with Marcel Breuer and SOM. He is best known for the circular Chancellery for the U.S. Embassy, Dublin (1958), and the Mummer's Theater, Oklahoma City (1970).

Johnson, Philip (1906–)
His New Canaan glass house (1949) saw the style of Mies Van der Rohe reach its ultimate development. It is a glazed box in which only the bathroom in enclosed. He designed the Seagrams Building (with Mies Van der Rohe) in New York City (1958). Other works include the Museum of Modern Art additions and sculpture garden, the New York State Theater at Lincoln Center, New York City (1964), and Kline Science Center (with Richard Foster) at Yale University, New Haven (1965). His works with John Burgee include the IDS Center, Minneapolis (1972); Boston Public Library addition, Boston (1972); and Pennzoil Place, Houston (1976).

Philip Johnson

He designed the Crystal Cathedral, Garden Grove, California (1980); PPG Place, Pittsburgh (1981). He also designed the Transco Tower (with Morris Aubrey), Houston (1983), and the AT&T Building (with John Burgee), New York City (1984).

Joint
The space between the stones in masonry or between the bricks in brick work. In concrete work, joints control the shrinkage on large areas and isolate independent elements.

angle joint
Any joint formed by uniting two members at a corner which results in a change of direction.

bevel joint
Any joint in which the ends of the two abutting elements are cut at an angle, especially when not forming a right angle.

blind joint
A joint that is invisible.

bridle joint
A carpentry joint connecting a slotted end of one timber to the double-notched end of another timber; used to connect a rafter to a tie beam or two rafters at a ridge.

broken joint
A pattern where the elements are installed so that the adjacent butt joints between pieces are not aligned, such as in flooring and brickwork.

butt joint
A plain square joint between two members, when the contact surfaces are cut at right angles to the faces of the pieces; the two are filled squarely against each other rather than lapped.

cogged joint
A carpentry joint formed by two crossed structural members, each of which is notched at the place where they cross.

construction joint
A separation provided in a building that allows its component parts to move with respect to each other; a joint where two placements of concrete meet.

control joint
A joint that is premolded, tooled, or sawed, and installed to prevent shrinkage of large areas. It creates a deliberately weakened section to induce cracking at the chosen location rather than at random.

dovetail joint
A splayed tenon, shaped like a dove's tail, broader at its end than at its base; the joint is formed by such a tenon fitting into the recess of a corresponding mortise.

end-lap joint
A joint formed between the ends of two pieces of timber, normally at right angles; each piece is notched equal to the width of the other piece, to form a flush surface in the assembled joint.

expansion joint
A joint designed to permit the expansion or contraction due to temperature changes. It generally extends through the entire structure from the footings to the roof.

finger joint
An end joint made up of several meshing fingers of wood, made with a machine and glued together.

flush joint
Any joint finished even or level with the surrounding surfaces.

indented joints
A joint used in joining timbers end to end; a notched fish-plate is attached to one side of the joint to fit into two corresponding notches in the joined timbers; the entire assembly is fastened with bolts.

interlocking joint
A form of joggle in which a protrusion on one member complements a slot or routed groove in another; a joint formed between sheet-metal parts by joining their pre-formed edges to provide a continuous locked piece.

isolation joint
A joint that separates one concrete section from another so that each one can move independently; found in floors, at columns, and at junctions between the floor and walls.

joggle joint
A notch or projection in one piece of material, which is fitted to a projection or notch in a second piece, to prevent one piece from slipping past the other.

lap joint
A joint in which one member overlaps the edge of another and is connected.

miter joint
A joint between two members at an angle to each other; each member is cut at an angle equal to half the angle of the junction, usually at right angles to each other.

mortise and tenon
A joint between two members, formed by fitting a tenon at the end of one member into a mortise cut into the other.

rigid joint
A joint that is capable of transmitting the full extent of force at the end of the member to the other members framing into the joint.

scarf joint
A wood joint formed by two members cut diagonally to overlap and interlock; pegs, glue, straps, or other devices are used to attach the members.

semirigid joint
A joint in either steel or concrete that is designed to permit some rotation; also called a partially fixed joint.

spline joint
A joint formed by inserting a spline of long strips of wood or metal in a slot cut into the two butting members.

standing seam joint
In metal roofing, a type of joint between the adjacent sheets of material, made by turning up the edges of two adjacent sheets and then folding them over.

straight joint
A line created by the meeting of two or more separate elements or pieces, often continuing in a straight line from one end to another.

tongue-and-groove joint
A joint formed by the insertion of the tongue of one member into the corresponding groove of another.

tooled joint
Any mortar joint finished with a tool, other than a trowel, that compresses and shapes the mortar; common types include a beaded joint, concave joint, and raked joint.

Jointing
In masonry, the finishing of joints between courses of bricks or stones before the mortar has hardened.

Joist
One of a series of parallel timber beams used to support floor and ceiling loads, and supported in turn by larger beams, girders, or bearing walls; the widest dimension is placed in the vertical plane.

ceiling joist
Any joist which carries a ceiling: one of several small beams to which the ceiling of a room is attached. They are mortised into the sides of the main beams or suspended from them by strap hangers.

floor joist
Any joist or series of joists which supports a floor.

trimming joist
A joist supporting one end of a header at the edge of an opening in a floor or roof frame, parallel to the other common joists.

Jones, Inigo (1573–1632)
London-born Royal Architect who first introduced the Palladian style to Jacobean England and started the Palladian revival. He worked on Old St. Paul's Cathedral, London (1631– 1671), adding Classical elements showing the power and scale of Roman architecture, which paved the way for Sir Christopher Wren when he began rebuilding the cathedral.

Jugendstil
A term meaning "youth style." The German version of Art Nouveau, named after the journal *Die Jugend* that publicized the style; was associated with the Sezession movement in Vienna, Munich, and Dresden; chief proponents were Endell, Hoffman, Olbrich, and Wagner.

Juxtaposition
The state or position of being placed close together or side by side, so as to allow comparison or to create contrast.

Kk

Kahn, Albert (1869–1942)
German-born American architect who formed a practice with his brothers Julius and Moritz, designed industrial buildings for automobile manufacturers Packard, Ford, and Chrysler.

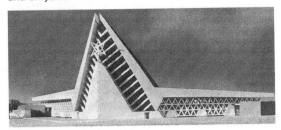

Kahn, Ely Jacques (1884–1972)
An American architect, trained in Paris, who designed many Art Deco skyscrapers in New York in the 1920s and 1930s.

Kahn, Louis (1901–1974)
Born in Estonia, he settled in the United States and became known for the monumentality, dignity and sculptural form of his buildings, including the Yale Art Gallery, New Haven (1951). The Salk Institute Laboratories (1959) was an important work, as was the Kimball Art Museum, Fort Worth (1967), and the Phillips Exeter Academy Library, Exeter, New Hampshire (1967). Richards Laboratories in Philadelphia (1957) has a bold silhouetting of towers. His last work was the National Assembly of Bangladesh, Dacca (1962–1974).

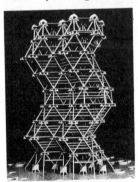

Kando
Main sanctuary of a Japanese Buddhist temple.

Keep
Inner tower of a castle.

Kent, William (1684–1748)
English architect and landscape designer, whose revolutionary informal gardens created a new relationship between a building and its natural setting.

Key
A tapered or wedge-shaped piece that locks pieces of timber together.

Key console
A console that acts as the keystone of an arch.

Key course
A continuous course of keystones in an arch, used in a deep archway where a single keystone will not suffice; a course of keystones used in the crown of a barrel vault.

Keystone
The central stone or voussoir at the top of the arch, the last part to be put into position to lock the arch in place, often embellished.

Keystone

Khan, Ali Mardan (1630–1653)
His design for the Taj Mahal is the most well known Islamic tomb monument.

Kiesler, Frederick (1890–1965)
Vienna-born American visionary architect; his "endless house" encapsulated his organic ideas of curves and continuous wall and ceiling planes as a contrast to the rectangular grid.

Kikutake, Kiyonori (1928–)
Japanese architect and leading light in Metabolism. His Sky House, Tokyo (1958), made his reputation. His proposed Marina City Project (1958), extending cities into the sea, was later partially realized at Aquapolis, Okinawa (1975).

Kiln
A large oven used for the artificial seasoning of lumber, for the firing of brick, and for the burning of lime.

Kinetic architecture
A style (1971–1985) depicted by forms that are dynamic, adaptable and responsive to the changing demands of the users. This broad category includes a number of other concepts, such as mobile architecture, which would not necessarily be constantly moving, only capable of being moved if required.

King closer See **Brick**

King truss See **Truss**

Kiosk
A small ornamented pavilion or gazebo, usually open for the sale of merchandise, or to provide cover or shelter to travelers.

Klenze, Leo von (1784–1864)
Versatile German architect who created dignified and monumental public buildings, some in the Greek style, others in the Renaissance style.

Klerk, Michael de (1884–1923)
A Dutch architect and member of the Amsterdam school who designed Elgen Haard Housing, Amsterdam, one of several housing estates, with his colleague Piet Kramer (1881–1961). It was built of brick and featured skillfully curved corners and details. He also designed the Navigation House (1916), and the De Dageraad housing complex (1920), both in Amsterdam.

Kling, Vincent (1916–)
Philadelphia-based architect; he designed the Municipal Services Building, Philadelphia (1965).

Knee
A bent or curved element used to stiffen a joint where two members meet at an angle, such as a timber frame column and beam.

Knee brace See **Brace**

Kneestone
A stone which is sloped on top and flat on the bottom that supports inclined coping on the side of a gable, or a stone that breaks the horizontal joint pattern to begin the curve of an arch.

Knob ornament See **Ornament**

Knot See **Wood**

Knot ornament See **Ornament**

Knotted column See **Column**

Knotwork ornament See **Ornament**

Kohn, Eugene
Partner in the firm Kohn, Pederson, Fox, with William Pederson and Sheldon Fox. They designed the Procter and Gamble General Offices, Cincinnati (1985); and 333 Wacker Drive, Chicago (1983); One Logan Square, Philadelphia; and the DG Bank, Frankfurt, Germany (1993), among many other office structures.

Koolhaas, Rem (1944–)
Dutch architect who formed the Office for Metropolitan Architecture (OMA) in 1975, producing a number of visionary and theoretical projects, including <u>Delirious New York</u>, later published as a book (1978). He was a publicist for Deconstructivism.

Kramer, Piet (1881–1961)
Dutch architect of the Amsterdam School, collaborated with de Klerk on the Navigation House (1916) and the De Dageraad housing complex (1925) in Amsterdam; both regarded as superb examples of Expressionism.

Krier, Leon (1946–)
Luxembourg-born architect and theorist: who championed Rational Architecture. His view of the city as a document of intelligence, memory, and pleasure is the antithesis of the concept of the disposable, adaptable, Plug-in City of Archigram and other advocates. He was critical of Post-modernism.

Krier, Rob (1938–)
Luxembourg-born Austrian architect, brother of Leon Krier, who built many housing projects in Berlin (1970s). He has been dubbed a devotee of Neo-Rationalism.

Kump, Ernest (1911–1991)
His most notable project was Foothill College, Los Altos Hills, California (1961), consisting of 40 buildings on a 122-acre campus, all designed and built as a unit.

Kurokawa, Kisho (1928–)
Japanese architect and member of the Metabolist group, who developed systems based on standardized units. Works include the Nakagin Capsule Hotel, Tokyo (1972); Sony Tower, Osaka (1976); Museum of Contemporary Art, Hiroshima (1988), and Ehime Museum of Science (1994).

LI

L'Enfant, Pierre Charles (1754–1825)
Designed a city plan for Washington, D.C.

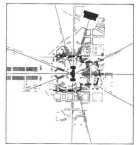

L'Orme, Philibert de (1514–1570)
Original and inventive, he was instrumental in creating a distinctive version of Renaissance classicism that drew on French traditions as well as Italian models. Works include Tuileries Palace, now destroyed.

Label stop
The termination of a hood-mold or arched dripstone in which the lower ends are turned in a horizontal direction away from the door or window opening.

Labrouste, Pierre Henri (1801–1875)
A French architect whose reputation rests on the Bibliotheque Ste-Genevieve, Paris (1838), in which an iron structure was slotted into a masonry cage. The reading room of the Bibliotheque Nationale, Paris, employed the same exposed iron and glass interior (1854).

189

Labyrinth
A maze of twisting passageways; a garden feature of convoluted paths outlined by hedges, often with a garden house at the center; in medieval cathedrals, the representation of a maze inlaid in the floor.

Lacework
Architectural patterns or decorations resembling lace.

Lacing course
A course of brick or tile inserted in a rough stone or rubble course as a bond course.

Ladder
A wooden object consisting of two side pieces connected to each other at regular intervals by rungs; used for climbing up or down during construction, or used as a temporary stair.

Lally column See **Column**

Lamb's tongue
The end of a handrail which is turned out or down from the rail and curved to resemble a tongue.

Lamella roof See **Roof**

Laminated beam See **Beam**

Laminated floor See **Floor**

Laminated glass See **Glass**

Laminated timber See **Wood**

Lanai
A living room or lounge area which is entirely, or in part, open to the outdoors.

Lancet arch See **Arch.**

Lancet window See **Window.**

Land use
The manner in which a particular piece of property or district is permitted to be used; typical usage includes residential, commercial, industrial, institutional, and agricultural.

Landing
The horizontal platform at the end of a stair flight or between two flights of stairs.

half-space landing
A stair landing at the junction of two flights, reversing its direction, making a turn of 180 degrees. Such a landing includes the width of both flights, plus the well.

quarter-space landing
A square landing connecting two flights of stairs that continue in a straight line

Landmark
Any building structure or place that has a special character or special historic or aesthetic interest or value as part of the heritage or cultural characteristics of a city, state, or nation.

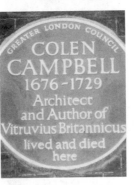

Landscape
The exterior environment of a site, district, or region, including landforms, trees and plants, rivers and lakes, and the built environment.

Landscape architect
A person trained and experienced in the design and development of landscape and gardens; a designation reserved for a person professionally licensed to perform landscape architectural services.

Landscape window See **Window**

Lantern
A tower or small turret with windows, crowning a dome or cupola.

Lantern light
A superstructure crowning a roof or dome, often glazed; provides light or ventilation to the space below.

Lap joint See **Joint.**

Lap splice See **Splice.**

Larch See **Wood**

Lateral brace See **Brace**

Lath
A thin, sawn strip of wood, fixed to the timber framing, leaving small gaps between adjacent laths, as a foundation for plastering. Also refers to other materials used for the same purpose, such as metal lath.

Latin cross
A cross which has an upright much longer than the cross beam; three arms are the same length, and the fourth lower arm is much longer.

Latrobe, Benjamin (1764–1820)
Trained in Europe, but emigrated to the United States, where he met George Washington, and built a number of public buildings, including work on the U.S. Capitol (1803–1814); advised Thomas Jefferson on the design of the University of Virginia campus (1817).

Lattice
A network of bars, straps, rods, or laths crossing over and under one another; the result is a rectangular or diagonal checkered pattern, which may be varied by the width of the bands and the spacing of the members.

Lattice dome See **Dome**

Lattice molding See **Molding**

Lattice structure
An open web joist, column, cylindrical shell, dome, or other structural type, built up from members that intersect diagonally to form a lattice.

Lattice truss See **Truss**

Latticed window See **Window**

Latticework
Reticulated or netlike work formed by the crossing of laths or thin strips of wood or iron.

Lautner, John (1911–1994)
American architect who studied with Frank Lloyd Wright and set up practice in Los Angeles designing original private homes. The most well known is the Malin House, (now Kuhn house), Los Angeles (1960), where the entire structure is carried on one pier; and the Elrod House, Palm Springs (1968), with massive roof frames and wedge-shaped windows.

Le Corbusier (1887–1965)
Pseudonym of Charles-Edouard Jenneret; the most influential of twentieth-century architects. The Villa Savoy, Poissy (1931), is typical of his residential designs, which was freely planned with geometric shapes and used modern construction techniques. He called such houses "machines for living." The Pavilion Suisse, Paris (1932), was built on stilts and featured the curved walls, cubist blocks, and a random rubble wall to contrast with the white concrete. The Unite d'Habitation, Marseilles (1946), shows his emphasis on mass and on untreated concrete. The proportions for his buildings were worked out on his "modular system." He designed Notre-Dame-du-Haut, Ronchamps, France (1954), which is molded in concrete, to create a huge sculptural form penetrated by windows placed at random. Chandigarh, East Punjab (1956) was planned as a new state capitol, but only three buildings were completed. His late work included the Carpenter Center, Harvard University, Cambridge (1963).

Lead See **Metal**

Leaded glass See **Glass**

Leaded light
A window having small diamond-shaped or rectangular panes of glass set into lead canes.

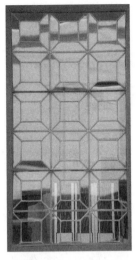

Lean-to
A shed or building having a single pitched roof, with its highest end against an adjoining wall or building.

Leaves
Hinged or sliding components, as in a door.

Ledoux, Claude-Nicholas (1736–1806)
His Neo-classical buildings combined simple shapes and austere treatments.

Leeward
The side of the structure that is sheltered from the wind.

Legorreta, Ricardo (1931–)
Mexican-born architect whose abstract forms and bold colors evoke images of his heritage. His work includes projects in both Mexico and Texas.

Leonardo da Vinci (1452–1519)
He built nothing, but he produced a number of influential architectural schemes and designs.

Lescaze, William (1896–1969)
His Savings Fund Building, Philadelphia, was an early skyscraper designed in the International style.

Lesche
In ancient Greece, a public portico or clubhouse, frequented by people for conversation or hearing the news; such buildings were numerous in cities, and their walls were decorated by celebrated painters.

Lescot, Pierre (1510–1578)
French architect; responsible for rebuilding the Louvre in Paris.

Lesene
Vertical strips resembling a pilaster, but without a base or capital; used to subdivide wall surfaces and domes into framed panels.

Libeskind, Daniel (1946–)
Polish-born American Deconstructivist architect, known for the Jewish Museum, Berlin (1989), and the Boilerhouse extension, Victoria and Albert Museum, London (1992).

Library
A room or set of rooms in a dwelling or public building, or an entire building devoted to housing collections of books and manuscripts for study.

Lierne
Short rib that runs from one main rib of a vault to another.

Life cycle costing
The analysis of the total cost of a building or structure over an extended period of time, including the initial cost, maintenance costs, and replacement costs based on the life expectancy of its components; usually compares alternative components and systems.

Lift slab
A reinforced or prestressed concrete flat plate cast at ground level and jacked up to its correct level after the concrete has hardened.

Lift-slab construction
Casting floor and roof slabs one upon another, then jacking or hoisting them into final position, saving on formwork for cast-in-place floors in a multistory structure.

Light
An opening through which daylight is admitted to the interior space of a building; a pane of glass, window, or compartment of a window.

Light fixture
A luminaire secured in place or attached as a permanent appendage or appliance. It consists of a lighting unit with lamps and components to protect the electrical circuits from the weather, and other devices to spread the light in a prescribed pattern.

Light fixture

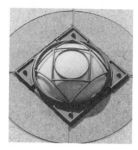

Light well
A small court commonly placed in large buildings to admit daylight to interior areas not exposed to an open view.

Lighthouse
A tower or other structure supporting one or more lights to assist in the navigation of ships into harbors or to warn of dangerous shoals; often, quarters for the lighthouse keeper may be within or adjacent to the structure.

Lightweight concrete
Concrete that is composed of lightweight aggregate, such as sand.

Limestone See Stone.

Line
The path of a point extended through space; it may be geometric (straight lines and arcs), free form (flowing and curving), or a combination of the two.

Lineal foot
A running foot, as distinct from a square foot or a cubic foot.

Lineal measure
One-dimensional measurement of a piece of material.

Lineal organization See Organization

Linear
Forms that describe a line, or are arranged in a line.

Linear diffuser
A device used in air-conditioning, which distributes air to a space from a linear slot, often at the terminals of the duct, but also along the run.

Linear grouping
An arrangements of units along one side of a gallery, or along both sides of a corridor.

Linen-scroll ornament See **Ornament**

Lining
Material which covers any interior surface, such as a framework around a door or window or boarding that covers interior surfaces of a building.

Link
The part of a building addition that connects to an existing building; often recessed from the facade and sometimes constructed of different materials, when the style of the addition is not similar to the existing building.

Linked organization See **Organization**

Linoleum
Floor covering made from jute or similar fabric, that has been impregnated with oxidized oils, resin, and a filler, such as cork.

Lintel
The horizontal beam that forms the upper structural member of an opening for a window or door and supports part of the structure above it.

Lintel course
In stone masonry, a course set at the level of a lintel, it is commonly differentiated from the wall by its greater projection, its finish, or thickness, which often matches that of the lintel.

Live load
A load that is not permanently applied to a structure, as compared with a dead load representing the building component's permanent weight.

Load bearing wall See **Wall**

Loading dock
The area of a building accessible from the street, and convenient to the transportation systems within the building, that provides for the loading and unloading of commercial vehicles.

Lobby
A space at the entrance to a building, theater, hotel, or other structure.

Lock
A device which fastens a door, gate, or window in position; may be opened or closed by a key or a dead bolt.

Locust See **Wood**

Loft
An open space beneath a roof often used for storage; one of the upper floors of a warehouse or factory, typically unobstructed except for columns, with high ceilings; the upper space in a church, choir or organ loft.

Log house
A house built of logs that are horizontally laid and notched and fitted at the ends to provide stability.

Loggia
An arcaded or colonnaded structure, open on one or more sides, sometimes with an upper story; an arcaded or colonnaded porch or gallery attached to a much larger structure.

Lombard architecture
A north Italian pre-Romanesque architecture (600–700) during the rule of the Lombards, based on early Christian and Roman forms, and characterized by the development of the ribbed vault shaft.

Long column See Column

Longhena, Baldassare (1595–1682)
Italian architect who designed St. Maria della Salute, Venice (1630–1687), sited at the head of the Grand Canal. It is the architect's masterpiece.

Longhouse
A communal dwelling characteristic of many early cultures consisting of a wooden bark-covered frame-work, often as much as 100 feet in length.

Longitudinal section See Projection drawing

Lookout
Rafter, bracket, or joist at the ridge of a roof that projects beyond an end wall of a building: may support an overhanging portion of the roof or cornice.

Loop window See **Window**

Loophole
Any opening in a parapet or wall to allow for vision, light, or air.

Loos, Adolf (1870–1933)
Viennese architect, primarily a designer of houses, disclaimed all forms of ornament. Designed the Kartner Bar, and the Gustav Sheu House, both in Vienna, a typically boxlike exterior with rectangular windows of various sizes.

Lot
Surveyed parcel of land, particularly one that is large enough to accommodate a single building.

Lotus
A fan-shaped decorative motif formed by symmetrically arranging lotus petals with a spreading curvature.

Lotus capital See Capital

Louis XIV –XVI style
A high classical style (1643–1792) typified in the architecture, decoration and furniture of France, culminating in the building of Versailles. It developed into the ornate Rococo style.

Louver
A window opening made up of overlapping boards, blades or slats, either fixed or adjustable, designed to allow ventilation in varying degrees without letting the rain come in.

 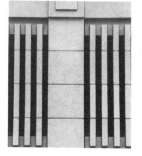

 Louvered door See **Door**

Low-emissivity glass See **Glass**

Low-rise
A relatively short multistory building, often described in building codes as not more than 75 feet tall, as opposed to a high-rise.

Lozenge
An equilateral four-sided figure with pairs of equal angles, two acute and two obtuse; a rhombic or diamond-shaped figure.

Lozenge window See **Window**

Lubetkin, Berthold (1901–1990)
Russian-born architect, who emigrated to England and founded Tecton, a practice producing International style modern buildings notable for their simplicity.

Lucarne window See **Window**

Luckman, Charles
Partner with William Periera in the firm of Periera and Luckman. They designed the space-age restaurant at the Los Angeles International Airport. Their most notable buildings are the Prudential Center, Boston (1965), and the Transamerica Building in San Francisco.

Lumber
Timber that is sawn or split in the form of beams, boards, joists, planks, or shingles; refers especially to pieces smaller than heavy timber.

Luminaire
A device for providing mechanical support and electrical connections to a lamp or lamps, and fixed to a support, such as a wall or ceiling.

Luminous ceiling
A lighting system in which the whole ceiling is translucent with lamps that are installed above and suspended from a structural ceiling.

Lundy, Victor (1923–)
He trained under Walter Gropius and worked with Marcel Breuer. His best known work was the I. Miller Shoe Salon, Fifth Ave., New York City (1961), employing timber ribs and mirrors.

Lunette
A semicircular window or wall panel framed by an arch or vault.

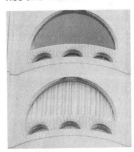

Luster glass See **Glass**

Lutyens, Sir Edwin Landseer (1869–1944)
Important English architect; he designed the plan for the city of New Delhi, India (1912). His later work includes many commercial bank buildings in London (1920).

Lyndon, Donlyn (1936–)
Partner in the firm of Moore, Lyndon, Turnbull in San Francisco.

M m

M roof See **Roof**

Machicolation
Openings formed by setting the parapets out on corbels so as to project beyond the face of the wall. Some parapets set out on corbels have a similar appearance, even if there are no openings.

Machine room
A space that houses machinery and equipment, such as elevator equipment, generators, boilers, or air-conditioning equipment.

Machu Picchu
The most celebrated Inca citadel, on a promontory 2,000 feet above the valley in the Andes in Peru. The site includes buildings which surround an oblong plaza. The houses were built around courts, with stairs, windows, interior niches, narrow doorways and thatch-covered gable roofs. Some houses were carved out of the rock; some connecting stairs were hewn out of the mountain.

Macintosh, Charles Rennie (1868–1928)
A highly original architect and designer who created his own version of Art Nouveau, combining logical planning and expressive ornament. His first major work was the Cranston Tea Room, Edinburgh, Scotland. He also designed the Glasgow School of Art, a highly original Art Nouveau design.

Charles Rennie Macintosh

Maderno, Carlo (1556–1679)
Italian architect who designed St. Susannah facade, Rome (1603), a Baroque elevation crowded with orders and set with niches rather than windows. One of his last works, the Pallazzo Barberini, Rome (1628), was completed by Bernini.

Mahogany See **Wood**

Maillart, Robert (1872–1940)
Structural engineer; he built his first of 40 reinforced-concrete bridges in 1901. He contributed to the design of mushroom slab construction in high structures, where the columns, beams, and floors are integrated.

Makovecz, Imre (1935–)
Hungarian architect influenced by the work of Rudolph Steiner. He designed the Hungarian Pavilion for Expo '92, Seville, Spain (1992), with seven churchlike spires rising through the roof.

Maltese cross
A cross that is formed by four equal triangles or arrowheads joined at their points; the outer edge of each arm is indented with an angle.

Manastaba
In Indian architecture, a freestanding upright pillar in front of a temple.

Mannerism
A style of Italian architecture (1530–1600) which was a reaction against the classical perfection of High Renaissance architecture, either responding with a rigorous application of classical rules and motifs or flaunting Classical convention in terms of shape and scale. It was a relaxed nonconformist style, using unnatural proportion and stylistic contradictions.

Mannerism

Manor house
The house occupied by the lord of a manor; the most important house in a country or village.

Mansard roof See Roof

Mansart, Francois (1598–1666)
French architect who designed in the French Classical style.

Mansion
A large and imposing dwelling.

Mantel
The frame and shelf surrounding the fireplace; often used to denote just the shelf.

Mantelpiece
The fittings and decorative elements of a mantel, including a cornice and shelf carried above the fireplace.

Manueline architecture
The last phase (1495–1521) of Gothic architecture in Portugal, so named after King Manuel.

Maple See Wood

Marbleized
Painted in imitation of the surface color and pattern of stone, especially veined marble; base materials may include slate, plain marble, cast iron, and plaster.

Marble See Stone

Margin Draft
A narrow dressed border along the edge of a squared stone, usually the width of a chisel, as a border surrounding the rough central portion,

Marmoset
An antic figure, usually grotesque, introduced into architectural decoration in the 13th century.

Marquee

A permanent projecting roof-like shelter over an entrance to a building, often displaying information about performances.

Marquetry

Inlaid pieces of a material, such as wood or ivory, fitted together and glued to a common background.

Mascaron

The representation of a face, a human, or partly human head, more or less caricatured, and used as an architectural element.

Mask

A corbel, the shadow of which bears a close resemblance to that of a human face. It was a favorite ornament under the parapet of a chancel.

Mask

Mason

A craftsman skilled in shaping and joining pieces of stone or brick together to form walls and other parts of buildings and structures.

Masonite See Wood

Masonry

Includes all stone products, all brick products and concrete block units, including decorative and customized blocks.

ashlar masonry

Smooth square stones laid with mortar in horizontal courses.

broken rangework

Stone masonry laid in horizontal courses of different heights, any one course of which may be broken into two or more courses.

cavity wall masonry

An exterior wall of masonry, consisting of an outer and inner course separated by a continuous air space, connected together by wire or sheet-metal ties; the dead air space provides improved thermal insulation.

Masonry

concrete masonry
Construction consisting of concrete masonry units laid up in mortar or grout.

coursed masonry
Masonry construction in which the stones are laid in regular courses, not irregularly as in rough or random stonework.

coursed rubble
Masonry construction in which roughly dressed stones of random size are used, as they occur, to build up courses; the spaces between them are filled with smaller pieces or with mortar .

cyclopean masonry
Often found in ancient cultures, characterized by huge irregular stones laid without mortar and without coursing.

diamondwork masonry
Masonry construction in which pieces are set to form diamond-shaped patterns on the face of the wall.

hollow masonry unit
Extruded block of concrete or burnt clay, which consists of voids and consequently is a good insulator. It is used for walls and as a backing for brick.

patterned block
Concrete block with a recessed decorative pattern on the front face.

pebble wall masonry
A wall built of pebbles set in mortar, or one faced with pebbles embedded in a mortar coating on the exposed surface, either at random or in a pattern.

pitch-faced masonry
In masonry, a surface in which all arrises are cut true and in the same plane, but the face beyond the arris edges is left comparatively rough, dressed with a chisel.

polygonal masonry
Masonry constructed of stones having smooth polygonal surfaces.

quarry-faced masonry
Squared blocks with rough surfaces that look as if they just came out of the ground.

random ashlar masonry
Ashlar masonry in which regular stones are set without continuous joints and appear to be laid without a drawn pattern, although the pattern may be repeated.

random coursed ashlar
An ashler masonry bond pattern with random-sized stones laid in horizontal courses of different heights, with varying-sized stones in each course.

Masonry

random rubble
Rubble masonry consisting of stones of irregular size and shape with roughly flat faces, set randomly in a wall.

rubble masonry
Very irregular stones, used primarily in the construction of foundations and walls where the irregular quality is desirable.

rubblework
Stone masonry built entirely of rubble.

rustic stone masonry
Any rough, broken stone that is suitable for rustic masonry, most commonly limestone or sandstone; usually set with the longest dimension exposed horizontally.

rusticated masonry
Coursed stone masonry where each unit is separated by deep joints; the surface of each unit is usually very rough.

square rubble masonry
Wall construction in which squared stones of various sizes are combined in patterns that make up courses at every third or fourth stone.

vermiculated masonry
A form of masonry surface, incised with discontinuous wandering grooves resembling worm tracks; a type of ornamental winding frets or knots on mosaic pavements, resembling the tracks of worms.

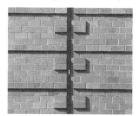

Masonry Field
In brickwork, the expanse of wall between openings, composed principally of stretchers.

Masonry wall See **Wall**

Mass
The physical volume or bulk of a solid body; or a grouping of individual parts or elements that compose a body of unspecified size.

Massing
The overall composition of the exterior of the major volumes of a building, especially when a structure has major and minor elements.

Mastaba
A freestanding tomb found in ancient Egypt, consisting of a rectangular superstructure with inclined sides, from which a shaft leads to underground burial chambers.

Master builder
An individual of broad experience and training, who is distinguished in the craft of building.

Master plan
A planning document designed to guide the future development on an entity; may be employed for the construction or remodeling of a building, site planning or access, or for a political jurisdiction indicating proposed land uses and public improvements.

Mastic
Any heavy-bodied, dough-like adhesive compound; a sealant with putty-like properties used for applying tiles to a surface or for weatherproofing joints.

Matched veneer
Wood or stone veneer pieces installed with the grain of adjoining pieces aligned at the edges; types include herringbone matched and bookmatched.

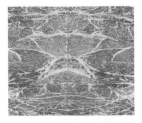

Matte surface
A surface that redistributes the incident light uniformly in all directions, so that the luminance is the same and without sheen, even when viewed from an oblique angle.

Mausoleum
A large and stately tomb, or a building housing such a tomb or tombs; originally the tomb for King Mausolos of Carla, about 350 B.C.

Mayan arch See **Arch.**

Mayan architecture
Sites such as Tikal in Guatemala, Copan in Honduras, and Palenque in Mexico represent the highest development of this style (600–900). It is characterized by monumental constructions, including soaring temple pyramids, palaces with sculptural facades, ritual ball courts, plazas and interconnecting quadrangles.

Buildings were erected on platforms, often with a roof structure. The lower section contained a continuous frieze carrying intricate decoration of masks, human figures, and geometric forms.

Decorative elements formed open parapets. Exterior surfaces were covered with a lime stucco and painted in bright colors, and interior walls were massive and decorated. The sites were totally rebuilt periodically, leaving previous structures completely covered and intact.

One of the most notable examples is Chichen Itza in Yucatan, the largest center of the Mayan civilization.

Mayan architecture

Maybeck, Bernard (1862–1937)
Designed the Christian Science Church, Berkeley, California, in a mixture of styles. He also designed the Palace of Fine Arts, San Francisco, for the Pan Pacific International Exposition of 1915. The Exposition buildings were demolished, but the Palace remains, now rebuilt out of permanent materials.

Mayekawa, Kunio (1905–1986)
Japanese architect and member of the Japanese group Werkbund. His Harimi Apartments, Tokyo (1957), carry over Japanese domestic traditions into the dimensions of a modern skyscraper.

Mayne, Thom (1944–)
Principal Deconstructivist architect in the firm Morphosis, whose work includes Salick Office Tower, Los Angeles (1990), and the Vintage Car Museum, Los Angeles (1991).

Maze
A confusing and intricate plan of hedges in a garden, usually above eye level, forming a labyrinth.

McKim, Charles F. (1847–1909)
An American architect, in partnership with William Mead and Stanford White, ran the largest architectural practice of its time in the U.S. His bold design is expressed best in Pennsylvania Station, New York City (1911), (now demolished). Another of his important works is the layout and design of the Columbia University campus in New York City (1901) and the Morgan Library (1903).

Mead, William R. (1846–1928)
Partner in the New York firm of McKim, Mead & White.

Meander
A running ornament consisting of a fret design with many involved turnings and an intricate variety of designs.

Measured drawing
An architectural drawing of an existing building, object, site, or detail that is accurately drawn to scale on the basis of field measurements.

Measuring line See **Perspective projection**

Mechanical code
Building code that governs the safe design of heating, ventilating, plumbing, and air-conditioning systems for a structure.

Mechanical room
A room devoted to mechanical equipment and controls, such as a boiler, furnace, ductwork, plumbing, and water heater.

Mechanical systems
Construction related to furnishing heating, ventilating, and air-conditioning, plumbing, and fire suppression system.

Medallion
An ornamental plaque, usually round or oval in shape, inscribed with an object in low relief, such as a head, flower or figure, and applied to a wall or frieze.

Medallion molding See **Molding**

Medieval architecture
The architecture of the European Middle Ages (400–1400); the use of Byzantine, Romanesque and Gothic elements spanned a millennium. It was an age of the fortified castle, where bishop's palaces rivaled cathedrals in splendor and served public and private functions.
As the population grew, smaller houses nestled around castle walls, creating medieval towns. As urban land grew more valuable, tall narrow houses with upper stories were common.

Medusa
In Greek mythology, the mortal one of the three Gorgons, who had snakes for hair and whose head was cut off by Perseus to present to Athena as an ornament for her shield.

Meeting house
A house of worship, especially that of the Society of Friends, or Quakers, and the Mormons.

Megalithic
Built of unusually large stones, used as found in nature or roughly hewn, especially as used in ancient construction.

Megalopolis
An urban area consisting of several large, densely populated cities that are adjacent to each other.

Megastructure
A type of structure that was popular from 1964 to 1976 in which individual buildings became merely components, or lost their individuality altogether. Vast new structures were proposed to replace existing cities; their overall purpose was to provide a total environment for work and leisure activities.

Megeron
A rectangular hall, fronted by an open, two-columned porch, traditional in Greece since Mycenaean times.

Meier, Richard (1934–)
Worked with Marcel Breuer and SOM, and was the most prolific of the New York Five. He persisted in using white in his buildings such as the Saltzman House, in East Hampton, New York (1967), and the Douglas House, Harbor Springs, Michigan (1971). His later works include the High Museum of Art, Atlanta, (1980), and the vast Getty Center, Los Angeles (1984), and the Barcelona art Museum (1996).

Melnikov, Konstandin (1890–1974)
Russian architect whose work anticipated certain aspects of Deconstructivism, which gained him popularity among the avant-garde. He is mostly associated with the Constructivists, however.

Melon dome See **Dome**

Member
Any individual element of a building, such as a framing member; also one of the individual shapes that make up a molding, such as a cornice or a water table.

Membrane
A thin, flexible surface such as a net or form with a fabric surface, supported by tension cables or by an air system.

Membrane structure
A roof of flexible membranes of canvas or plastic, supported by cables or ropes.

Membrane structure

Memento mori
An image meant to serve as a reminder of death, usually a human skull or skeleton.

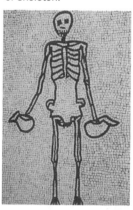

Memorial
An architectural or sculptural object or plaque commemorating a person or an event.

Memorial arch
An arch commemorating a person or event, popular during the Roman Empire and again at the time of Napoleon.

Memorial plaque
A flat inscribed stone commemorating a special event or to serve as a memorial; set into or fixed to the surface of a wall.

Mendelsohn, Eric (1887–1953)
German architect who designed the Einstein Tower in Potsdam (1921), a highly plastic building. Its design is an outcome of Expressionist demands. He also designed the Luckenwalde Hat factory (1923) and the Schoken Department stores at Stuttgart, Germany (1928), using bold new forms to express a new function.

Mengoni, Guiseppe (1829–1877)
Italian architect and designer of the Galleria Vittorio Emanuelle, Milan, Italy (1871), the largest shopping arcade of its type in Europe, and the architect's most famous project.

Merlon
One of the solid alternates between two crenels, or open spaces, in a battlement parapet,

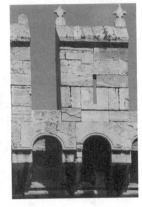 

Merrill, John (1896–1975)
Partner in the firm of Skidmore, Owings and Merrill (SOM).

Meshrebeeyeh
An elaborately turned or carved wood screen or wood lattice that encloses a balcony window, as found in Islamic countries.

Mesoamerican architecture
A characteristic feature of this architecture (1300–500 B.C.) is the great temple pyramids of pre-Columbian America, which are equivalent in complexity to those of ancient Egypt and the Middle East.

The main centers in Mexico and Peru are divided into four main cultures: Mayan, Toltec, Aztec, and Inca. All four of these civilizations conceived of their architecture in monumental terms characterized by strong grid plans, huge walled enclosures, and vast stone cities.

Mesolithic Era
The cultural period between the Paleolithic and Neolithic eras, marked by the appearance of cutting tools.

Mesopotamian architecture
A massive architecture (3000–500 B.C.) constructed of mud, bricks set with clay mortar; producing heavy walls articulated by pilasters and recesses and faced with glazed brick. Columns were seldom used, and openings were infrequent and small.

Metal roofing
Any of the various sheet-metal roof coverings; types include batten roof and standing-seam roof.

Metal-clad door See Door

Metals
Any of a class of elementary substances which are crystalline when solid and characterized by opacity, ductility and conductivity; mined in a form called "ore" and manufactured to specific applications.

Metals

aluminum
A lightweight metal which is malleable and non-magnetic and has good conductivity; it is a good reflector of heat and light and is resistant to oxidation; it is often anodized for better corrosion resistance, color and surface hardness.

brass
Any copper alloy having zinc as the principal alloying element, but often with small quantities of other elements.

bronze
An alloy of copper and tin, bronze in color, having a sub-stantial admixture of copper to modify the properties of the principal element, as aluminum bronze and magnesium bronze.

cast iron
A hard, nonmalleable iron alloy containing carbon and silicon, which is poured into a sand mold and then machined to a desired architectural shape.

cast iron

copper
A metal with good electrical conductivity, used for roofing, flashing, hardware and plumbing applications; when exposed to air, copper oxidizes and develops a greenish "patina" that halts corrosion.

ferrous metal
Metal in which iron is the principal element.

iron
A metalic element found in the earth's crust, consisting of a malleable, ductile, magnetic substance from which pig iron and steel are manufactured.

lead
A soft, malleable, heavy metal that has a low melting point and a high coefficient of thermal expansion; very easy to cut and work.

stainless steel
A high-strength, tough steel alloy: contains chromium with nickel as an additional alloying element and is highly resistant to corrosion and rust.

Metals

steel
A hard and malleable metal when heated; produced by melting and refining it according to the carbon content; used for structural shapes due to its alloy of iron and carbon which has a malleable high tensile strength.

tin
A lustrous white, soft, and malleable metal having a low melting point; relatively unaffected by exposure to air; used for making alloys and solder, and in coating sheet metal.

weathering steel
A high-strength, low-alloy steel that forms an oxide coating when exposed to rain or moisture, which adheres to the base metal and protects it from further corrosion.

wrought iron
A commercially pure iron of fibrous nature, valued for its corrosion resistance and ductility; used for water pipes, water tank plates, rivets, and other forged work.

zinc
A hard bluish-white metal, brittle at normal temperatures, very malleable and ductile when heated; not subject to corrosion; used for galvanizing sheet steel and iron, in various metal alloys.

Metope
A panel, either plain or decorated with carvings, between the triglyphs in a Doric frieze.

Mews
An alley or court in which stables are or once were located or have been converted into residences.

Mezzanine
A low-ceilinged story located between two main stories, it is usually constructed directly above the ground floor, often projecting over it as a balcony.

Mezzo-relievo See **Relief**

Michelangelo Buonarroti (1475–1564)
Architect, sculptor, painter, and poet, representing the Italian Renaissance at its height. In 1546, he was appointed architect of St. Peters, Rome.

Mid-wall column See **Column**

Miesian
Designed in the style of Mies van der Rohe, German-born architect who designed many International Style buildings; typical elements include exposed structural supports, reveals at joints between materials, and a total lack of applied ornament.

Milling
In stonework, the processing of quarry blocks, through sawing, planing, turning, and cutting, to produce finished stone.

Mills, Robert (1781–1855)
Designed the Washington Monument, the tallest obelisk that epitomized the romantic Classical ideals.

Millwork
Wood products, such as cabinets, door and window frames, moldings, panels, and stair components that are manufactured by machines.

Minaret
The tall slender tower of a mosque with stairs leading up to one or more balconies from which followers are called to prayer.

Minoan architecture
A Bronze Age civilization (1800–1300 B.C.) that flourished in Crete, whose gate buildings with porches provided access to unfortified compounds. Foundation walls, piers and lintels were stone with upper walls framed in timber.

Rubble wall masonry was faced with stucco and decorated with colorful wall frescoes. Ceilings were wood, as were the many columns with balloon capitals, and featured a distinct downward tapering shaft, as in the Palace of King Minos at Knossos, in Crete.

Miralles, Enric (1955–)
Spanish architect; designed the Olympic Archery Range in Barcelona (1991).

Mirror
A surface capable of reflecting light without appreciable diffusion.

Mission
A diplomatic office in a foreign country; a small church or monastic order.

Mission architecture
The church and monastery architecture of the Spanish religious orders in Mexico and California In the eighteenth century.

Mission parapet
A low free-standing wall at the edge of a roof, frequently curved; as found in many Spanish missions of the southwestern U.S.

Mission style
A characteristic of this style (1890–1920) is its simplicity of form. Round arches supported by piers form openings in the thick stucco walls, with roof eaves that extend beyond the wall surface. Towers, curvilinear gables and small balconies were used on large buildings. The only ornamentation is a plain stringcourse that outlines arches, gables or balconies.

Mission tile See Tile

Mitchell, Ehrman (1924–)
An American architect and partner with Romaldo Guirgola.

Miter
The line formed by the meeting of moldings or other surfaces that intersect each other at an angle; each member is cut at exactly half the angle of the junction

Miter arch See Arch

Mixtec architecture
An architecture (700–1000) characterized by great mass, use of interior stone columns, and emphasis on horizontal lines, developed in Oaxaca, Mexico. The minutely detailed fretwork of the interior and exterior paneled friezes, was produced by assembling thousands of small decorative elements, and setting them into clay. At Mitla there are free-standing buildings surrounding large courts oriented toward cardinal points of the compass.

Moat
A broad, deep trench, filled with water, surrounding the ramparts of a town or fortress.

Mobile
A type of sculpture made of movable parts that can be set in motion by the movement of air currents.

Model

A three-dimensional representation of a building or part of a building, executed at a small scale for the purposes of studying the massing or details of a proposed project.

Modeling

The shaping of three-dimensional forms in a soft material, such as clay; also, the gradations of light and shade reflected from the surfaces of materials.

Modelscope

Device that attaches to the lens of a camera; allowing users to view a model from the level of a pedestrian.

Modern architecture

Building design in the currently fashionable architectural style; originally used to describe a movement that combined functionalism with ideals that rejected historical design concepts and forms; included styles such as Art Deco, International Style, Organic Architecture, and Prairie Style.

Modernism

A term meaning "just now." The Modern Movement (1960–1975) exemplified a conscious attempt to find an architecture tailored to modern life, and one that made use of new materials.

It rejected the concept of applied style and the use of any ornament. It used concrete, steel and glass to help evolve an architecture directly related to construction methods. Exterior and interior forms were conceived and expressed as a single entity.

Modernism

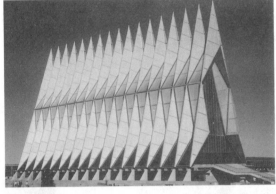

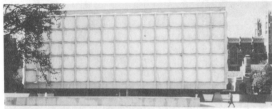

Modernistic style

A style (1920–1940) characterized by a mode of ornamentation combining rectilinear patterns and zigzags with geometrical curves. One of the distinctive forms consisted of polychrome low-relief frames.

Ornamentation around doors and windows and on panels stresses the verticality in skyscraper designs. Stepped setbacks are also common, reflecting local urban zoning ordinances.

Modernistic style

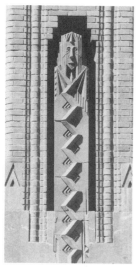

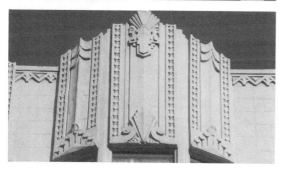

Modillion
A horizontal bracket or console, in the form of a scroll with acanthus, supporting the corona under a cornice.

block modillion
A modillion in the form of a plain block.

Modular brick See **Brick.**

Modular grid
Reference grid in which the grid lines are spaced at exact multiples of the module.

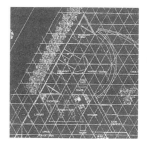

Modular system
A method of designing or constructing buildings and equipment in which standardized modules are widely used.

Modulation
To measure, to adjust to, or regulate by a certain proportion; to temper or to soften in passing from one element, form, or material to another.

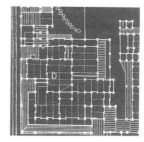

Module
A simple ratio by which all parts of a building are related as part of an ordered system.

Modulor
A system of proportion developed by Le Corbusier in 1942. It was based on the theories of early civilizations and on the human form, and was related to the golden section.

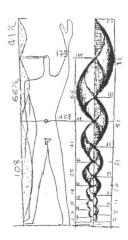

Mogul architecture
The later phase of Indian Islamic architecture, named after the Mogul dynasty, typified by monumental palaces and mosques and detailed decorative work. The Taj Mahal is the most famous example.

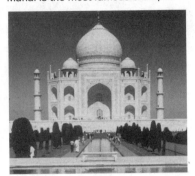

Molded brick See Brick.

Molding
A decorative profile that is given to architectural members and subordinate parts of buildings: whether cavities or projections, such as cornices, bases, door and window jambs and heads.

backband molding
A piece of millwork used around a rectangular window or door casing to cover the gap between the casing and the wall, or used as a decorative feature.

band molding
A small broad, flat molding, projecting slightly, of rectangular or slightly convex profile, used to decorate a surface, either as a continuous strip or formed into various shapes.

bar molding
A rabbeted molding applied to the edge of a bar or counter to serve as a nosing.

base molding
Molding used to trim the upper edge of an interior baseboard.

bead molding
A narrow wood drip molded on one edge against which a door or window closes, a stop bead; a strip of metal or wood used around the periphery of a pane of glass to secure it in a window frame.

bead-and-reel molding
A classical molding consisting of alternate small, egg-shaped beads and semicircular disks set edgewise.

beak molding
A molding ornamented with carved birds or fantastic animal-like heads or beaks.

bed molding
A molding or group of moldings that support the corona of a classical style entablature, often made up of a bottom ogee, a band, a quarter round, and a top band; a similar molding used as the bottom of a cornice or as a rake molding.

beveled molding
Milled molding with an inclined plane surface.

billet molding
A common Norman or Romanesque molding formed by a series of circular cylinders, arranged alternately with notches in single or multiple rows.

bolection molding
A molding projecting beyond the surface of the work which it decorates, such as between a panel and the surrounding stiles and rails; often used to conceal a joint when the joining surfaces are at different levels.

cable molding
An ornamental molding formed like a cable showing twisted strands; the convex filling of the lower part of the flutes of classical columns.

calf's-tongue molding
A molding consisting of a series of pointed tongue-shaped elements all pointing in the same direction or toward a common center when around an arch.

cant molding
A square or rectangular molding having the outside face beveled.

cap molding
Trim at the top of a window or door; above the casing trim.

cavetto molding
A hollow member or round concave molding used in cornices and column bases, containing at least one quadrant of a circle in its profile.

chain molding
A molding carved with a representation of a chain.

corner bead
A vertical molding used to protect the external angle of two intersecting wall surfaces; a perforated metal strip used to strengthen and protect an external angle in plaster work or gypsum wallboard construction.

cove molding
A concave or canted interior corner molding, especially at the transition from the wall to a ceiling or floor.

cover molding
Any plain or molded wood strip covering a joint, as between sections of paneling, or covering a butt joint.

crenellated molding
Molding notched or indented to represent merlons and embrasures in fortifications.

crown molding
Any molding serving as a corona or otherwise forming the crowning or finishing member of a structure.

cyma molding
A molding that has a profile with a double curvature, or ogee.

cyma recta molding
A molding of double curvature, that is concave at the outer edge, and convex at the inner edge.

cyma reversa molding
A molding of double curvature, that is convex at the outer edge, and concave at the inner edge.

cymatium molding
The crowning molding of a Classical cornice, especially in the form of a cyma.

dovetail molding
A molding consisting of decorated fretwork in the form of dovetails.

drip molding
Any molding so formed and located as to act as a drip.

drop molding
A panel molding recessed below the surface of the surrounding stiles and rails.

egg-and-dart
An egg-shaped ornament alternating with a dart-like ornament used to enrich ovolo and echinus moldings and also on bands.

fillet molding
A molding consisting of a narrow flat band, often square in section; the term is loosely applied to almost any rectangular molding, usually used in conjunction with other moldings or ornaments.

flush molding
An applied door or window molding that is flush with or below the surface of the rails and stiles.

flush bead molding
A molding whose surface is on the same plane as that of the wood member or assembly to which it is applied.

guilloche
An ornament in the form of two or more bands that are twisted together in a continuous series, leaving circular openings that are filled with round ornaments.

guilloche

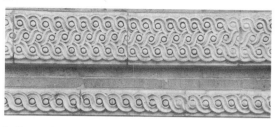

half-round molding
A convex strip or molding of semicircular profile.

hollow molding
A concave, often circular molding; a cavetto.

Hollow square molding
A common molding consisting of a series of indented pyramidal shapes having a square base, found often in Norman architecture.

hoodmold
The projecting molding of the architrave over a door or window, whether inside or outside; also called a dripstone.

indented molding
A molding with the edge toothed or indented in triangular tooth-like shapes.

lattice molding
A wood molding, rectangular in section and broad in relation to its projection, resembling the wood strips used in latticework.

medallion molding
A molding consisting of a series of medallions, found in the later examples of Norman architecture.

notched molding
An ornament produced by notching the edges of a band or fillet.

ovolo molding
A common convex molding consisting of a quarter circle in section.

pellet molding
Any small, round decorative projection; one of a series of small, flat disks or hemispherical projections.

quarter-round molding
A convex molding, with a projection that is exactly or nearly a quarter of a circle.

quirk bead molding
A molding containing a bead with a quirk on one side, as on the edge of a board.

quirked molding
A molding characterized by a sudden and sharp return from its extreme projection or set off and made prominent by a quirk running parallel to it.

raised molding
A molding that extends above the adjoining surface, such as applied door moldings that overlaps, and covers, the joints between panels and the rails and stiles.

raking molding
Any molding adjusted at a slant, rake, or ramp; any overhanging molding which has a rake or slope downward and outward.

reed molding
A small convex molding, usually one of several set close together to decorate a surface.

reticulated molding
A molding decorated with fillets interlaced to form a network or mesh-like appearance.

roll molding
Any convex rounded molding, which has a cylindrical or partially cylindrical form.

rover molding
Any member used as a molding that follows the line of a curve.

scotia molding
A deep concave molding, especially one at the base of a column in Classical architecture.

scroll molding
An ornamental molding consisting of a spiral design or a terminal similar to the volutes of the Ionic capital or the "S" curve on consoles.

square billet molding
A Norman molding consisting of a series of projecting cubes, with spaces between the cubes.

struck molding
A molding cut into rather than added to or planted onto another member.

sunk fillet molding
A molding slightly recessed behind the surface on which it is located; a fillet formed by a groove in a plane surface.

tresse molding
Flat or convex bandelets that are intertwined, especially such interlacing ornamentation used to adorn moldings.

Venetian molding
Molding with repetitive individual projecting elements: similar to dentils.

wave molding
A molding decorated with a series of stylized representations of breaking waves.

Monastery
A building complex that houses a monastic order.

Monitor
A superstructure that straddles the ridge of a roof or crowns a dome: often glazed to provide light or louvered to provide ventilation.

Monochromatic
Consisting of only one color.

Monolith
An architectural member such as an obelisk, the shaft of a column, consisting of a single stone.

Monolithic
Shapes usually formed of a single block of stone, or cast in one piece without construction joints; they are massive and uniform.

Monolithic column See **Column**

Monopteral
Describes a temple the roof of which is supported by columns, but without walls.

Monostyle
Having the same style of architecture throughout the structure; a single shaft applied to medieval pillars.

Montage
A composition made by overlapping parts or objects.

Monterey Style
An architectural style found in the southwest U.S., especially California, that combines Spanish Colonial and Greek Revival style features; includes adobe or stuccoed stone walls, pitched roofs with shingles or clay tiles, Greek Revival wood trim at doors and windows, and cantilevered second-story porches.

Monument
A stone, pillar, megalith, structure or building erected in memory of the dead, an event, or an action.

Monumental scale See **Scale**

Moon gate See **Gate**

Moore, Charles (1925–1993)
A leading figure of Postmodernism, who was also notable as a university teacher and writer.. Architectural history played a part in his designs, which are tempered with fancy, myth, and evocative motifs. These are typified in the Piazza d'Italia, New Orleans, Louisiana (1975). Other work includes houses at Sea Ranch, California (1970), and the Beverly Hills Civic Center (1985).

Moorish arch See **Arch**

Moorish architecture
Prevalent in Spain and Morocco, the style (500–900) was influenced by Mesopotamian brick and stucco techniques with frequent use of the horseshoe arch, along with Roman marble columns and limestone carved capitals. Vaults developed into highly complex ornate forms. Brick was used decoratively and structurally in combination with marble, with extensive use of stucco to build up the richly molded surfaces, painted with bright colors and sometimes gilded.

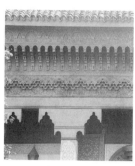

Moorish capital See **Capital**

Moorish revival
A revival style using horseshoe arches and multifoil window tracery.

Moretti, Luigi (1907–1973)
Italian architect whose early work was in the Neo-classical style of Rationalist architecture. His most notable later work is the Watergate complex in Washington, D.C. (1960).

Morgan, Julia (1872–1957)
American architect and engineer; the first woman to study at the Ecole des Beaux Arts, Paris; and California's first licensed woman architect. Her work includes several buildings for Mills College, Oakland, California, including the reinforced concrete campanile (1903) and the Library and Gymnasium (1907). She designed the buildings at San Simeon, California (1919), for William Randolph Hearst.

Morphosis
A California firm of architects, led by Thom Mayne (1944-) and Michael Rotondi (1949-), whose aim is to absorb the idiosyncratic by drawing on the more terrifying aspects of technology. Their Venice, California, house has a system of weights and pulleys controlling sun-sails that constantly change the appearance of the building.

Mortar joints

beaded joint
Recessed mortar joint in the form of a quirked bead: a joint with a raised bead in the center that projects past the surface of the brick or stone.

bed joint
The horizontal joint between two masonry courses; one of the radial joints in an arch.

concave joint
A recessed masonry joint, formed in mortar by the use of a curved steel jointing tool; because of its curved shape it is very effective in resisting moisture.

flush joint
A masonry joint finished flush with the surface.

ground joint
A closely fitted joint in masonry, usually without mortar: also a machined metal joint that fits tightly without packing or employing a gasket.

head joint
A vertical joint between two masonry units that are perpendicular to the face of a wall.

raked joint
A joint made by removing the surface of mortar with a square-edged tool while it is still soft; produces marked shadows and tends to darken the overall appearance of a wall; not a weather-tight joint.

Mortar joints

rustic joint
In stone masonry, a deeply sunk mortar joint that has been emphasized just by having the edges of adjacent stones chamfered or recessed below the surface of the stone facing.

struck joint
A masonry joint from which excess mortar has been removed by a stroke of the trowel, leaving a flush joint; a weather-struck joint.

tooled joint
Any masonry joint that has been prepared with a tool before the mortar in the joint has set rigidly.

troweled joint
A mortar joint finished by striking off excess mortar with a trowel.

v-shaped joint
A horizontal V-shaped mortar joint made with a steel jointing tool; very effective in resisting the penetration of rain.

weather-struck joint
A horizontal masonry joint in which the mortar is sloped outward from the upper edge of the lower brick, so as to shed water readily; formed by pressing the mortar inward at the upper edge of the joint.

Mortice
A rectangular slot cut into one piece of timber, into which a tenon or tongue from another piece is fitted to form a joint.

Mortise and tenon joint See **Joint**

Mosaic
A process of inlaying small pieces of stone, tile, glass or enamel into a cement or plaster matrix, making a pattern, design, or representational picture.

Mosaic

Florentine mosaic
A kind of mosaic made with precious and semiprecious stones, inlaid in a, surface of white or black marble or similar material, generally displaying elaborate floor patterns.

Venetian mosaic
A type of terrazzo topping, containing primarily large chips, with smaller chips filling in between.

Mosque
A Muslim house of worship.

Moss, Eric Owen (1943–)
Deconstructivist architect whose projects include the Petal House, Los Angeles (1984), Hayden Tower, Culver City (1992), and The Box, Culver City (1995).

Motif
A part or element repeated in an ornamental design.

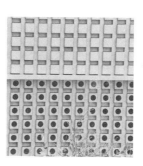

Mouchette
Gothic tracery and derivatives, a typical small motif: pointed, elongated, and bounded by elliptical and ogee curves, a dagger motif with a curved axis.

Mouse tooth gable See Gable

Mozarabic architecture
A northern Spanish style (800–1400) built by Christian refugees from Moorish domination, characterized by the horseshoe arch and retaining all other Moorish features.

Mudejar architecture
A Spanish style (1200–1300) created by the Moors while under Christian domination, characterized by a fusion of Romanesque and Gothic styles but retaining some Islamic elements, such as the horseshoe arch.

Mulgardt, Louis Christian (1866–1942)
American architect of German descent, influenced by the Arts and Crafts movement. In the 1920s, he produced a series of fantastic proposals for San Francisco, including habitable piers and bridges connected by 24-lane tiered motorways. None were ever realized.

Mullion
A dividing piece between the lights of windows, taking on the characteristics of the style of the building.

Multicentered arch See Arch

Multicurved gable See Gable

Multifoil See Foil

Multiple dwelling
A building for residential use that houses several separate family units.

Multistory frame
A building framework of more than one story, in which loads are carried to the ground by a system of beams and columns.

Muntin
A secondary framing member to hold panes in a window, window wall, or glazed door; an intermediate vertical member that divides panels of a door.

Muqarnas
An original Islamic design involving various combinations of three-dimensional shapes featuring elaborate corbeling.

Mural
A wall painting; fresco is a type of mural technique.

Murphy, Charles F. (1890–1985)
Worked with Daniel Burnham and the Chicago school. He produced several Chicago office buildings, and with partner Helmut Jahn designed O-Hare International Airport (1965) and the Exhibition building at McCormick Place (1971).

Museum
An institution for the assembly and public display of any kind of collection: especially one of rare or educational value.

Mushroom column See Column

Muslim architecture
In this style (600–1500) a new domed mosque was developed from the Christian basilica. There were many variations of the basic elements such as arches, domes, cross ribs, and crenellations. Surfaces are covered with an abundant geometric, floral and calligraphic decoration, executed in stone, brick, stucco, wood and glazed tile.

Mutule
A sloping flat block on the soffit of the Doric cornice; usually decorated on the underside with rows of six guttae each, which occurs over each triglyph and metope of the frieze.

Mycenaean architecture
The earliest phase (1600–1200 B.C.) was exemplified by masonry sidewalls and a timber roof. Monumental beehive-like tombs were constructed of superimposed layers of corbelled stones to create a parabolic vault.

Stone-faced, inclined access passages led to the entrance, which had sloping jambs; overhead, a stone lintel supported a characteristic triangular sculptured panel.

N n

Naos
Inner sanctuary of a Greek temple.

Nara
A period in Japanese history (710-794) characterized by the adoption of Chinese culture and form of government, named after the first permanent capital and the chief Buddhist center in ancient Japan.

Narthex
An arcaded porch or entrance hall to an early Christian basilican church.

Nash, John (1753–1835)
Planned Regent Park and Regent Street, London, as a picturesque scheme. He also designed the Brighton Pavilion (1815) for the Prince of Wales in a mixture of Indian, Chinese, and Gothic styles.

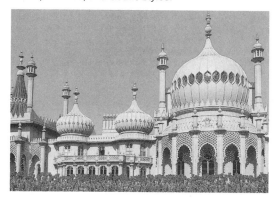

National Trust for Historic Preservation
A nonprofit organization that promotes the cause of preservation; it owns a limited number of historic properties and administers preservation programs.

National Historic Landmark
A designated district, site, building, structure or object of exceptional significance to the country as a whole, rather than just to a particular state or locality; each is listed in the National Register of Historic Places.

Natural forms
Refers to those forms that include artificial foliage as well as derivations of the acanthus leaf, flowers and fruit festoons; also animal forms, such as the lion and eagle, and human forms, such as heads and figures.

Natural forms

Natural stone See **Stone**

Natural ventilation
Ventilation without the use of mechanical power. It is achieved by the suitable location and arrangement of windows and doors.

Nave
The principal or central part of a church; by extension, both middle and side aisles of a church, from the entrance to the crossing of the chancel; that part of the church intended for the general public.

Neck
In the Classical orders, the space between the bottom of the capital and the top of the shaft, usually marked by a sinkage, or a ring of moldings.

Neo-classicism
A revival style (1900–1920) based primarily on Greek and to a lesser extent on Roman orders, producing symmetrically arranged buildings of monumental proportions. Colossal pedimented porticos were flanked by a series of pilasters.
   The arch was not used, and enriched moldings are rare. The preference was for simple geometric forms and smooth surfaces. The design was based on the assembly of separate volumes, each dedicated to a single function.

Neo-expressionism
Structures which express continuity of form by sweeping curves characterize this style (1964–1975). These structures were primarily the result of using reinforced concrete to create smooth shapes and seamless soaring forms.

Neo-expressionism

Neo-formalism
A style (1964–1970) which combines the Classical symmetrical forms and smooth wall surfaces with arches of precast concrete and decorative metal grilles, very often delicate in appearance.

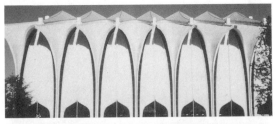

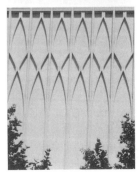

Neolithic era
The last phase of the Stone Age (9000–8000 B.C.), characterized by the cultivation of crops and the use of technically advanced stone implements.

Neon lamp
A lamp containing neon gas at low pressure; a discharge of electricity through the neon produces an intense glow, which is used for signs.

Nervi, Pier Luigi (1891–1979)
Italian civil engineer; he was best known for reinforced-concrete structures. He created a structure for the Exhibition Hall, Turin, Italy (1947), and the Palazzo Dello Sports (1958) in Rome, where an immense concrete dome floats over the space.

Net vault See **Vault**

Network
Any set of interconnected elements that form an overall organization; also a diagram representing a series of interconnected events, as in the representation of the critical tasks in a building project.

Neumann, Johann Balthasar (1687–1753)
German Rococo architect, whose work exhibits swirling curves, fluid spaces, and rich but delicate decoration. Work includes the Bishop's Palace (Residenz) Wurzburg, Germany.

Neutra, Richard (1892–1970)
Vienna-born architect working with Adolf Loos and Eric Mendelsohn. He met Louis Sullivan and Frank Lloyd Wright, and in 1925 formed an association in Los Angeles with Rudolph Schindler. He designed many homes for notable Hollywood names.

New Brutalism
This style (1953–1965) was representative of buildings which expressed materials, structure and utilities honestly, in the tradition of Le Corbusier's beton brut; it featured rough, honest brickwork and exposed concrete imprinted with the grain of the wooden forms.

New Classicism

A final phase of Post-modernism (1982–) that led to a new form of Classicism, a freestyle version of the traditional language. It shares traditional assumptions of previous revivals, such as relating ideas to the past and using universal figures of representation as the design vocabulary.

It combines two purist styles – Classicism and Modernism – and adds new forms based on new technologies and social usage. Previous rules of composition are not disregarded but rather extended and distorted.

Among those architects identified with this style are James Stirling, Robert Venturi, Michael Graves, Hans Holleln, Charles Moore and Arata Isozaki.

New England Colonial style

A local style (1600–1700) characterized by a use of natural materials in a straightforward manner. The box-like appearance is relieved by a prominent chimney, and a sparse distribution of small casement-type windows.

The characteristic shape, formed by extending the rear roof to a lower level than the front roof, was called a "saltbox." In larger structures the upper floor projected beyond the lower floor, creating an overhang called a "jetty".

Newel

The central post or column which provides support for the inner edges of the steps in a circular staircase and around which the steps wind.

Newel cap

The terminal feature of a newel post, often molded or turned in a decorative manner.

Newel post

A tall post at the head or foot of a stair supporting the handrail, often ornamental.

Niche

A recess in a wall; usually semicircular at the back, terminating in a half-dome, or with small pediments supported on consoles, often used as a place for a statue.

angle niche

A niche formed at a corner of a building; common in medieval architecture.

Niemeyer, Oscar (1907–1989)

Brazilian architect who designed the Ministry of Health and Education, Rio de Janeiro (1945), a Modern-style tower block modified by louvers, devised by Le Corbusier, the consultant architect. Niemeyer was interested in buildings as sculpture. Brasilia, Brazil (1960), was planned in the shape of a bird, with the Parliamentary Building at its head. The influence of Le Corbusier is evident.

Nogging

Brick or miscellaneous masonry material used to fill the spaces between the wooden supports in a half-timber frame.

Nominal size of timber
The size of timber before it is dressed, and usually before it is seasoned. Size of timber is usually given in nominal size, and the actual size is slightly smaller.

Noncombustible
In building construction a material that will not ignite, burn, support combustion, or release flammable vapors when subjected to fire or heat.

Nonconforming building
A building that does not meet the current requirements of a regulation in the building code or restrictions in the zoning code.

Non-load-bearing wall See **Wall**

Norman architecture
A Romanesque form of architecture (1066–1180), that predominated in England from the Norman Conquest to the rise of the Gothic style. It was plain and massive, with moldings confined to small features; archways were plain and capitals devoid of ornament. As the style advanced, greater enrichment was introduced, and later examples exhibit a profusion of ornament. Windows resemble small doors without mullions. Pillars were slender and channeled.

Norman cottage
A large asymmetrical house in the style of the farmhouses of Normandy, France, built in the early 1930s; typical elements include a round tower with a conical roof, steeply pitched roof with dormers, mixed brick, stone, and stucco walls, multipaned casement windows; often employs half-timbering.

Nosing
The rounded edge of a horizontal surface that projects beyond the vertical surface below, such as the projection of the tread beyond the riser.

Notched molding See **Molding**

Nouvel, Jean (1945–)
French architect whose most well known work is the Institut du Monde Arabe, Paris (1987).

Nowicki, Matthew (1910–1951)
Polish architect who designed the Norton Arena, North Carolina State Fair, Raleigh (1948), with two intersecting hyperbolic parabolas. He is regarded as a pioneer of such structural design. He also worked with Saarinen on the master plan for Chandigarh, India.

Noyes, Eliot (1910–1977)
American architect and industrial designer; he worked with Gropius and Breuer, as well as IBM and Westinghouse. Work includes the Bubble houses (1953), created by spraying concrete on a large balloon; United States Pavilion, Expo 67, Montreal; and the IBM Management Development Center, Armonk, New York (1980).

Nursing home
A building used for the lodging, boarding, and nursery care for patients of mental or physical incapacity who require care and related medical services less intense than those given in a hospital.

Nylon See **Plastic**

Nympheum
A Classical building or room with a fountain, statues, and plants, used as a place for relaxation.

O o

Oak See **Wood**

Obata, Gyo (1923-)
Partner in the firm of Hellmuth Obata and Kassabaum,
noted for the Chapel Priory of St. Mary, St. Louis (1962);
the National Air and Space Museum, Washington, D.C.
(1976); the renovation of Union Station, St. Louis (1985),
and the Dallas/Ft. Worth Airport (1973).

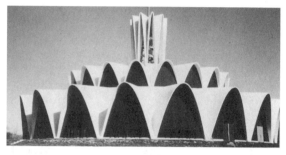

Obelisk
A four-sided stone shaft,
either monolithic or
jointed, tapering to a
pyramidal top.

Oblique projection See **Projection drawing**

Oblique section See **Projection drawing**

Oblong
A right-angle plane figure with unequal pairs of sides;
it can approach the dimensions of a square, on the one
hand, or stretch out to express a band on the other.

Obscure glass See **Glass**

Observatory
A structure in which astronomical observations are
carried out: a place such as an upper room that affords
a wide view, a lookout.

Obsidian See **Stone**

Obtuse angle arch See **Arch**

Octagonal
Refers to those plane geometric figures containing
eight equal sides and
eight equal angles.

Octagonal house
An eight-sided house,
usually two-to-four stories
high.

Octahedral
Forms that exhibit the characteristics of a regular
polygon having eight sides.

Octastyle
A portico having eight
columns in front.

Oculus
A roundel or bull's eye
window opening, or an
opening at the crown of
a dome.

Oculus

Office building
A building used for the transaction of public or private business, especially clerical work associated with business, government, legal or other professions.

Offset
Surface or piece forming the top of a horizontal projection on a wall.

Ogee
A double curve resembling an S in shape, formed by the union of a convex and concave line.

Ogee arch See **Arch.**

Ogee pediment See **Pediment**

Ogee roof See **Roof**

Olhbrich, Joseph (1867–1908)
Cofounder of the Vienna Sezession movement. He designed the Ernst Ludwig Haus, Darmstadt, in the Art Nouveau style, and the Wedding Chapel and Exhibition Hall, Darmstadt, Germany.

Olive leaf cluster See **Ornament**

Olmec architecture
This architecture (1200–500 B.C.) flourished in the tropical lowlands of the Mexican Gulf Coast; characterized by temple- pyramids and vast ceremonial centers.

Olmsted, Frederick Law (1822–1903)
One of the most important landscape architects of the time, and an innovator in the design of public parks, much influenced by John Paxton's work in England. He designed Prospect Park in Brooklyn and Central Park in New York City. His last large scheme was the World's Columbian Exposition, Chicago (1893), where he created a sylvan setting for the Neo-classical buildings of McKim, Mead & White, Daniel Burnham, and others.

One-point perspective See **Perspective projection**

Onigawara
Ornamental tiles at the ends of the main roof ridge of a traditional Japanese structure, at the lower ends of the roof slopes, and at the corner ends. The most common is an ogre mask, from which it gets its name.

Onion dome See **Dome.**

Opacity
Quality of being impenetrable by light: not reflecting light, or transmitting light, neither transparent nor translucent.

Opal glass See **Glass**

Opalescent glass See **Glass**

Open cornice See **Cornice**

Open eaves
Overhanging eaves where the rafters and underside of the roof are visible from below.

Open pediment See **Pediment**

Open plan
A floor plan in which there are no internal walls or a minimum number of internal walls that subdivide the space, usually at a reduced height.

Open space
The area within a community that is not occupied by buildings or transportation networks; may be contained in a plaza, park, farmland, or part of the natural environment.

Open stair See **Stair**

Open-space easement
Easement requiring that a certain section of property remain undeveloped.

Open-string stair See **Stair**

Open-timbered
Heavy timber work which is exposed and not concealed by sheathing, plaster, or other covering.

Open-timbered roof See **Roof**

Open-web beam See **Beam**

Open-web joists
A lattice joist welded from light steel sections and mass-produced to certain standard lengths, used to support floor or roof loads.

Open-well stair See **Stair**

Openwork
Any work characterized by perforations, especially of an ornamental nature.

Opera house
A theater intended primarily for the performance of opera.

Operable transom
A panel of glass light above a door, which may be opened for ventilation.

Operable window See **Window**

Opus incertum
Ancient Roman masonry consisting of small stones set irregularly in mortar.

Opus quadratum
The Ancient Roman term for ashlar, or squared stones, frequently laid without mortar.

Opus reticulatum
Permanent formwork for Ancient Roman concrete, consisting of stones or bricks set diagonally.

Opus spicatum
Ancient Roman brickwork set in a herringbone pattern.

Opus testaeceum
Ancient Roman facing of broken tiles set horizontally in mortar.

Orb
A plain circular boss, used as a decorative accent, where two or more ribs of a vault cross each other.

Orchestra
A circular area in a Greek theater, where the chorus sang and danced.

Orchestration
To organize and combine harmoniously so as to achieve a desired or effective combination of form, color and texture of the materials used.

Order
A logical and regular arrangement among the separate components or elements of a group: a unity of idea, feeling and form.

Orders
In classical architecture, a style of columns and capitals with standard details appearing on the entablatures. Greek orders are the Doric, Ionic, and Corinthian; the Romans added the Tuscan and the Composite.

Organic
Refers to forms that have a structure that perfectly fulfills their own functional requirements; intellectually integrated by a systematic connection and coordination of the parts to the whole.

Organic architecture
The principles of organic architecture (1985–) rely on the integration of form and function, in which the structure and appearance of a building is based on a unity of forms that stresses the integration of individual parts to the whole concept, relating it to the natural environment in a deliberate way, with all forms expressing the natural use of materials.

Organic architecture

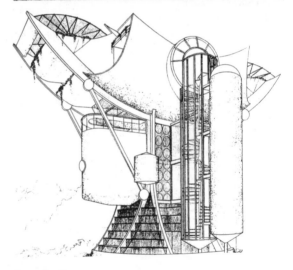

Organization
An arrangement of elements or interdependent parts with varied functions into a coherent and functioning entity.

centralized organization
Spaces gathered around or coming together at a large or dominant central area.

clustered organization
Spaces that are grouped, collected, or gathered closely together and related by proximity to each other.

embedded organization
A space incorporated as an integrated and essential part of a larger space.

226

Organization

grid-based organization
Spaces that are organized with reference to a rectangular system of lines and coordinates.

interlocking organization
Two spaces interwoven or fit into each other so as to form an area of common space.

linear organization
Spaces that are extended, arranged, or linked along a line, path, or gallery.

linked organization
Two spaces that are joined or connected by a third intervening space.

radial organization
Spaces arranged like radii or rays from a central space or core.

Oriel window See Window

Oriental style
Adaptations of Middle Eastern or Asian architecture built in the U.S., typically employing variations of the Italianate style using hipped roofs with multifoil arches; oriental features may include a Turkish dome, structural polychromy, and Moorish ornamentation.

Orientation
The placement of a structure on a site with regard to local conditions of sunlight, wind, drainage, and an outlook to specific vistas.

Ornament
Anything that embellishes, decorates, or adorns a structure, whether used intentionally and integrated into the structure or applied separately to enhance the building's form and appearance.

acorn ornament
A small ornament in the shape of a nut of the oak tree; used in American Colonial architecture as a pendant, finial, carved on a panel, or as an element in the center of a broken pediment.

Ornament: animal forms
The use of animals in a natural or idealized form for ornamental details, such as sculptured or relief figures on friezes, capitals of columns, and bas-relief panels.

aegricranes
Sculptured representations of the heads and skulls of goats and rams, once used as decoration on altars and friezes.

227

Ornament: animal forms

bestiary
A collection of medieval allegorical fables about animals, each with an interpretation of its significance to good or evil; in medieval churches, a group of highly imaginative and symbolic carved creatures.

birds
Any member of the class Aves, which includes warm-blooded, feathered, vertibrates, with forelimbs modified to form wings.

bovine
Any of the bovine mammal species, such as the ox and cow.

bovine

bucranium
A sculptural ornament representing the head or skull of an ox, often garlanded, and most frequently used on Roman Ionic friezes.

canine
Any member of the dog family, including wolves and foxes.

Ornament: animal forms

centaur
In classical mythology, a monster, half man and half horse: a human torso on the body of a horse.

chimera
A fantastic assemblage of animal forms so combined as to produce a single but unnatural design: a creation of the imagination.

eagle
Any of various large birds of prey, characterized by a powerful hooked bill, and long broad wings; used as emblems, insignias, seals, and ornamental sculpture.

eagle

feline
Belonging to the cat family; includes lions, tigers, and jaguars.

griffin
A mythological beast with a lion's body and an eagle's head and wings, used decoratively.

Ornament: animal forms

griffin

horse
A large hoofed mammal, having a short-haired coat, a long mane, and a long tail, and domesticated since ancient times for riding and to pull vehicles or carry loads.

VIRTUS

owl
Any of various nocturnal birds of prey, with hooked and feathered talons, large heads with short hooked beaks and eyes set in a frontal facial plane.

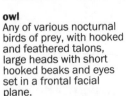

owl

sphinx
An Egyptian figure having the body of a lion and a male human head; the Greek version featured a female monster represented with the body of a lion, winged, and the head and breasts of a woman.

Ornament: animal forms

sphinx

wivern
A two-legged dragon having wings and a barbed and knotted tail, used often in heraldry.

Ornament

banderole
A decorative representation of a ribbon or long scroll, often bearing an emblem or inscription.

bouquet
The decorative ornament at the top of a finial or other projection in a floral or foliated form; similar to the anthemion.

Ornament

bow knot
A decorative element in the stylized shape of a ribbon tied in a bow; often in the form of repetitive open loops which contain rosettes.

corner drop
A hand-carved or turned wood ornament that is attached to the bottom of an overhanging second-story post; often found in early American Colonial houses.

cornucopia
A goats horn overflowing with fruits, flowers and corn, signifying prosperity; a horn of plenty; any cone-shaped receptacle or ornament.

crocket
In Gothic architecture and derivatives, an upward-oriented ornament, often vegetal in form, regularly spaced along sloping or vertical edges of emphasized features such as spires, pinnacles and gables.

dog tooth
One of a series of projecting pyramidal ornaments resembling a row of teeth; used in Gothic Revival and Early English architecture.

fleur-de-lis
A stylized three-petaled flower representing the French royal lily, tied by an encircling band, and used as an ornamental device in late Gothic architecture and in later derivatives.

Fret
An ornament; usually in bands, but also covering broad surfaces, consisting of interlocking geometric motifs.

Ornament

grapevine
A running ornament or carved panel which consisted of grapevines with bunches of grapes and grape leaves; popular in communities along the Rhine and elsewhere in Germany.

hip knob
A finial or other similar ornament placed on the top of the hip of a roof or at the apex of a gable.

hollyhock
A tall plant, widely cultivated for its showy spike of large variously colored flowers; used as an ornamental motif by Frank Lloyd Wright on the Barnsdall residence in Los Angeles.

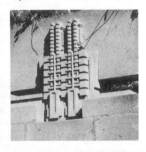

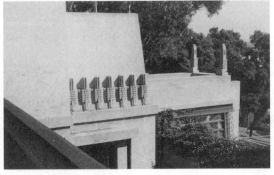

honeysuckle
A common name for the anthemion, commonly used in Greek decorative sculpture.

knob
A protuberance, whether useful or ornamental, that forms the termination of an isolated member; also, a handle that is more or less spherical, used for operating the mechanism for opening a door.

knot
In medieval architecture, a bunch of leaves, flowers, or a similar ornament, such as bosses at the intersection of ribs, and bunches of foliage in capitals; an ornamental design resembling cords that are interlaced.

knotwork
A carved ornamental arrangement of cord-like figures joined together to form a type of fringe; used to decorate voussoirs and moldings.

linen scroll
A form of ornament for filling panels.

olive leaf cluster
Bunches of olive leaves sculpted to form the decoration of the Composite order.

palmette
A decorative motif based on the fan-shaped leaf of a palm tree.

Ornament

pine cone
Oval drop that occurs in the open corner of the dentil course in the Composite order.

pineapple
A decorative carved ornament representing a pineapple, used as a terminal or finial for a hipped roof or as the central element of an ogee pediment.

rose
A stylized carving of a wild rose; used in Gothic style ornamentation and on Corinthian capitals.

scroll
Ornamentation that consists of a spirally wound band or a band resembling a partially rolled scroll of paper; S scrolls are found in ornamental brackets, window and door surrounds, and in other ornamental bands.

strapwork
Decoration formed by interlaced strips, either applied or carved in wood, stone, or plaster; used in screens, ceilings and cornices.

tooth
One of a series of carved ornaments, typically a pyramidal shape or a four-petal flower, usually set in a concave molding band; used in both the Romanesque and Gothic Revival styles.

trefoil
An architectural ornament resembling a three-leaf clover.

wreath
A decorative element in the form of a garland or band of foliage; often intertwined with flowers, fruits, and ribbons.

Ornament in relievo
Decorative elements carved so that they are above the surface of a molding, such as scrolls or flowers and leaves.

Ornamental
Refers to forms that adorn or embellish a surface or any other part of a structure.

Ornamental cast iron
Decorative railings, brackets, spears and architectural elements molded from cast iron; popular in the lower Mississippi Valley.

Ornamental iron
Cast iron used for grilles, gates, finials, hardware, and innumerable architectural accessories.

Ornamental metals
Bronze, brass, copper, aluminum and stainless steel, not used for major construction, but as infill materials, including copper panels, sheet aluminum, stainless steel, and baked enamel metal alloy panels.

Ornamental plaster
Decorative moldings and ornamentation applied to plain plaster surfaces or used as integral designs.

Ornamental stone
Any type of stone used for ornamentation or interior finish work, as opposed to building stone.

Ornamentation
Any adjunct or detail used to adorn, decorate, or embellish the appearance or general effect of an object.

Orthographic projection See Projection drawing

Ostberg, Ragner (1866–1945)
Swedish architect and designer; known internationally for one work, the Stockholm Town Hall (1923).

Otto, Frei (1925–)
German architect and pioneer of the suspended tent roof. He used the idea for the West German Pavilion, Expo '67, Montreal, Canada (1967), and for the Olympic stadium, Munich, Germany (1972). He published the book Tensile Structures in 1991.

Ottoman style
The phase of Turkish Islamic architecture (1350–1550) much influenced by Byzantine forms, under the rule of the Ottoman sultans in the Balkans, Anatolia, and the Middle East.

Ottonian architecture
The pre-Romanesque round-arched style (960–1000) in Germany during the rule of the Ottonian emperors, characterized by the development of forms derived from Carolingian and Byzantine styles.

Oud, Jacobus J. P. (1890–1963)
His Hook of Holland Housing Estate in Rotterdam expresses the rigid discipline of the de Stijl artists.

Outbuilding
Any building that is detached from the main house or structure; typically includes carriage houses, garages, sheds, stable or wood storage shed.

Outlooker
A member that projects beyond the face of a gable and supports the overhanging portion of a roof.

Outrigger
A beam that extends from the ridge of a roof beyond the wall of the building; often serves as a support for hoisting tackle or for ornamentation.

Oval
Resembling an egg in shape, ellipsoidal or elliptical; it is duocentric with a long and short axis.

Oval window See Window

Overdoor
A wall area directly above a doorway containing a panel ornamented with carvings or figures.

Overhang
The horizontal distance that the upper story or roof projects beyond the story immediately below.

Overhanging
Projecting or extending beyond the wall surface below.

Overlapping
Forms extending over and covering part of an area or surface that has a common alignment; it may be slight or significant, as long as there is a common surface between the elements.

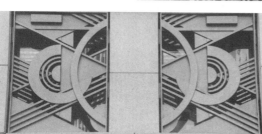

Overlapping counterpoint See **Counterpoint**

Oversailing
A process by which an arch, or course of bricks or stone, is made to project over a similar arch or course below; a type of repeated corbeling.

Overthrow
An ironwork hoop supporting a lantern, forming an arch in front of the door.

Ovolo molding See **Molding**

Ovum
An egg-shaped ornamental motif, used in ornamental bands in found in Classical architecture and Classical Revival styles.

Owings, Nathaniel (1903–1984)
Partner in the firm of Skidmore, Owings and Merrill (SOM). Noteworthy projects of the firm are Lever House, New York City (1952); Inland Steel Building, Chicago (1958); One Chase Plaza New York City (1962); Beinecke Rare Book Library, Yale University, New Haven (1963); Air Force Academy Chapel, Colorado Springs (1963); Circle Campus, University of Illinois, Chicago (1965); John Hancock Center, Chicago (1970); Weyerhauser Headquarters, Tacoma (1971), and Sears Tower, Chicago (1974).

Owl See **Ornament: animal forms**

Ox-eye window See **Window**

Ozenfant, Amedee (1886–1966)
French painter and cofounder with Le Corbusier of Purism.

P p

Pagoda
A multistory shrine-like tower: originally a Buddhist monument crowned by a stupa.

Pai-lou See **Gate**

Paint
A protective finish for architectural elements, most often composed of a coloring agent ground in linseed oil or other synthetic base.

Painted glass See **Glass**

Painter
A craftsman skilled in the preparation and application of paint, lacquer, and varnishes to wood, plaster, and other surfaces.

Paired brackets
Two brackets spaced close together to form a pair; also called coupled brackets.

Paired gables See **Gable**

Palace
Official residence of an important dignitary: often an elaborate structure with many rooms.

Palazzo
In Italy, a palace: or any impressive public building or private residence.

Paleolithic Era
The cultural period beginning with the first chipped stone tools, about 75,000 years ago, and continuing until the beginning of the Mesolithic era, about 15,000 years ago.

Palladian motif
A door or window opening in three parts, divided by posts, featuring a round-headed archway flanked by narrow openings with a flat lintel over each side; the arched area rests on the flat entablatures.

Palladian style
A style (1508–1586) named after Andrea Palladio, an Italian Renaissance architect, whose _Four Books of Architecture_ set out the classic orders in detail, establishing the proportions between the various components in each one.

He studied the Roman architect Vitruvius and the laws of harmonic proportions. His villas were an inspiration for many of the later country houses, especially in England.

Palladianism
A mode of building following strict Roman forms, particularly popular in England, as set forth in the publications of the Italian Renaissance architect Andrea Palladlo (1508–1580).

Palladio. Andrea (1508–1580)
St. Giorgio Maggore and Il Rendentore are his two notable buildings in Venice (1566). His Villa Capra Vicenza (1569) is the most symmetrical of his villas, with porticoes on each side. His _Four Books on Architecture_ was published in 1570.

Palm capital See **Capital**

Palmette ornament See **Ornament**

Pancharam
One of a number of miniature shrines located on the roof, cornices, or lintels of a Hindu temple, used as a decorative feature.

Pane
A relatively small piece of window glass set in an opening; also known as a light.

Panel
A portion of a flat surface recessed below the surrounding area, set off by moldings or some other distinctive feature.

Panel

 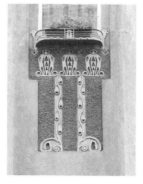

Panel divider
A molding that separates two wooden panels along their common edge.

Panel tracery See **Tracery**

Panel truss See **truss**

Panel vault See **Vault**

Panelboard
A metal box that encloses the electric wiring connections between the main feeder supply and the branch circuits; typically has a hinged door and contains a series of circuit breakers.

Paneled door See **Door**

Paneling
A finished surface composed of multiple thin wood panels held by rails, stiles, or moldings.

Pantheon
Temple dedicated to all the gods of a people; specifically the temple built in 25 B.C. in Rome by Emperor Hadrian, with a coffered concrete dome illuminated by an oculus at the top, set on a very thick circular drum, and having an octastyle portico attached to the drum outside.

Pantile
A roofing tile in the shape of an "S" laid on its side and overlapped in courses running up the slope of the roof.

Pantograph
A drafting instrument for copying drawings, or plans, either at the same scale or an enlarged or reduced scale.

Paper-mache
A material used for model making composed principally of paper; prepared by pulping a mass of paper and adding glue, to produce a dough-like consistency, and molding it into a desired form.

Papyriform capital See **Capital**

Parabolic
Forms which resemble a parabola in outline.

Parabolic arch See **Arch**

Paraline drawing See **Projection**

Parallel
Always the same distance apart; thus two parallel lines never meet.

Parallel counterpoint See **Counterpoint.**

Parallelogram
A quadrilateral having both pairs of the opposite sides parallel to each other.

Parapet
A low protective wall or railing along the edge of a raised platform, terrace, bridge, roof, balcony, and above cornices,

Parapet gutter
A gutter that is located behind a parapet wall.

Parapeted gable See **Gable**

Parasol
An umbrella form on top of a Chinese pagoda.

Pargetting See **Plaster**

Park
Public land used for outdoor recreation, ranging from a small urban plot to vast natural areas, such as the Grand Canyon.

Parking area
An area, usually paved, set aside for the parking or storage of vehicles.

Parking garage
A garage for passenger vehicles only, exclusively for the purpose of parking or storing of automobiles and not for automobile repairs or service work.

Parking lot
An area on the ground surface used for parking vehicles; may be paved or unpaved.

Parlor
A multipurpose room for sitting and formal entertainment, situated on the main floor of most dwellings.

Parquet
A flat inlay pattern of closely fitted pieces, usually geometrical, for ornamental flooring or wainscoting; often employing two or more colors or materials such as stone or wood.

Parquetry
Small pieces of wood fitted together to form a geometrical design.

Parthian architecture
The architecture (400 B.C.–200 A.D.) developed while under Parthian rule in Iran and western Mesopotamia, combining Classical with indigenous features.

Parti See **Design drawing**

Particle board See **Wood**

Partition wall See **Wall**

Party wall See **Wall**

Passage
Any interior corridor connecting room in a building; also called a hallway.

Passageway
A space that connects one area of a building with another.

Passive solar energy system
A system by which energy is collected from the sun and stored; then distributed throughout the structure by natural means of conduction convection or radiation.

Pastiche
Inappropriate architectural ornament added after the original work is completed.

Patera
A representation of a flat round or oval disk found in friezes.

Patina
A greenish-brown crust produced by oxidation that forms on the surface of copper and bronze, often multicolored and considered decorative; any thin oxide film which forms on a metal or other material.

Patio
An outdoor area, often paved and shaded, adjoining or enclosed by the walls or arcades of a house.

Pattern
The juxtaposition of repetitive elements in a design, organized so as to produce an arrangement of parts that are viewed as an unit; may occur at various scales and sizes.

Pattern book
A book on architectural practice that serves as a builder's manual, buyer's guide, or handbook, containing plans and details for common building element such as columns, cornices, and doors and windows.

Patterned block See **Masonry**

Patterned brickwork
Bricks with more than one color or texture that are laid in different directions, so as to form decorative designs.

Patterned brickwork

Patterned glass See **Glass**

Pavement

The durable surface of a sidewalk or other outdoor area, such as a walkway or open plaza.

Pavement light
Thick, translucent glass disks or prisms, set into a section of pavement to transmit light to a space below.

Pavilion
An open structure or small ornamental building, shelter or kiosk used as a summer house, or as an adjunct of a larger building. It is usually found as a detached structure for specialized activities, and is often located as a terminal structure with a hipped roof on all sides so as to have a pyramidal form.

Pavilion porch
Gazebo type structure projecting out of a veranda or porch.

Pavilion roof See Roof

Paving tile See Tile

Paxton, Sir Joseph (1801–1865)
English architect who designed the Crystal Palace, London (1851), the first prefabricated building in iron, glass, and laminated wood.

Peak-head window See Window

Pebble pavement
Pavement with a surface composed of water-rounded pebbles closely set in clay or concrete; different colors are often used in decorative designs.

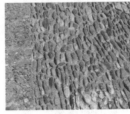

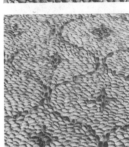

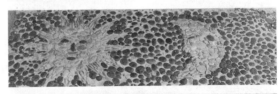

Pebble wall masonry See Masonry

Pebbledash
Small round stones applied to a fresh coat of plaster on an exterior wall to create a textured appearance.

Pedestal

A support for a column, urn, or statue, consisting of a base and a cap or cornice.

Pediment

A low-pitched triangular gable above a facade, or a smaller version over porticos above the doorway or above a window: a triangular gable end of the roof above the horizontal cornice, often decorated with sculpture.

Pediment

broken pediment

A pediment with its raking cornice split apart at the center, and the gap often filled with a cartouche, urn, or other ornament.

ogee pediment

Pediment in the shape of an ogee.

open pediment

A broken pediment

Pediment

round pediment
A round or curved pediment, used ornamentally over a door or window.

segmental pediment
A pediment above a door or window that takes the form of an arc of a circle.

swan's neck pediment
A broken pediment having a sloping double S-shaped element on each side of the pediment; used often in the Georgian style.

Peg
A tapered cylindrical wooden pin that is driven through a hole to hold two or more members together.

Peg-braced frame
A timber frame featuring pegged mortise-and-tenon joints and diagonal corner braces.

Pei, Ieoh Ming (1917–)
A Chinese-born American architect who studied with Walter Gropius at Harvard and worked with William Zeckendorf's contracting firm in New York City. His notable later works include Mile High Center, Denver (1955); National Center for Atmospheric Research, Boulder (1967); Christian Science Service Center, Boston (1971); John Hancock Tower, Boston (1975); Dallas Municipal Center (1977); National Gallery of Art, East Wing, Washington, D.C. (1978); Kennedy Library, Boston (1979); Jacob Javits Convention Center, New York City (1986); Holocaust Museum, Washington, D.C. (1986); Bank of China, Hong Kong (1990); the entrance pyramid at the Louvre Museum, Paris (1993), and the Rock 'n' Roll Hall of Fame, Cleveland (1995).

Pellet molding See **Molding**

Pelli, Cesar (1926–)
Argentine-born American architect who worked for Eero Saarinen before becoming director of design for Daniel, Mann, Johnson & Mendenhall in1964, and later the design partner, Gruen Associates. He set up his own practice in New Haven (1977). The Pacific Design Center, Los Angeles (1971), brought his name to notice. He designed the Winter Garden and World Financial Center at the World Trade Center, New York City (1981), the Canary Wharf Tower, London (1986), and the huge Petronas Twin Towers, Kuala Lampur, Malaysia (1997).

Pendant
A hanging ornament or suspended feature on ceilings or vaults.

Pendentive
The curved triangular surface that results when the top corner of a square space is vaulted so as to provide a circular base for a dome.

Pendentive bracketing
Corbeling in the general form of a pendentive; common in Moorish and Muslim architecture.

Pendil
The projecting and exposed lower end of a post of the overhanging upper story or jetty, often carved.

Penitentiary
Place for the imprisonment of inmates and for their reformation through discipline and work.

Pennsylvania barn
A bank barn found throughout Pennsylvania, employing an overshoot on the side opposite the bank; the livestock are housed in the masonry lower level, and the timber frame haymow occupies the upper levels.

Pent roof See **Roof**

Pentagonal
A plane figure with five equal sides and five equal angles, commonly found in nature.

Pentastyle
A portico having five columns in front.

Penthouse
A structure on a fiat-roofed building: occupying usually less than half the roof area.

Pereira, William (1910–1990)
Founder of the Los Angeles-based firm of Pereira and Luckman, with Charles Luckman.

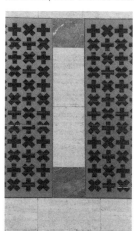

Perforated
Forms that exhibit holes or a series of holes in a pattern; formed by combining elements to produce voids, or through carving or casting materials containing pierced openings.

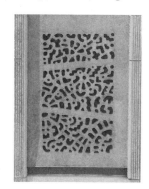

Pergola

A garden structure that consists of an open wooden-framed roof, often latticed and supported by regularly spaced posts or columns and covered by climbing plants to shade a walk or passageway.

Peripteral

Surrounded on the outside perimeter by a single row of columns.

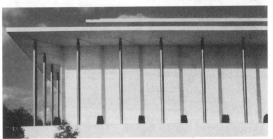

Peripteral temple

A temple surrounded by a single row of columns.

Perkins, Lawrence (1907–1982)

Founder of the Chicago-based firm of Perkins and Will.

Perpendicular

Line or plane that meets another at right angles.

Perpendicular style

The last and longest phase of Gothic architecture in England (1350–1550), was characterized by a vertical emphasis and elaborate fan vaults displaying perpendicular tracery.

Perpendicular tracery See Tracery

Perrault, Claude (1613–1688)

French architect, one of the designers of the Louvre, Paris (1665), notably the east facade.

Perret, Auguste (1874–1955)

His 25 Rue Franklin apartment house in Paris (1903) was an early example of reinforced-concrete frame construction. He designed the Garage Ponthiew in Paris (1906) and Notre-Dame le Raincy (1922), a hall-church design built with reinforced-concrete vaults and walls glazed with stained glass.

Perron

A formal terrace or platform, especially one centered on a gate or doorway; an outdoor flight of steps, usually symmetrical, leading to a terrace.

Persian architecture

Architecture (550–330 B.C.) developed under the kings who ruled ancient Persia during the Achaemenid dynasty, it was characterized by a synthesis of architectural elements from surrounding countries, such as Assyria, Egypt and Greece.

Persona

A mask of terra-cotta, stone or marble, designed to imitate the human face or the head of an animal, usually in the form of a grotesque; employed as an antic or as a gargoyle for discharging water.

Perspective drawing
Any one of a variety of techniques to represent three-dimensional objects and spatial relationships on a two-dimensional surface in the same manner as they would appear to the eye.

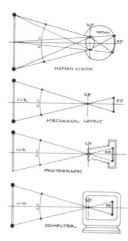

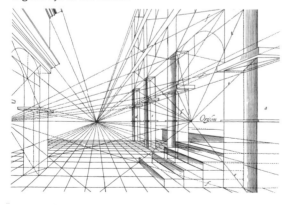

Perspective projection
A method of projection in which a three-dimensional object can be represented by projecting points upon a picture plane using straight lines converging at a fixed point, representing the eye of the viewer.

central visual axis
The sightline, which is perpendicular to the picture plane, indicating the direction in which the viewer is looking.

center of vision
A point representing the intersection of the central axis of vision and the picture plane in linear perspective drawing.

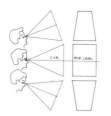

cone of vision
The field of vision radiating outwardly from the eye of the viewer in a more or less conical shape along the central visual axis.

ground line
A horizontal line representing the intersection of the ground plane and the picture plane.

ground plane
A horizontal plane of reference in linear perspective from which vertical measurements can be taken; usually it is the plane supporting the object depicted or the one on which the viewer stands.

horizon line
A horizontal line in linear perspective representing the intersection of the picture plane and a horizontal plane through the eye of the viewer.

measuring line
Any line coincident with or parallel to the picture plane, as the ground line, on which measurements can be taken.

one-point perspective
A rendition of an object with a principal face parallel to the picture plane; all horizontal lines parallel to the picture plane remain as is, and all other horizontal lines converge to a pre-selected vanishing point .

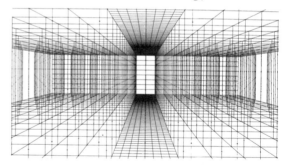

picture plane
An imaginary transparent plane, coexistent with the drawing surface, on which the image of a three-dimensional object is projected and on which all lines can be measured and drawn to exact scale.

station point
A fixed point in space representing a single eye of the viewer.

three-point perspective
A perspective of an object with all faces oblique to the picture plane; the three sets of parallel lines converge to three different vanishing points: one left, one right, and one above or below the horizon line.

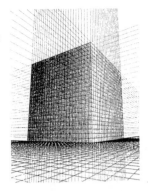

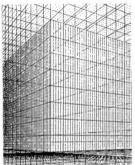

two-point perspective
A perspective of an object having two faces oblique to the picture plane. The vertical lines parallel to the picture plane remain vertical, and two horizontal sets of parallel lines oblique to the picture plane appear to converge to two vanishing points: one to the left and one to the right.

vanishing point
A point toward which receding parallel lines appear to converge, located at the point where a sight line parallel to the set of lines intersects picture plane.

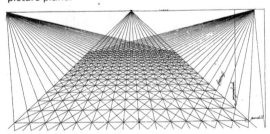

Peruzzi, Baldassare (1481–1536)
High Renaissance and Mannerist Italian architect; designed the Villa Farnesina, Rome (1505). Inside are brilliant frescoes by Raphael, Peruzzi, and others.

Photogrammetry
The process of producing accurate maps by tracing outlines of contours produced by stereo aerial photographs with specialized stereoscopic plotters.

Piano nobile
The principal, great or noble, floor, usually containing state rooms on the first floor above the ground or basement.

Piano, Renzo (1937–)
Italian architect; worked with Richard Rogers designing the high-tech Centre Pompidou, Paris (1971). His later work included the Kansai International airport, Osaka, Japan (1994), one of the longest structures in the world. He was very much influenced by Futurism, Archigram and Constructivism.

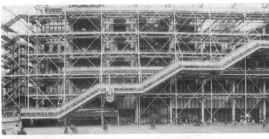

Piazza
A public open space or square surrounded by buildings.

Pictograph
A stylized illustration used for communication; also includes symbols that were scratched or painted on rock surfaces by prehistoric people.

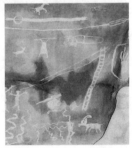

Picture plane See **Perspective projection**

Picture window See **Window**

Picturesque movement
A reaction to the Classical Revival Style architecture that included irregularly planned landscapes, follies, grottos, and asymmetrical buildings, mostly in the Italianate style.

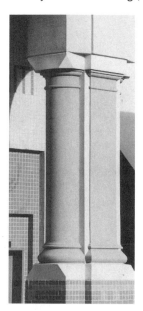

Pier
A free-standing support for an arch, usually composite in section and thicker than a column, but performing the same function; also, a thickened part of a wall to provide lateral support or bear concentrated loads.

Pier arch See **Arch**

Pier buttress
A pier which receives the thrust of a flying buttress.

Pierced work
Decoration which consists mainly of perforations, such as a non-bearing masonry wall in which an ornamental pierced effect is achieved by alternating rectangular or any other shaped blocks with open spaces.

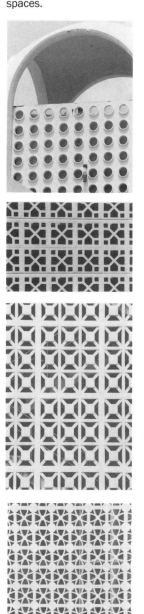

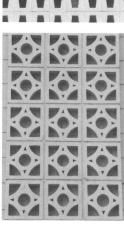

Pilaster
A partial pier or column, often with a base, shaft and capital, that is embedded in a flat wall and projects slightly; may be constructed as a projection of the wall itself.

grouped pilaster
Three or more closely spaced pilasters forming a group, often on one pedestal.

Pilaster face
The front surface of a pilaster that is parallel to the wall.

Pilaster face

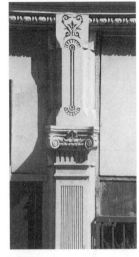

Pilaster mass
An engaged pier built up with the wall, usually without a capital or base.

Pilaster side
The form of the side surface of a pilaster perpendicular to the wall.

Pilaster strip
A slender pier of minimal projection.

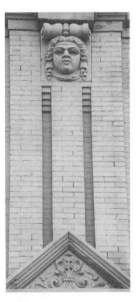

Pile
One of a series of large timbers or steel sections driven into soft ground down to bedrock to provide a solid foundation for the superstructure of a building.

Pillar
A column or post support-
ing an arch or other superimposed load. Clustered
or compound pillars
consist of a central shaft
with smaller shafts that
are grouped around it.

Pilotis
The free-standing columns, posts, or piles that support a building, raising it above an open ground level.

Pin
A peg or bolt of wood, metal, or any other material, which is used to fasten or hold something in place, or serve as a point of support.

Pin connection
A structural connection of
a truss or bridge made by
a pin in an eyebar, rather
than a rivet or turnbuckle.

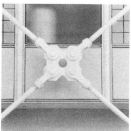

Pine cone ornament See **Ornament**

Pineapple ornament See **Ornament**

Pinnacle
An apex or small turret,
that usually tapers toward
the top as a termination
to a buttress.

Pinwheel
Shapes that are fixed at the center with identical radiating arms, either angular or curvilinear, and repeated any
number of times within the circumference of the circle
from which they are generated.

Pipe column See **Column**

Pipework
An assembly of pipes
and fittings used for the
conveyance of fluids.

Piranesi, Giovanni Battista (1720–1788)
Published *Della Magnificenza de Architectura de' Ro-
mani*, and *Invenzioni Capric di Carceri*, the "Prisons"
(c. 1745).

Pisé
A building whose walls are made of compressed earth, usually stiff clay formed and rammed into a movable framework; the building material itself; i.e., stiff earth or clay, rammed until firm to form walls and floors.

Pit dwelling
A excavated residence that is either partially or wholly below grade; found in the southwest U.S. and northern Mexico.

Pitch
Angle of a roof, or the proportion between the height and span of the roof.

Pitched roof See **Roof**

Pitch-faced masonry See **Masonry**

Pivoted door See **Door**

Pivoting window See **Window**

Plaid
A pattern created by regularly spaced bands at right angles to one another; the resultant checkered effects vary widely, depending on the relationship and intervals between lines and bands.

Plain
Unadorned; without any pattern or ornamentation.

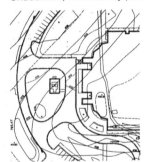

Plan
A two-dimensional graphic representation of the design and dimensions of the project, or parts thereof, viewed in a horizontal plane from above.

Plane
The simplest kind of two-dimensional surface, generated by the path of a straight line and defined by its length and width; the fundamental property of a plane is its shape and surface characteristics.

Plank
A long, flat piece of wood measuring at least two inches in thickness and more than eight inches in width; used for flooring and sheathing.

Plank house
A type of timber construction consisting of sawn planks laid horizontally and notched at the corners.

Plank-frame
A type of house in colonial America constructed of heavy wood planks erected vertically into grooves in a sill plate, and drilled and pegged together.

Planned Unit Development (PUD)
A zoning process that allows a developer to offer public amenities, such as building roads, schools, or providing open space in exchange for looser restrictions on density or building heights.

Planning
The process of studying the layout of spaces within a building or other facility, or installations in open spaces, in order to develop the general scheme of a building or group of buildings.

Planning grid
An arrangement of one or more sets of regularly spaced parallel lines, with the sets at right angles or any other selected angles to each other, and used like graph paper.

Plantation house
The principal house of a southern plantation on which cash crops were cultivated; typically two stories with very tall windows, with a veranda across the entire front facade, supported by two-story columns.

Planter
A permanent, ornamental container to receive planted pots or boxes, often nonmovable and integral with the finish of a building

Plaque
A tablet, often inscribed, added to or set into a surface on the exterior or interior wall.

Plaster
A mixture of lime or gypsum, sand, portland cement and water to produce a paste-like material which can be applied to the surfaces of walls and ceilings and which later sets to form a hard surface.

daubing
A rough coating of plaster given to a wall by throwing plaster against it.

intonaco
The fine finish coat of plaster made with white marble dust to receive a fresco painting.

pargetting
A decorative feature in which flat wet plaster is ornamented by patterns either scratched or molded into it; sometimes decorated with figures either in low relief or indented.

rendering
A coat of plaster directly on an interior wall or stucco on an exterior wall; a perspective or elevation drawing of a project or portion thereof with artistic delineation of materials, shades, and shadows.

scagliola
Plaster work that imitates stone, in which mixtures of marble dust, sizing, and various pigments are laid in decorative figures routed into the surface.

shikkui
A plaster, mortar, stucco, or whitewash, made from a mixture of lime and clay and having the consistency of glue, used in traditional Japanese construction.

Plaster of paris
A gypsum substance especially suitable for fine ornamental plasterwork: because it fills a mold completely and dries quickly.

Plasterboard
A building board made of a core of gypsum or plaster, faced with two sheets of heavy paper.

Plastic
Any of the various synthetic complex organic compounds produced by polymerization; can be molded, extruded, or cast into various shapes or drawn into fibers.

acrylic fiber
A synthetic polymer fiber.

fiberglass
The generic term for a material consisting of extremely fine filaments of glass that are mixed with a resin to give the desired form in a mold. Layers of this combination are laid or sprayed into the mold.

nylon
A class of thermoplastics characterized by extreme toughness, strength, and elasticity and capable of being extruded into filaments, fibers and sheets.

plexiglass
Used for windows and lighting fixtures.

polystyrene plastic
A hard, tough, stable thermoplastic that is easily colored, molded, expanded, or rolled into sheeting.

polyethelene
A tough, light, flexible thermoplastic used in the form of sheeting and film for packaging, damp-proofing, and as a vapor barrier.

vinyl
Any of various tough, flexible plastics made from polyvinyl resin.

Plastic laminate
A laminate consisting of paper, cloth or wood covered with a phenolic resin; used for countertops and cabinets that require a washable finish.

Plastic wood See Wood

Plasticizer
Admixture to mortar or concrete which increases its workability.

Plate
In wood frame construction, a horizontal board connecting and terminating posts, joists, or rafters; a timber laid horizontally on the ground to receive other timbers or joists.

Plate girder See Beam

Plate glass See Glass

Plate tracery See Tracery

Plateresque architecture
The richly decorative style of the Spanish Renaissance in the sixteenth century; also referred to as Isabelline architecture, after Queen Isabella (1474–1504).

Platform
A raised floor or terrace, open or roofed; a stair landing.

Platform framing
A system for framing wooden structures in which the studs are only one-story high; the floor joists rest on the top plates of the story below, and the bearing walls and partitions rest on the subfloor of each story.

Plaza
An open square or market place having one or more levels, approached in various ways by avenues, streets, or stairs or a combination.

Plenum
The air space in an integrated ceiling, which may be above atmospheric pressure if used for the air supply, or below atmospheric pressure if used for the air exhaust.

Plenum chamber
An air compartment maintained at a pressure slightly above atmospheric, to deliver and distribute the air to one or more ducts or outlets.

Plenum system
A method of heating or air-conditioning whereby the air forced into the building is at a pressure slightly above atmospheric.

Plexiglass See **Plastic**

Plinth
A square or rectangular base for column, pilaster, or door framing to support a statue or memorial; a solid monumental base, often ornamented with moldings, bas-reliefs, or other inscriptions.

Plinth block
A flat, plain member at the base of a pillar, column, pedestal, or statue.

Plot
A parcel of land consisting of one or more lots or portions thereof, which is described by reference to a recorded plot by survey.

Plot ratio
The gross floor area of a building divided by the area of its site. The basic ratio permitted is frequently modified by providing a bonus for arcades, setbacks, plazas, and the incorporation of existing buildings of architectural significance.

Plug-in architecture
A new type of architecture (1964–1970) proposed by the group Archigram. It consisted of a basic structure to contain transportation and communication services and a series of separate units–domestic environments, shops, and leisure activities–that are plugged into a central module.

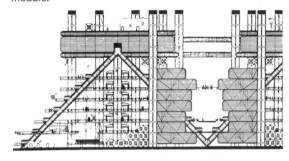

Plumb
Any method of lining up the building elements in a true vertical direction.

Plumber
A craftsman skilled in the fitting of pipes, both for the supply of water and gas as well as for waste, soil, fire protection, and drainage.

Plumbing system
The combination of supply and distribution pipes for hot water, cold water, and gas and for removing liquid wastes in a building which includes: the water-supply distribution pipes; fixtures and traps; the soils, waste, and vent pipes; the building drain and building sewer; storm-drainage pipes; and all connections within or adjacent to the building.

Ply
A thickness of material, used for building up several layers, as in plywood and built-up roofing.

Plywood See **Wood**

Pneumatic architecture
A term referring to a style (1850–1880) of structures that are air-inflated, air-supported, and air-controlled. Structures generally consist of curved forms, domes or half cylinders. Their rounded forms are organic and responsive to the technology which utilizes fabric and cables supported from within by air pressure.

Pneumatic structure
A structure held up by a slight excess of internal air pressure above the pressure outside; it must be sufficient to balance the weight of the roof membrane and must be maintained by air compressors or fans.

Pocket door See **Door**

Podium
Any elevated platform; the high platform on which Roman temples were generally placed; a low step-like projection from a wall or building, intended to form a raised platform for placing objects.

Poelzig, Hans (1869–1936)
Berlin-born architect, who as city architect of Dresden, Germany, designed the Grosse Schauspielhaus, Berlin (1919), and Chemical Plant, Luban (1912). As a professor, he produced several fantastic Expressionist designs, all unrealized.

Point
The smallest unit in a composition, depending on the scale of the work; it may be composed of straight lines and arcs, forms (flowing and curvilinear), or a combination of all.

Pointed arch See Arch

Pointed work
The rough finish that is produced by a pointed tool on the face of a stone.

Pointing
The finishing operation on a mortar joint, without the addition of surface mortar; pressing surface mortar into an existing raked joint.

Pole
A slender log used as a structural member, with or without the bark removed.

Pole structure
A building or structure with a roof supported by round wood columns

Polk, Willis (1867–1924)
An American architect working in San Francisco; influenced by McKim, Mead & White. He assisted Daniel Burnham in the city plan for San Francisco (1904). The Hallidie Building, San Francisco (1917), is his most distinctive work, having a fully glazed curtain wall hung from the main framed structure, the first of its kind.

Polshek, James Stewart (1930–)
Most noted for the New York State Bar Center, Albany (1971), and most recently designer of the new Rose Planetarium at the Museum of Natural History, New York City (2000).

Polygonal
Forms characteristic of a closed plane figure having three or more straight sides.

Polychromatic
Having or exhibiting a variety of colors.

Polychromy
The practice of decorating architectural elements or sculpture in a variety of colors.

Polyethelene See **Plastic**

Polygonal masonry See **Masonry**

Polygonal vault See **Vault**

Polyhedron
A solid geometric figure bounded by plane faces.

Polymer concrete
A concrete in which a plastic is used as a binder, instead of portland cement.

Polystyle colonnade
Colonnade with many columns, such as one situated around a building.

Polystyrene See **Plastic**

Polysulfide
A thermosetting resin, used as a building sealant.

Polyurethane
A group of plastics used mainly as a light insulating material in the form of flexible or rigid foam and as a sealant.

Polyvinyl chloride
A synthetic vinyl resin commonly used for the manufacture of PVC pipe; used for plumbing and waste lines.

Pompeii (1592)
The date that ruins of the city buried by the eruption of a volcano in 79 A.D. was first discovered. Excavations of the ruins did not begin until 1709.

Pompeii

Ponti, Gio (1891–1979)
Italian architect and designer, influenced by the Sezession movement and Otto Wagner. He was the founder-director of _Domus_ magazine (1928). He worked with Nervi in the design of the Pirelli Tower in Milan, Italy (1956), and designed the Museum of Modern Art in Denver (1972).

Pop architecture
A style (1962–1974) which refers to structures that symbolically represent objects, to fantastic designs for vast sculptures on an architectural scale, or to any architecture produced more as metaphor than building.

Pope, John Russell (1874–1937)

Disciple of McKim, Mead & White; he trained at the Ecole des Beaux Arts, Paris. Designed the Jefferson Memorial (1937) and the National Gallery of Art (1937), both in Washington, D.C., and the Sculpture Hall, Tate Gallery, London (1937). The latter contains the sculpture from the Parthenon in Athens – the Elgin Marbles.

Poppelmann, Daniel (1662–1736)

German architect, who designed the Zwinger Palace, Dresden, Germany (1722), with Marcus Dietze. It is a Baroque structure with rich sculptural decoration.

Porcelain enamel

A glassy metal oxide coating bonded to a metal panel at an extremely high temperature and baked onto steel panels for large architectural applications. It is a very durable material that is scratch resistant.

Porch

A roofed entrance, either incorporated in a building or as an applied feature on the exterior.

Porta, Giacomo della (1533–1604)

Italian Mannerist architect; who completed the dome of St. Peter's and also completed other designs by Michelangelo.

Portal

An entrance, gate, or door to a building or courtyard, often decorated, it marks the transition from the public exterior to the private interior space.

Portico

A range of columns or arches in front of a building, often merged into the facade, including a covered walkway of which one or more sides are open. It includes every kind of covered ambulatory.

Portman, John, Jr. (1924–)

American architect/developer known for his large urban buildings, including Peachtree Center (1961) and the Hyatt Regency Hotel (1967), both in Atlanta. He also designed Rockefeller West in San Francisco (1975); and an office tower, One Peachtree Center, Atlanta (1992).

Post

Any stiff, vertical upright, made of wood, stone, or metal, used to support a superstructure or provide a firm point of lateral attachment.

angle post

The corner post in half-timbered construction.

crown post

Vertical member in a roof truss, especially a king post.

king post

A vertical member extending from the apex of the inclined rafters to the tie beam between the rafters at the lower ends of a truss, as well as in a roof.

queen post

One of the two vertical supports in a queen-post truss.

Post, George B. (1837–1913)

American architect and engineer, designed early skyscrapers of 10 stories; his best-known work is the New York Stock Exchange.

Post-and-beam

A type of framing in which horizontal members are supported by a vertical post rather than by a bearing wall: or a system of arches and vaults.

Post-and-lintel

A type of construction characterized by the use of vertical columns, posts and a horizontal beam, or lintel to carry a load over an opening, in contrast to structural systems employing arches or vaults.

Postmodernism

A reaction against the International style and Modernism was evidenced in this style (1980–). It reintroduced ornament and decorative motifs to building design, often in garish colors and illogical juxtaposition.

It is an eclectic borrowing of historical details from several periods, but unlike previous revivals is not concerned with scholarly reproduction. Instead, it is a light-hearted compilation of esthetic symbols and details, often using arbitrary geometry, and with an intentional inconsistency of scale.

The most prevalent aspect is the irony, ambiguity and contradiction in the use of architectural forms. Those connected with the beginning of this movement include Aldo Rossi, Stanley Tigerman, Charles Moore, Michael Graves, Robert Krier, and Terry Farrell.

Postmodernism

Prairie style

A style (1900–1940) that is typical of the low horizontal house associated mostly with the work of Frank Lloyd Wright and his followers. Horizontal elements were emphasized in these one- or two-story houses, built with brick or timber and covered with stucco.

The central portion that rises above the flanking wings were separated by clerestory windows. The eaves of the low-pitched roof extend well beyond the wall. A large chimney is located at the axis of intersecting roof planes. Casement windows are grouped into horizontal bands continuing around the corners.

Exterior walls are highlighted by dark wood strips against a lighter stucco finish or by a coping of smooth stucco at the top of brick walls.

Prandtauer, Jacob (1660–1726)

Rebuilt Melk Abbey (1702), which is dramatically sited above the Danube River; its facade is undulating Baroque in a mixture of white and cream-colored bands.

Pratt truss See **Truss**

Precast
A building material that is molded before it is incorporated into a building; used for both structural and ornamental elements.

Pre-Columbian architecture
The design and construction of Native American structures prior to the voyage of Columbus and contact with any European culture.

Predock, Antoine (1936)
New Mexico–based architect using stark, abstract forms and natural desert materials, whose most well known works are the Nelson Fine Arts Center, Arizona State University, Tempe, Arizona (1989), and the Las Vegas Library and Discovery Museum (1990).

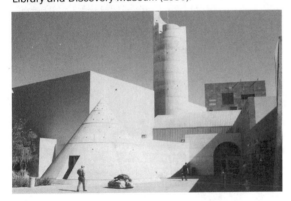

Prefabricated house
A house assembled from components cut to size at a factory, or assembled from entire building modules shipped to the construction site.

Prefabrication
The manufacture of standardized units or components, usually at a mill or plant away from the site, for quick assembly and erection on the job site.

Prehistoric architecture
Design of buildings before written records were kept.

Prehistoric era
The era before written or recorded human events, knowledge of which is gathered through archaeological investigations, discoveries and research.

Presentation drawing See **Design drawing**

Preservation
Protection of a material from physical deterioration due to natural elements or human activity; by various technical, scientific, and craft techniques

Preservative
A substance that inhibits decay, infection, or attack by fungi and insects in timber.

Pressed brick See **Brick**

Pressed-metal ceiling
A thin sheet metal that is embossed with a decorative pattern and coated with a layer of tin or lead or prepared with an undercoat of paint to prevent oxidation; used as ceiling panels by nailing to the underside of beams or furring strips.

Prestressed concrete See **Concrete**

Pretensioning
Prestressed concrete in which the tendons are tensioned before the concrete has hardened, and generally before it is cast; the concrete is cast around the wires which are flame-cut after the concrete has hardened.

Primary colors
Hues red, yellow, and blue. From these three colors, with the addition of white, it is possible to create the full color spectrum.

Prince, Bart (1947–)
American architect who studied under Bruce Goff, proponent of organic architecture, designed the Prince House, Albuquerque (1984), and the Price House, Corona Del Mar (1989).

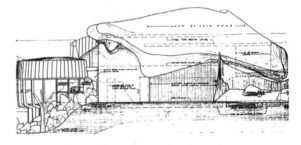

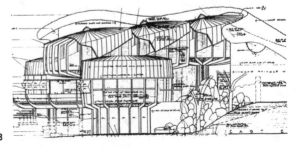

Principal purlin
A massive wood purlin that runs parallel to the ridge of the roof about midway between the ridge and top plate: it is framed into the principal rafters and supports a number of common rafters.

Principal rafter
One of several such wooden rafters that extend from the ridge uninterrupted down to the wall plate; more massive than common rafters, and framed into a tie beam that makes the assembly more stable.

Prism
Geometric solid with regular polygons at its ends and parallelograms on its sides connecting the ends.

Prismatic
Characteristic of a solid figure in which the two ends are similar and parallel, with parallelograms for sides: used extensively in space frames covering open areas or large atrium areas.

Prismatic glass See **Glass**

Prison
A place used to confine persons either for punishment or rehabilitation.

Pro forma
A statement of the economic analysis of the costs and value of a proposed real estate development; usually includes land costs, hard and soft costs, equity, financing and sales price.

Profile
An outline of a form or structure seen or represented from the side, or one formed by a vertical plane passed through an object at right angles to one of its main horizontal dimensions.

Program
A written document that defines the intended functions and uses of a building, or site, and is used to initiate and control an architectural design or preservation project.

Progression
A gradual increase in the size or shape of a form or design, keeping the same basic theme or Idea.

Project management
The practice of developing, planning, procuring and controlling the services and activities required for the satisfactory completion of a project according to an agreed time and cost.

Projecting window See **Window**

Projection
Any component, member, or part that juts out from a building; in masonry construction, stones or bricks that are set forward off the general wall surface to provide a rugged appearance.

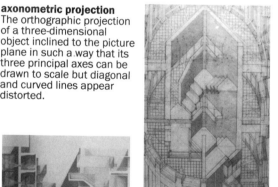

Projection drawing
The process or technique of representing a three-dimensional object by projecting all its points by straight lines, either parallel or converging to a picture plane.

axonometric projection
The orthographic projection of a three-dimensional object inclined to the picture plane in such a way that its three principal axes can be drawn to scale but diagonal and curved lines appear distorted.

cutaway
A drawing or model having an outer section removed to display the interior space.

dimetric projection

An axonometric projection of a three-dimensional object to the picture plane in such a way that two of its principal axes are equally foreshortened, and the third appears longer or shorter than the other two.

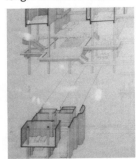

exploded view

A drawing that shows the individual parts of a structure or construction separately, but indicates their proper relationship to each other and to the whole.

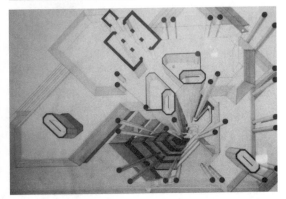

isometric projection

An axonometric projection of a three-dimensional object is created by having its principal faces equally inclined to the picture plane; so that its three principal axes are all equally foreshortened.

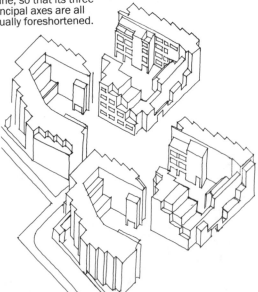

longitudinal section

An orthographic projection of a section made by cutting through the longest axis of an object.

oblique projection

A method of projection in which a three-dimensional object, having one principal face parallel to the picture plane, is represented by projecting parallel lines at some angle other than 90 degrees.

oblique section

An orthographic projection of a section made by cutting with a plane that is neither parallel nor perpendicular to the long axis of an object.

orthographic projection

A method of projection in which a three-dimensional object is represented by projecting lines perpendicular to a picture plane.

paraline drawing

Any of various single-view drawings characterized by parallel lines remaining parallel to each other rather than converging as in linear perspective.

section

An orthographic projection of an object or structure as it will appear if cut through by an intersecting plane to expose its internal configuration.

transverse section
An orthographic projection of a section made by cutting through an object along the shortest axis.

trimetric projection
An axonometric projection of a three-dimensional object inclined to the picture plane in such a way that all three principal axes are foreshortened at a different rate.

Promenade
A suitable place for walking for pleasure, as in a mall.

Pronaos
Vestibule in a Greek temple that stands in front of the doorway to the naos.

Prophyrios, Demetri (1949–)
Greek-born architect most well known for his classically inspired designs and publications on the Classical Style.

Propylaeum
The monumental gateway to a sacred enclosure: specifically, the elaborate gateway to the Acropolis in Athens.

Proportion
The ratio of one part to another, or its relationship to the whole; a comparison of parts as to size, length, width, and depth.

Proposal
A written offer from a contractor to perform work and/or supply materials; typically describes the extent of the work and its cost.

Propylon
A monumental gateway, usually between two towers, in ancient Egyptian architecture. One, or a series, stood in front of the actual entrance or pylon of most temples and other important buildings.

Proscenium
The portion of a theater stage between the drop curtain and the orchestra.

Proscenium arch See **Arch**

Prostyle
Having a portico featuring columns at the exterior front of a building only.

Pseudoperipteral
A Classical temple or other building which has columns all the way around; those on the flanks and rear are engaged rather than freestanding.

Public garden
An urban ground laid out with walks, plantings, and buildings, which offer a variety of entertainment and recreation to the public.

Public housing
Low-cost housing, owned, sponsored, or administered by a municipal or other government agency.

Pueblo
A communal dwelling and defensive structure of the Pueblo Indians of the southwestern United States, built of adobe or stone, typically multistoried and terraced, with entry through the flat roofs by ladder.

Pueblo architecture
Houses of thick adobe construction, built by the Pueblo Indians in New Mexico and Arizona, featuring multistoried units with stepped back roof lines, access to which was by wooden ladders.

Pueblo Revival style
A style loosely based on the adobe pueblos of the southwestern U.S.; typical elements include irregular massing, flat roofs with projecting beams, and rounded parapets and corners.

Pueblo style
A style (1905–1940) characterized by battered walls, rounded corners, and flat roofs with rounded ends of projecting roof beams. Windows had straight heads set deep into the walls. The second and third floors are terraced, resembling the Indian pueblos of the southwest.

Purcell, William (1880–1965)
Scottish-born American architect who, with partner George Grant Elmslie (1871–1952), helped establish the Prairie School Style as applied to the many homes they designed. He had previously worked with Adler and Sullivan on the ornamentation for the Cage Building (1898) and the Carson Pirie Scott Store (1904), both in Chicago.

Purism
A movement linked to the painter Ozenfant and architect Le Corbusier, to adapt lessons inherent in the precision of machinery, influencing the architectural theories of Constructivism and the teachings of the Bauhaus.

Purlin
A piece of timber laid horizontally on the principal rafters of a roof to support the common rafters on which the roof covering is laid.

Putto
A decorative sculpture or painting representing chubby, usually naked infants; used in Renaissance architecture and classical derivatives.

Putty
A heavy paste used to fill holes and cracks prior to painting, also used to secure glass panes.

Pylon
A monumental gateway in the form of a truncated pyramid or other vertical shaft that marks the entrance approach to a structure.

Pyramid
A polyhedron with a polygonal base and triangular faces meeting at a single common apex.

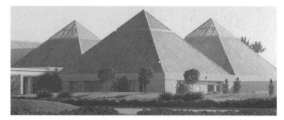

Pyramidal roof See **Roof**

Q q

Quadra
Square border or frame enclosing a wall panel or painting; also refers to a square base or plinth at the bottom of a pedestal or podium.

Quadrafron
Having four fronts or faces looking in four directions.

Quadrafron capital See **Capital**

Quadrangle
A rectangular courtyard or grassy area enclosed by buildings, most often used in conjunction with academic or civic building groupings.

Quadrant
Arc of a circle, forming one quarter of its circumference.

Quadratura
In Baroque interiors and derivatives, painted architecture, often continuing into the three-dimensional trim, executed by specialists in calculated perspective.

Quadrilateral
A plane figure bounded by four straight lines. If two of the lines are parallel, it is a trapezium. If two pairs of lines are parallel, it is a parallelogram. An equilateral parallelogram is a rhombus. A right-angled rhombus is a square.

Quadro-riportato
The simulation of a wall painting for a ceiling design in which painted scenes are arranged in panels that resemble frames on the surface of a shallow, curved vault.

Quaint
A term used to refer to antique or old-fashioned styles, such as English style cottages and Queen Anne houses.

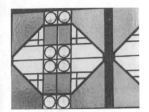

Quarry
A small, square or diamond-shaped pane of glass used in leaded windows.

Quarry-faced masonry See **Masonry**

Quarry tile See **Tile**

Quartered
Lumber that is sawn from a log at a perpendicular angle to the growth rings; the lumber sawn in this manner is easier to dry without warping and shrinking, and is used for flooring and weatherboards.

Quarter-round molding See **Molding**

Quartrafoil See **Foil**

Quattrocento
In the style of the early Italian Renaissance during the fifteenth century; from the Italian for four hundred, referring to dates starting with the number 14, that is, 1400 to 1499.

Quartzite See **Stone**

Queen closer See **Brick**

Queen post See **Post**

Quirk
An indentation separating one element from another, such as between moldings.

Quirk bead molding See **Molding**

Quirked molding See **molding**

Quoin
One of a series of stones or bricks used to mark or visually reinforce the exterior corners of a building; often through a contrast of size, shape, color or material, which may be imitated in non-load-bearing materials.

rustic quoin
A quoin treated with sunken joints, with its face generally roughened and raised above the surface of the masonry.

Quoin header
A quoin which serves as a header in the face of a wall and a stretcher in the face of the return wall.

Quoining
Any material that forms a quoin.

Quonset hut
A prefabricated military structure in the form of a barrel vault with flat ends, and composed of corrugated sheet steel that is reinforced with steel ribs.

R r

Rabbet
A long groove or channel that is cut into the edge or face of a board to receive another board that is fitted into the groove at a right angle to it.

Rabbeted
Two members joined together by interlocking grooves cut into each one.

Radial
Forms radiating from or converging to a common center or developing symmetrically about a central point.

Radial dome See **Dome**

Radial organization See **Organization**

Radial symmetry See **Symmetry**

Radiant heat
Heat transmitted to a body by electromagnetic waves, as distinct from heat transferred by thermal conduction or convection.

Radiating chapels
Chapels added to an apse and fanning out in a radial pattern.

Rafter
One of a series of inclined members that support the sheathing to which a roof covering is fixed.

hip rafter
A rafter located at the junction of the sloping sides of a hip roof.

jack rafter
Any rafter shorter than the full length of the sloping roof, such as one beginning or ending at a hip or valley.

valley rafter
In a roof framing system, the rafter in the line of the valley; connects the ridge to the wall plate along the meeting line of two inclined sides of a roof that are perpendicular to each other.

Rafter plate
A plate that supports the lower end of rafters and to which they are fixed.

Rafter tail
Portion of a rafter that projects beyond the exterior wall to support the eaves.

Rail
A bar of wood or other material passing from one post or support to another support; a horizontal piece in the frame or paneling, as in a door rail or in the framework of a window sash.

Railing
Any open construction or rail used as a barrier, composed of one or a series of horizontal rails supported by spaced upright balusters.

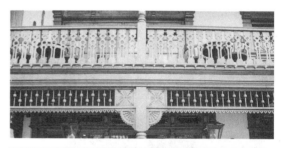

Railroad station
The structure where a train stops to load and unload passengers or freight; types range from a simple platform at grade to a large building with access to multiple raised covered platforms, including additional functions in the terminal itself.

Rainproof
Constructed, protected, or treated to prevent rain from entering a building.

Raised floor See **Floor**

Raised molding See **Molding**

Raised skylight
A skylight with the glazing frame supported on a curb above the roof surface.

Rake
The slope, or angle of inclination; the context usually indicates whether it is measured from the horizontal or the vertical axis.

Raked mortar joint See **Joint**

Raking bond See **Bond**

Raking coping See **Coping**

Raking cornice See **Cornice**

Raking molding See **Molding**

Ramp
An inclined plane.

Rampant arch See **Arch**

Rampant vault See **Vault**

Rampart
An earthen wall located on the inner side of a ditch surrounding a bastion for purposes of defense.

Random ashlar masonry See **Masonry**

Random coursed ashlar See **Masonry**

Random rubble See **Masonry**

Range
In masonry, a row or course of stonework, or a wall laid up in courses.

Rapson, Ralph (1914–)
Minneapolis-based architect, whose career began working with Eero Saarinen. Notable works include: Cedar Square West, Minneapolis (1974), and the Tyrone Guthrie Theater, Minneapolis (1963).

Ratio
A relationship in magnitude, quantity, or degree, between two or more similar things.

Razing
The process of demolishing a structure without possibile reconstruction.

Ready-mixed concrete
Concrete that is mixed at a central plant and transported to the building site.

Rear arch See **Arch**

Recess
Receding part or space, such as a cavity in a wall for a door, an alcove, or a niche.

Recessed
Forms created by indentations or small hollows in an other- wise plain surface or straight line; can be angular, rectilinear or curvilinear.

Recessed arch See **Arch**

Recessed dormer See **Dormer**

Recessed luminaire
A luminaire recessed into a ceiling, so that its lower edge is flush with the ceiling, as compared with surface mounting.

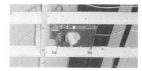

Reconstruction
The process of duplicating the original materials, form, and appearance of a historic building that no longer exists based on historical research; most often located at the original site.

Record drawings
Construction drawings revised to show significant changes made during the construction process, usually based on marked-up prints, drawings, and other data furnished by the contractor to the architect.

Rectangle
A plane four-sided parallelogram with four right angles; may be nearly square or stretched out to be nearly a band.

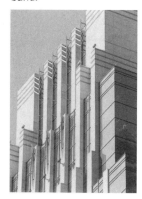

Rectilinear
Forming, formed by, or characterized by straight lines.

Rectilinear style
Similar to the Perpendicular style; it is characterized by perpendicular tracery and intricate stonework.

Redwood See **Wood**

Reed molding See **Molding**

Refectory
A room for dining in a monastery, college, or other institution.

Reflected ceiling plan
The plan of a ceiling as if it were reflected onto a flat surface directly below.

Reflection
The action on the part of surfaces of throwing back rays of light or sound falling upon them.

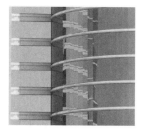

Reflection

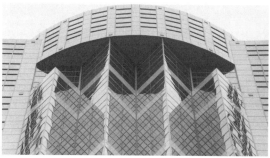

Reflective glass See **Glass**

Reflective insulation
Metal that reflects infrared radiation and therefore reduces the amount of heat entering a building, particularly through the roof; aluminum foil is the most commonly used type.

Regence style
The decorative and elegant Rococo style (1715–1723) flourishing under the regency of Philip of Orleans during the rule of Louis XV.

Regency style
A colorful Neo-classical style, often combined with oriental motifs (1811–1820), prevalent in England during the reign of George IV, characterized by close imitation of ancient Greek and Roman, Gothic, and Egyptian forms.

Regula
In the Doric entablature, one of a series of short fillets beneath the taenia; each corresponding to a triglyph above.

Rehabilitation
To repair an existing building to good condition with minimal changes to the building fabric; may include adaptive reuse or restoration; also called rehab.

Reinforced concrete
Concrete masonry construction, in which steel reinforcement is embedded in such a manner that the two materials act together in resisting forces.

Reinforcing
Steel or iron bars or wire mesh used to increase the tensile strength of reinforced concrete.

Reinforcing bar
A steel bar used in concrete construction that provides additional strength; the bars are deformed with patterns made during the rolling process.

Relief
Carved or embossed decoration of a figure or form, raised above the background plane from which it is formed.

bas-relief
Sculptural decoration in low relief, in which none of the figures or motifs are separated from their background, projecting less than half their true proportions from the wall or surface.

alto-relievo
Sculptural relief work in which the figures project more than half their thickness from the base surface.

cavo-relievo
Relief which does not project above the general surface upon which it is carved.

diaglyph
A relief engraved in reverse, an intaglio; a sunken relief.

anal glyph
An embellishment carved in low relief.

glyph
A sculptured pictograph: a grooved channel, usually vertical, intended as an ornament.

high relief
Sculptural relief work in which the figures project more than half their thickness from the base.

in cavetto
The reverse of relief; differing from intaglio in that the designs are pressed into plaster or clay.

mezzo-rellevo
Casting, carving, or embossing in moderate relief, intermediate between bas-relief and high relief.

stiacciato
Extremely flat bas-relief sculpture, from the Italian for "flattened out."

sunk relief
Relief in which the highest point of the forms does not project above the general surface from which it is modeled; also called cavo-relievo.

Relieving arch See **Arch**

Relocation
The process of moving a building or structure to a new location, usually placing it on a totally new foundation.

Remodeling
The process of modifying an existing building or space for current use; usually involves replacing some of the existing building fabric or adding new components.

Renaissance architecture
An architecture (1420–1550) that developed during the rebirth of Classical art and learning in Europe and evolved through several periods. It was initially characterized by the use of the Classical orders, round arches and symmetrical proportions.

It represented a return to the models of Graeco-Roman antiquity, and was based on regular order, symmetry, and a central axis with grandiose plans and impressive facades. Silhouettes were clean and simple, with flat roofs replacing Gothic spires. Walls of large dressed masonry blocks gave buildings an imposing sense of dignity and strength.

Gothic verticality was replaced with an emphasis on horizontality. Semicircular arches appeared over doors and windows and in freestanding arcades. Columns were used decoratively on facades and structurally in porticos, and ornamentation was based on pagan or Classical mythological subjects.

Renaissance Revival style
A revival style (1840–1890) characterized by a studied formalism, their symmetrical compositions are reminiscent of early sixteenth-century Italian elements. Ashlar masonry is accented with rusticated quoins, architrave framed windows, and doors supporting entablatures or pediments. A belt or string course often divides the ground or first floor from the upper story, and small square windows were used on the top story.

Rendering See **Plaster**

Renovation
The process of repairing and changing an existing building for modern use to make it functionally equivalent to a new building.

Repetition
The recurrence of rhythmic patterns, forms or accents, that are separated by spaces of repeated formal elements or different forms.

Replica
Exact copy of an original building or any building component.

Repose
Harmony in the arrangement of parts or colors that is restful to the eye.

Respond
A pier or pilaster projecting from a wall as a support for an arch at the end of an arcade.

Restaurant
A commercial establishment where meals to order are served to the public: either in a separate building or within a hotel or other facility.

Restoration
The process of returning an existing site, building, or object to its condition at a particular time in its history, using the same construction materials and methods as the original; may include removing later additions and replacing missing period components.

Retaining wall See **Wall**

Retarder
In concrete work, an additive that slows down the setting time, allowing for more time to place the concrete.

Reticulated
Refers to surfaces that are marked with lines, resembling or forming a network of squares arranged on the diagonal.

Reticulated molding See **Molding**

Reticulated tracery See **Tracery**

Reticulated work
Masonry that is constructed with diamond-shaped or square stones placed diagonally or crossing in a network.

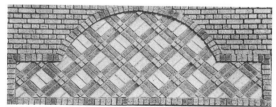

Retrofit
To make an improvement to an existing building, or to adapt it to a new use.

Retrofitting
The process of installing new mechanical, fire protection, and electrical systems or equipment in an existing building; most often required to meet current building code requirements.

Return
The continuation of a molding, projection, member, or cornice in a different direction, usually at right angles.

Return air
The air that is brought in from an air-conditioned space and recirculated in order to reduce the energy that would be consumed by using only fresh air as a source.

Reveal
The visible side of an opening for a window or doorway between the framework and outer surface of the wall; where the opening is not filled with a door or window, the whole thickness of the wall.

Revell, Viljo (1910-1964)
A Finnish architect who studied with Alvar Alto and made his name with the "Glass Palace" office building in Helsinki, Finland. He won the competition in 1958 for the Toronto City Hall, whose two curvilinear towers contrast with the neighboring office structures.

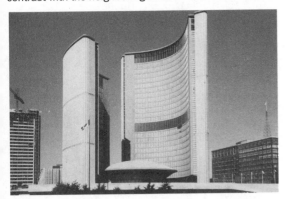

Revival architecture
The use of older styles in new architectural movements, most often referring to the Gothic, Roman, Egyptian, Etruscan, Greek, Colonial, or revival styles of the eighteenth and nineteenth century.

Revolving door See Door

Rhythm
Any kind of movement characterized by the regular occurrence of elements, lines, shapes and forms; the flow of movement shown by light and heavy accents, similar to recurring musical beats.

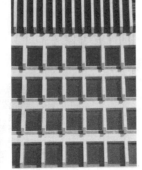

Rib
Any curved structural member supporting a curved shape or panel; a molding that projects from the surface and separates the various roof or ceiling panels.

Ribbed arch See Arch

Ribbed fluting
Flutes alternating with fillets.

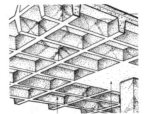

Ribbed slab
A panel composed of a thin slab reinforced by ribs in one or two directions, usually at right angles to one another; also called a waffle slab due to its appearance.

Ribbed vault See Vault

Ribbing
An assemblage or arrangement of ribs, as timberwork that sustains a vaulted ceiling.

Ribbon window See Window

Richardson, Henry Hobson (1838–1886)
American architect, pupil of Labrouste in Paris; was renowned for his massive Romanesque buildings. He designed Trinity Church, Boston (1877), inspired by French and Spanish Romanesque styles.

Richardsonian style
Named for Henry Hobson Richardson, this style (1870–1900) featured a straightforward treatment of stone, broad roof planes and a select grouping of door and window openings. It also featured a heavy, massive appearance with a simplicity of form and rough masonry.

The effect is based on mass, volume, and scale rather than decorative detailing, except on the capitals of columns. The entry includes a large arched opening without columns or piers for support.

Ridge
The horizontal lines at the junction of the upper edges of two sloping roof structures.

Ridgebeam
A horizontal beam at the upper edge of the rafters, below the ridge of the roof.

Ridgeboard
A longitudinal member at the apex of a roof that supports the upper ends of the rafters.

Ridgecap
Any covering such as metal, wood, or shingles used to cover the ridge of a roof.

Ridge course
The last or top course of roofing tiles, roll roofing, or shingles.

Ridge crest
A linear ornamental device; usually composed of metal, attached to the crest of a roof, providing a transition to the sky.

Ridge rib
A continuous, projecting rib connecting the apexes of the intermediate ribs of a rib vault with the center of the vault.

Ridge roll
A wood strip, rounded on top, which is used to finish the ridge of a roof, often covered with lead sheathing; a metal or tile covering which caps the ridge of a roof.

Ridge tile See **Tile**

Rietvelt, Gerrit (1888–1964)
Architect and member of the de Stijl group of artists which included painter Piet Mondrian. Their buildings were intricate, delicately balanced compositions of line and plane. The Schroder House, Utrecht (1924), was small but unusual, reminiscent in its intersecting planes and angles of a Mondrian painting.

Rigid arch See **Arch**

Rigid frame
A structural framework in which all columns and beams are roughly connected; there are no hinged joints and the angular relationship between beam and column members are maintained under load.

Rigid joint See **Joint**

Rinceau
An ornamental band of undulant and curving plant motifs, found in Classical architecture.

Ring stone
One of the stones of an arch that shows on the face of the wall or at the end of the arch: one of the voussoirs of the face forming the archivolt.

Rio Bec style
A style of Mayan architecture (550–900) that was the transitional style between that of sites at Tikal and at Uxmal; it was characterized by lavishly decorated structures flanked by soaring temple pyramids with steeply raked steps.

Riprap
Irregularly broken and random-sized large pieces of quarry rock used for foundations; a foundation or parapet of stones thrown together without any attempt at regular structural arrangements.

Rise
Vertical height of an arch, roof truss, or rigid frame.

Riser
The vertical board under the tread of a step; a vertical supply pipe for a sprinkler system; a pipe for water, drainage, steam, gas, or venting that extends vertically through one or more stories and services other pipes.

Risk assessment
An environmental survey of an existing building to determine the extent of hazardous materials that may be present, such as lead paint or asbestos.

Risk management
The management of an activity, accepting a level of risk which is balanced against the benefit of the activity, usually based on an economic assessment.

Rivet
A shank with a head which is inserted into holes in the two pieces being joined and closed by forming a head on the projecting shank. The rivets must be red hot to be formed in such a manner and have generally been replaced by welding or bolting.

Rocaille
A small ornament combining forms based on water-worn rocks, plants and shells, characteristic of the eighteenth-century Rococo period, especially during the reign of Louis XV.

Roche, Eamonn Kevin (1922–)
Irish-born American architect, formed the successor firm to Eero Saarinen in the 1950s with John Gerald Dinkeloo (1918–1981). Their first work was the Oakland Museum (1961) a vast structure covering four city blocks. The best known is the Ford Foundation Headquarters, New York (1963), with a 12-story indoor atrium. The later work includes the extension to the Metropolitan Museum of Art, New York, including the Pavilion for the Ancient Egyptian Temple of Dendur.

Roche, Martin (1853–1927)
American architect, a partner with William Holabird, designed the Tacoma Building, Chicago (1889, but later demolished). It included a structure of cast-iron columns and wrought-iron beams, clad in terra-cotta and glass, establishing the skeletal structure for the Chicago School style.

Rock rash
A patchwork applique of oddly shaped stone slabs used on edges as a veneer, often further embellished with small cobbles or geodes.

Rock-cut
Said of a temple or tomb excavated in natural rock; usually represents an architectural front with dark interior chambers, of which sections are supported by masses of stone left in the form of solid pillars.

Rockwork
Quarry-faced masonry: any stonework in which the surface is left irregular and rough

Rococo style
A style of architecture and decoration (1720–1790), primarily French in origin, representing the final phase of the Baroque. It was characterized by a profuse, semi-abstract ornamentation of shell work and foliage. It was associated with lightness, swirling forms, flowing lines, ornate stucco work, arabesque ornament, and the blending of separate members into a single molded volume.

Rod
A thin metal strip used as a stiffener or fastener.

Rodilla, Simon
Italian-born mason who built an artistic fantasy on the outskirts of Los Angeles, consisting of steel-framed, free-form towers, constructed of concrete-covered reinforcing rods encrusted with inlaid tile, shells, and fragments of broken bottles (1954).

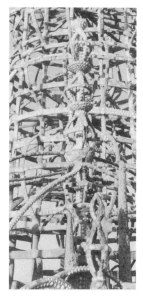

Rogers, Richard (1933–)
Italian-born English architect who was in partnership with Renzo Piano (1971–1981), and completed the high-tech Centre Pompidou, in Paris, and set up his own practice in London. Work includes Lloyds Building, London (1986), and Terminal 5 Heathrow Airport London (1989).

Roll molding See Molding

Rolled glass See Glass

Rolled steel section
Any hot-rolled steel section, including joists, angles, channels, and rails.

Rolling door See Door

Roll-up door See door

Roman arch See Arch

Roman architecture
An architecture (300 B.C.–365 A.D.) influenced by the Etruscans, combining the use of the arch with Greek columns. The invention of concrete led to a system of vaulting and the development of the dome used to roof a circular area, demonstrated sophisticated engineering skills.

The pilaster was used decoratively on walls instead of half-columns. Colonnades and arcades were both in use, and occur one above the other at times. Doorway headers were both square and semicircular and became decorative features of importance in the exterior design of large public buildings. Window headers were generally semicircular.

Orders were sometimes superimposed, and pedestals were developed to give the column additional height. The Romans relied on the abundant carving on their moldings rather than on the contours. Marble, granite and alabaster were the primary facing materials, as well as stucco and mosaics.

The emphasis was on monumental public buildings, reflecting the grandeur of the empire. Many had very sophisticated building services, such as plumbing, heating and water supply. On an urban scale the Romans also produced an impressive array of planning elements: formal axial planning with whole communities and towns constructed on a grid plan were typical.

Romanesque architecture

The style (800-1180) emerged from Roman and Byzantine elements; characterized by massive articulated wall structures, semicircular arches and vaults. It showed an evolution of stone vaulting and of the rib method of construction.

It was characterized by heavy masonry construction, sparse ornament, and smooth plain walls; with decoration derived from the structure. It also featured thick molded piers, assembled from small stones Individually carved to fit.

Romanesque Revival style

A style (1840–1900) characterized by monochromatic brick or stone buildings, highlighted by semicircular arches over window and door openings. The arch was also used decoratively to enrich corbel tables along the eaves and courses marking horizontal divisions. The arches and capitals of columns are carved with geometrical medieval moldings. Facades are flanked by polygonal towers and covered with various roof shapes.

Romano, Guilio (1492–1546)

Italian architect and painter who manipulated the rules of the Classical styles toward the Mannerist style. Works include the Palazzo Ducale, Mantua (1538).

Rood

A large crucifix set above the chancel entrance.

Rood arch

The central arch in a rood screen.

Rood beam

A horizontal beam across the chancel to support the screen.

Rood loft

A gallery in which the rood is kept.

Rood screen

A carved wood or stone separating the nave and chancel.

Rood spire

A spire located over the crossing of the nave and transepts.

Rood stairs

Provides access to a rood loft.

Rood tower

A tower located at the crossing and above the rood.

Roof

The external covering on the top of a building, usually of wood shingles, slates, or tiles on pitched slopes, or a variety of built-up membranes for flat roofs.

barrel roof
A roof of semi-cylindrical section: capable of spanning long distances, parallel to the axis of the cylinder.

bell roof
A roof whose cross section is shaped like a bell.

bell-cast roof
A form of mansard roof in which the lower roof slopes downward in a straight line, then curves outward at the eaves.

built-up roofing
Flat roof covered with multiple layers of roofing felt, secured with layers of hot tar, and topped with a layer of crushed stone.

butterfly roof
A roof shape that has two surfaces that rise from a valley at the roof's center-line to the eaves.

canopy roof
A roof that is in the shape of a suspended cloth canopy; often used over a balcony or porch.

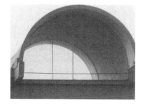

compass roof
A convex-shaped roof formed either by curved rafters or by a combination of beams arranged in a vault.

conical roof
A roof in the shape of an inverted cone on top of a cylindrical tower; used in the Chateauesque and Queen Anne styles; also called a witches' hat.

curb roof
A pitched roof that slopes away from the ridge in two successive planes, as in a gambrel or mansard roof.

277

Roof

double-gable roof
A roof composed of two parallel gables forming the shape of the letter M on the end wall.

double-hipped roof
A hipped roof having a double slope.

double-pitched roof
A roof having two flatter slopes on each side of a steep central ridge; similar to a gambrel roof.

Dutch roof
A gable roof divided into two sections of unequal slope; the flatter slope is from the top of the ridge, the steeper slope connects to the top plate.

Dutch gambrel roof
A type of gambrel roof that has two flat surfaces on each side of the ridge, each at a different pitch; the top slope is the flatter of the two, while the lower slopes often end in a flared eave.

flat roof
A roof having no slope, or one with only a slight pitch so as to drain rainwater: a roof with only sufficient slope to effect drainage.

Roof

gable roof
A roof having a gable at one or both ends: a roof sloping downward in two opposite directions from a central ridge, so as to form a gable at each end.

gambrel roof
A roof which has two pitches on each side.

hammer-beam roof
A roof without a tie beam at the top of the wall.

helm roof
Four faces rest diagonally between the gables and converge at the top.

hip roof
A roof which slopes upward from all four sides of a building, requiring a hip rafter at each corner.

hip-and-valley roof
A hip roof on a building with an irregular plan, with valleys at the inside corners.

Roof

jerkinhead roof
A combination of a gable roof and a hipped roof: the gable rises about halfway up the ridge, then the roof is tilted back at a steep incline.

lamella roof
A roof frame consisting of a series of skewed arches, made up of relatively short members, fastened together at an angle so that each is intersected by two similar adjacent members at its midpoint, forming a network of interlocking diamonds.

M roof
A roof formed by the junction of two parallel gable roofs with a valley between them.

mansard roof
A roof with a steep lower slope and a flatter upper slope on all sides, either of convex or concave shape.

Roof

ogee roof
A roof whose section is an ogee

open-timbered roof
A roof construction in which there is no ceiling so that the rafters and roof sheathing are visible from below.

pavilion roof
A roof hipped equally on all sides, so as to have a pyramidal form; a similar roof having more than four sides, a polygonal roof.

pent roof
A small sloping roof, the upper end of which butts against a wall of a house, usually above the first-floor window; if carried completely around the house, it is called a skirt roof.

Roof

pitched roof
A roof having one or more slopes, surfaces.

pyramidal-hipped roof
Same as a pavilion roof.

rotunda roof
A circular roof with a low slope and overhanging eaves.

saddle roof
A roof having a concave-shaped ridge with gables at each end of the roof, the configuration suggesting a saddle.

saddleback roof
A ridged roof, with short gable ends and a straight ridge, typically found on the top of a tower.

single-pitch roof
A roof that slopes in only one direction, such as a shed or lean-to roof.

sawtooth roof
A roof system having a number of small parallel roof surfaces with a profile similar to the teeth in a saw; usually the steeper side is splayed and faces north; usually asymmetrical with the shorter slope glazed.

shed roof
A roof shape having only one sloping plane.

sod roof
A roof composed of a thick layer of grassland containing roots; frequently it is pitched or barrel-shaped, and supported by logs or other wall structure.

Roof

square roof
A roof where rafters on opposite sides of the ridge meet at a 90-degree angle; each side of the roof has a slope of 45 degrees.

stepped roof
A roof constructed of stones which are arranged in a stair-stepped fashion, diminishing towards the top in a peak.

suspended roof
One whose load is carried by a number of cables which are under tension from columns or posts that are in compression and that transmit the loads to the ground.

terrace roof
A roof that has been truncated so as to form a flat horizontal surface without a ridge.

thatched roof
A roof made of straw, reed, or similar materials fastened together to shed water and sometimes to provide thermal insulation.

Roof

truncated roof
A roof with sloped sides and a flat top for a terrace; may have a balustrade around the flat center section.

umbrella-shell roof
A shell roof formed by four hypar shells.

visor roof
A relatively small section of roof that projects on brackets from a flat wall surface; sometimes appearing below a parapet, as in the Mission style.

Roof balustrade
A railing with supporting balusters on a roof; often near the eaves or surrounding a widows' walk.

Roof-comb
A wall along the ridge of a roof that makes the roof appear higher.

Roof cornice
A cornice immediately below the eaves; also called an eaves cornice.

Roof curb
A pitched roof that slopes away from the ridge in two successive planes, as a gambrel or mansard roof.

Roof drain
A drain designed to receive water collecting on the surface of a roof and to discharge it into a leader or a downspout.

Roof garden
A rooftop terrace with planters and potted plants, especially when on a tall building.

Roof guard
Any of various devices installed near the bottom of a sloped roof to prevent snow from sliding off.

Roof gutter
A channel of metal or wood at the eaves or on the roof of a building for carrying off rainwater

Roof pitch
The slope of a roof usually expressed as a ratio of vertical rise to horizontal run, or in inches of rise per foot of run.

Roof plate
A wall plate that receives the lower ends of roof rafters.

Roof rake
A slope or inclination; the incline from the horizontal of a roof slope.

Roof ridge
The horizontal line at the junction of the upper edge of two sloping roof surfaces.

Roof ridgebeam
A beam at the upper ends of the rafters, at the ridge of the roof.

Roof ridgecrest
The ornamentation of the roof ridge.

Roof ridgecap
Any covering such as metal, wood, shingles, or tile used to cover the top course of materials at the ridge.

Roof ridgeroll
A wood strip, rounded on top, which is used to finish the ridges of a roof; often covered with lead sheeting; a metal, tile, or asbestos-cement covering which caps the ridge of a roof.

Roof scupper
An opening in a wall or
parapet that allows water
to drain from a roof.

Roofing felt
Waterproof felt, soaked in asphalt, bitumen, or tar,
and used in built-up roofing.

Root, John Wellborn (1850–1891)
American architect who, in a partnership with Daniel
Burnham, influenced the development of the glass
curtain wall typical of the Chicago School and defined
the characteristics of the skyscraper. Works include the
Monadnock building (1891) and The Rookery (1886).

Rose ornament See **Ornament**

Rose window See **Window**

Rosette
A round pattern with a carved conventionalized floral
motif; a circular decorative wood plaque used in joinery,
such as one applied to a wall to receive the end of a
stair rail.

Rossi, Aldo (1931–1997)
Italian architect, and the most eminent protagonist of
Rational Architecture. His work embraced aspects of Inter-
national Modernism and a surrealism reminiscent of the
paintings of Giorgio de Chirico, in projects such as the
Carlo Felice Opera House, Genoa (1982), IBA Social
Housing, Berlin (1989), and the Bonnefantin Museum,
Mastricht (1994).

Rotated
Refers to forms created by
revolving a shape on an
axis and duplicating it in
another location with the
same relationship to the
central point; as the forms
are rotated they may be
transformed in some
manner.

Roth, Emery (1871–1948)
Designed the Helmsley Palace Hotel, New York City
(1980), and the Pan Am building, now the Met Life
building, in New York City, with Walter Gropius and
Pietro Belluschi (1963).

Rotunda
A building that is round
both inside and outside,
usually covered with a
dome.

Rotunda roof See **Roof**

Rough arch See **Arch**

Rough carpentry
The wood framing and sheathing of a building; including
blocking, joists, rafters, stringers, studs, and subflooring.

Round arch See **Arch**

Round barn
A barn having a circular plan.

Round horseshoe arch See **Arch**

Round pediment See **Pediment**

Rounded
Refers to forms that may be spherical, globular, shaped like a ball, or circular in cross section.

Roundel
A small circular panel or window; in glazing, a bull's-eye or circular light like the bottom of a bottle.

Roundel window See **Window**

Rover molding See **Molding**

Row house
One of an unbroken line of houses sharing one or more side walls in common with its neighbors, usually consisting of uniform plans, fenestration and other architectural treatments.

Rowlock
A brick laid on its edge so that its end face is visible; one ring of a rowlock arch.

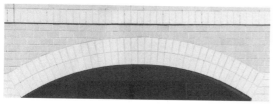

Rowlock arch See **Arch**

Rubbed
A decorative finish obtained by rubbing bricks with a stone, brush, or abrasive tool, so as to produce a smooth surface of consistent color; used to highlight door, window, and arcade openings, arches, bands, medallions, and corners of facades.

Rubble
Rough stones of irregular shapes and sizes, used in rough, uncoursed work in the construction of walls, foundations, and paving.

Rubble wall
A rubble wall, either coursed or uncoursed.

Rubblework
Stone masonry built of rubble.

Rudolph, Paul (1918–1997)
Studied with Walter Gropius at Harvard. He was the chairman of Architecture at Yale University and designed the monumental Art and Architecture Building at New Haven (1958–1965), which was typical of his Brutalist architecture. Other works include the Government Center, Boston (1962), and other college structures. Most of his later work was done in Indonesia.

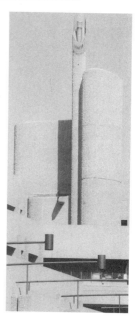

Paul Rudolph

Running bond See **Bond**

Running measure
One-dimensional measurement of a piece of material; also called lineal measurement.

Running ornament
Any ornamental molding in which the design is continuous through intertwined or flowing lines, as in the representation of foliage and meanders.

Ruskin, John (1819–1900)
Wrote the *Seven Lamps of Architecture*, an influential book advocating functional planning and honesty in the use of materials in construction.

Russo- Byzantine architecture
The first phase of Russian architecture (1000–1500) derived from the Byzantine architecture of Greece; it consisted mainly of stone churches characterized by cruciform plans and multiple bulbous domes.

Rust
A substance, usually in powder form, accumulating on the face of steel or iron as a result of oxidation; it will ultimately weaken or destroy the steel or iron on which it forms.

Rustic
Descriptive of rough, hand-dressed building stone, intentionally laid with high relief; used frequently in modest rural structures.

Rustic arch See **Arch**

Rustic brick See **Brick**

Rustic mortar joint See **Joint**

Rustic quoin
A stone quoin, projecting out from the main surface of the wall with rough, split faces and chamfered edges, to give the appearance of rugged strength.

Rustic slate
One of a number of slate shingles of varying thicknesses, yielding an irregular surface when installed.

Rustic stone
Any rough broken stone suitable for rustic masonry, most commonly limestone or sandstone, usually set with the longest dimension exposed horizontally.

Rustic stone masonry See **Masonry**

Rustic style
A broad term applied to hunting lodges, ranger stations, or log cabins in mountainous areas, featuring log-cabin siding, peeled logs, and rough-cut lumber, a fieldstone chimney, a steep roof covered with hand-split shingles, and an overhanging roof with exposed rafters.

Rustic woodwork
Decorative or structural work constructed of unpeeled logs or poles.

Rustic Work
In ashlar masonry, grooved or channeled joints in the horizontal direction, to render them more conspicuous.

Rusticate
To give a rustic appearance by beveling the edges of stone blocks to emphasize the joints between them; used mainly on the ground floor level.

Rusticated masonry See **Masonry**

Rusticated wood
Wood incised in block shapes to resemble rough stone.

Rustication
Masonry that is cut into large blocks with the surface left rough and unfinished, separated by deep recessed joints. The border of each block may be beveled or rabeted on all four sides or top and bottom. It is used mainly on the lower part of a structure to give a bold, exaggerated took of strength.

Ss

Saarinen, Eero (1910–1961)
Finnish-born American architect, and son of Eliel Saarinen. Projects include General Motors Technical Institute, Warren, Michigan (1951); Kresge Auditorium, MIT, Cambridge (1952); David S. Ingalls Ice Hockey Rink, Yale University, New Haven (1953); TWA Terminal at Kennedy International Airport, New York City (1956); Ezra Stiles and Morse College, Yale University, New Haven (1958), and Dulles International Airport, Washington, D.C. (1958).

Saarinen, Eliel (1873–1950)
Designed the Helsinki Railway Station, built of rugged granite and inspired by the designs of the Vienna Sezession.

Saddle roof See **Roof**

Saddleback roof See **Roof**

Safde, Moshe (1938–)
Israeli-born Canadian architect who designed the Habitat Housing, Montreal, Canada (1967), for Expo '67, which consisted of prefabricated concrete housing units fitted together in an experimental design. Later work includes Vancouver Library Square (1991).

Safety glass See **Glass**

Sailor course bond See **Bond**

Sakha
In the architecture of India, a door jamb or door frame.

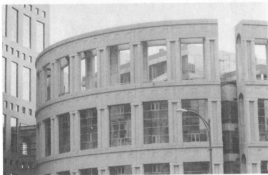

Salient
Any part or prominent member projecting beyond a surface.

Salon
French word for a formal room in which exhibitions of art were held.

Saltbox
A wood-framed house, common to colonial New England, which has a short roof pitch in front and a long roof pitch sweeping close to the ground in the back.

Sanctis, Francesco de (1693–1740)
Along with Alessandro Specchi, designed the Spanish Steps in Rome, which consist of an elegant ensemble of the piazza, the triple set of steps, and Bernini's fountain.

Sanctuary
In a church, the immediate area around the principal altar.

Sand finish
Colored, textured plaster surface, similar in appearance to sandpaper.

Sandblasting
Abrading a surface, such as concrete, by a stream of sand ejected from a nozzle by compressed air; used for cleaning up construction joints, or carried deeper to expose the aggregate.

Sanding
Finishing surfaces, particularly wood, with sandpaper or some other abrasive.

Sandstone See **Stone**

Sandwich construction
Composite construction consisting of a light core of insulation and outer layers of higher density materials with greater strength.

Sangallo, Antonio de (1485–1546)
Designed the Palazzo Farnese, the largest in Rome, and one of the most magnificent Renaissance palaces.

Sant'Elia, Antonio (1888–1916)
Italian architect who designed cities for the future, complete with skyscrapers, pedestrian precincts, and overhead roads; he planned the publication *Citta Nuova*. He studied architecture in Milan and was influenced by Otto Wagner's Vienna School. He exhibited work with fellow student Mario Chiattone and published a manifesto on Futurism in the exhibition catalog.

Sanzio, Raphael (1483–1520)
High Renaissance architect and painter of great distinction. After Bramante's death, he was appointed master of works of St. Peters, Rome, and proposed a basilican version of Bramante's plan.

Sarcophagus
An elaborate coffin for an important person, of terracotta, wood, stone, metal or other material, decorated with painting, carving, and large enough to contain only the body. If larger, it becomes a tomb.

Sash
Any framework of a window; may be movable or fixed.

Sash bars
The strips of wood that separate the panes of glass in a window composed of several panes; also called muntins.

Sash window See **Window**

Sassanian architecture
This architecture (200–600) was prevalent in Persia, primarily in palace complexes. It featured extensive barrel vaults and parabolic domes set on squinches and stuccoed with plaster mortar. The massive walls were covered with pilasters and cornices. The most notable example is the Palace at Ctesiphon.

Satinwood See **Wood**

Saturation
The purity of a hue; the higher the saturation the purer the color.

Saucer dome See **Dome**

Sawtooth roof See **Roof**

Scaffold
A temporary platform to support workers and materials on the face of a structure and to provide access to work areas above the ground; any elaborated platform.

Scaffold crane
A small self-contained motorized crane attached to the scaffolding for lifting relatively small loads.

Scagliola See **Plaster**

Scale
The relationship of one part of an object to an outside measure, such as a human body or some standard reference; a system of representing or reproducing objects in a different size proportionately in every part.

Scale

human scale
The size or proportion of a building element or space, or article of furniture; relative to the structural or functional dimensions of the human body.

monumental scale
Impressively large, sturdy and enduring.

Scallop
One of a continuous series of curves resembling segments of a circle, used as a decorative element on the outer edge of a strip of wood used as a molding.

Scalloped capital See **Capital**

Scarf joint See **Joint**

Scarp
A steep slope constructed as a defensive measure in a fortification.

Scarpa, Carlo (1906–1978)
Italian architect practicing in Venice, who subscribed to the Modern movement. Later, his work focused on exhibitions, galleries, and museums.

Scharoun, Han (1893–1972)
German architect influenced by Expressionism. His most celebrated work is the Hall for the Berlin Philharmonic Orchestra (1963), which illustrates his commitment to Organic architecture.

Schematic design phase
The first phase of the architect's basic services. The architect prepares schematic design studies, consisting of drawings illustrating the scale and relationship of the projected components for approval by the owner.

Scheme See **Design**

Schindler, Rudolph (1887–1953)
Born in Vienna, he was influenced early by Otto Wagner. He later worked for Frank Lloyd Wright in Chicago, but his work remains reminiscent of the de Stijl movement, as shown in his Lovell Beach house, Newport Beach, California (1926).

Schinkel, Karl Friedrich (1781-1841)
German architect of original Neo-classical buildings; his work was stylistically eclectic, but lyrical and logical. Schinkel's funeral in 1841 was a national event, his grave marked by a stele of his own design. King Friedrich Wilhelm IV (reigned 1840–1861) decreed that all of Schinkel's work be purchased by the state.

Schoolhouse
A building used for a school, especially an elementary school.

Scissors truss See **Truss**

Sconce
An electric lamp, designed and fabricated for mounting on a wall, resembling a candlestick or a group of candlesticks.

Scotia molding See **Molding**

Screed
A wooden or metal guide for leveling plaster or concrete, typically placed along the edge of the work at the desired level.

Screen
Any construction whose essential function is merely to separate, protect, seclude, or conceal, but not to support.

Screen facade
A nonstructural facing assembly used to disguise the form or overall size of a building.

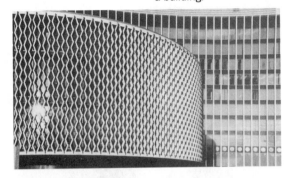

Screen wall See **Wall**

Scribbled ornament
A decorative effect produced by irregularly distributing lines and scrolls over a surface or on a panel.

Scroll molding See **Molding**

Scroll ornament See **Ornament**

Scrollwork
Ornamental work of any kind in which scrolls, or lines of scroll-like character are an element.

Sculpture

The art of shaping figures or designs in the round or in relief by carving wood, chiseling marble, modeling clay or casting in metal; any work of art that is created in this manner.

Sculpture in the round

Freestanding figures carved or molded in three dimensions.

Scuttle

A small opening in a ceiling or roof; usually installed on top of a built-up frame.

Season

To dry wood through exposure to the air or the heat of a kiln, thus lowering its moisture content.

Seat

A chair, stool, or bench on which to sit; may be built in, such as a window seat.

Secondary colors

The colors green, orange, and purple that result from a mixture of pairs of primary colors.

Section

The representation of a building or portion thereof, cut vertically at some imagined plane, so as to show the interior of the space or the profile of the member.

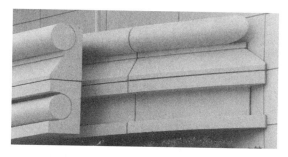

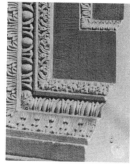

Segmental arch See **Arch**

Segmental pediment See **Pediment**

Seismic code

A building code that defines the minimum earthquake resistance of a structure: usually requires seismic reinforcing of existing buildings that are being altered.

Seismic load

The design load for potential seismic forces acting on a building during an earthquake that is used to determine the extent of seismic reinforcing.

Seismic reinforcing

The structural strengthening of a building to resist seismic forces, using shear walls or partition trusses or increasing the size of structural members.

Self-closing door See **Door**

Seljuk architecture
An early phase of Turkish Muslim architecture (1000–1200), Influenced by Persian architecture, consisting mainly of mosques and minarets.

Semiarch See **Arch**

Semicircular
Describing a form that exhibits an arrangement of objects in the shape of a half-circle, as divided by its diameter.

Semicircular arch See **Arch**

Semicircular dome See **Dome**

Semidetached house
One of a pair of houses with separate entrances that share a party wall between them.

Semidome See **Dome**

Semiglyph
Half glyphs at the edge of a triglyph.

Seminary
A school, academy, college, or university, especially a school for the education of men for the priesthood.

Semirigid joint See **Joint**

Seraph
A celestial being or angel of the highest degree, usually represented with six wings.

Serpentine
A form that resembles a serpent, showing a sinuous winding movement; a greenish brown or spotted mineral used as a decorative stone in architectural work.

Serpentine flutes
The flutes that wind around a Solomonic column shaft.

Serpentine wall See **Wall**

Serrated
Consisting of notches on the edges, like a saw.

Sert, Josep Luis (1902–1983)
Catalonian architect who worked with Le Corbusier; he settled in the United States in 1939 and became dean of faculty at the Graduate School of Design, and chairman of Architecture at Harvard University (1953). He designed the U.S. Embassy, Baghdad, Iraq, and the Miro Foundation Building, Barcelona, Spain (1972).

Service core
A vertical element in a multistory structure, containing the elevators, vertical runs of most of the mechanical and electrical services, and the fire stairs. It is generally the first element to be constructed, and then is used for vertical transportation during construction.

Service stair See **Stair**

Service switch
Main disconnect switch at the location where the electric service cable enters a building.

Setback
The upper section of a building, successively recessed, that produces a ziggurat effect, admitting light and air to the streets below.

Sexfoil
A foil having six points called cusps.

Sezession
A term adopted by several groups of artists in Germany who seceded from the traditional conservative academies to show their work; the most celebrated was the one founded in Vienna in 1897, and included the artist Gustav Klimt and the architects Joseph Olbrich and Otto Wagner.

Sgraffito
Decoration produced by covering a surface, such as plaster or enamel, of one color with a thin coat of a similar material of another color and scratching through the outer coat to show the color beneath.

Shaft
The main body of a column, pilaster, or pier between the capital and the base, or a thin vertical member attached to a wall or pier, supporting an arch or vaulting rib.

Shafting
In medieval architecture, an arrangement of shafts, combined in the mass of a pier or jamb, so that corresponding groupings of archivolt moldings above may start from their caps at the impost line.

Shake See **Wood products**

Shear wall See **Wall**

Sheathing
The wood covering placed over the exterior studding or rafters of a building, to provide a base for the application of wall or roof cladding.

Shed
A rough structure for shelter, storage or a workshop; it may be a separate building or a lean-to against another structure, often with one or more open sides.

Shed dormer See **Dormer**

Shed dormer window See **Window**

Shed roof See **Roof**

Sheet glass See **Glass**

Sheet metal
A flat, rolled metal product, rectangular in cross section and formed with sheared, slit, or sawn edges.

Sheet pile
A pile in the form of a plank, driven in close contact with others to provide a tight wall to resist the lateral pressure of water or adjacent earth.

Sheetrock
A proprietary name for gypsum wallboard.

Shell
The basic structure and enclosure of a building, exclusive of any interior finishes and mechanical, plumbing, and electrical systems; often describes a deteriorated structure that has lost much of its original fabric.

Shell construction
A thin, curved, structural outer layer that distributes loads equally in all directions; most commonly used for roofs composed of concrete; also called thin-shell concrete.

Shell ornament
Any decoration where a shell form is a characteristic part; coquilage.

Shells
Hollow structures in the form of thin curved slabs, plates or membranes that are self-supporting. They are called form-resistant structures because they are shaped according to the loads they carry.

Shikkui See **Plaster**

Shingle See **Wood products**

Shingle style
A style (1880–1895) that featured an eclectic American adaptation of New England forms to the structuralism of the Victorian era. Structures were de-emphasized by a uniform covering of entire surfaces of the roof and walls with monochromatic shingles; the eaves of the roofs are close to the walls so that they emphasize the homogeneous shingle covering. The houses in this style were rambling and horizontal and featured wide verandas and hipped roofs.

Shiplap siding See **Wood**

Shipporeit-Heinrich
Originally from the office of Mies van der Rohe, G.D. Shipporeit and John C. Heinrich designed the first skyscraper entirely enclosed in glass, the Lake Point Towers in Chicago (1968).

Shoe
A piece of timber, stone, or metal, shaped to receive the lower end of any member, also called a "soleplate"; a metal base plate for an arch or truss shaped to resist the lateral thrust.

Shoji
A very lightweight sliding partition used in Japanese architecture, consisting of a wooden lattice covered on one side with translucent white rice paper. The lattice is most often composed of small horizontal rectangles.

Shopping center
A group of retail stores and service establishments in a suburban area, with parking facilities usually at grade level.

Shopping mall
A shopping center enclosed within a large structure and placed around a central atrium; may have numerous stores, entertainment facilities such as movie theaters, fast-food outlets, restaurants, and public areas.

Shore
A temporary support used in compression as a temporary support for excavations, formwork, or for propping up unsafe structures.

Shoro
A small structure in a Japanese temple compound, from which a bell is hung.

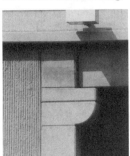

Shoulder
A projection or break changing the thickness or width of a piece of shaped wood, metal, or stone.

Shouldered arch See **Arch**

Shreve, Raymond (1877–1946)
Partner in the firm of Shreve, Lamb and Harmon, designers of the Empire State Building, New York City (1932).

Shrine
A place, building, or structure made sacred by association with a historic event or holy personage; an altar, tomb, or chapel.

Shrinkage reinforcement
Secondary reinforcement designed to resist shrinkage stresses in concrete.

Shutter
One of a pair of movable panels used at window openings to provide privacy and protection when closed.

Shutter bar
A hinged bar that can be fastened across the interior side of a pair of shutters, providing a measure of security.

Shutter box
A pocket or recess located along the interior side of a window to receive shutters when folded.

Shutter fastener
A pivoted device often made of decorative wrought iron that holds a shutter in the open position on the exterior side of a window.

Shutters
Protective covering for the outside of windows; louvered shutters are used for ventilation.

Siamese (Thai) architecture
An architecture (1350–1500) consisting of stupas and temples. The most characteristic forms are the eaves of overlapping roof planes, which are terminated with sculptural finials. The Temple of the Emerald Buddha in Bangkok is the most notable example.

Siamese fixture
A plumbing fixture with a Y-shaped end, found on the exterior of the building for connecting a fire hose to a standpipe.

Sibyl
A woman in Greek and Roman mythology reputed to possess powers of prophecy and divination.

Side aisle
One of the corridors parallel to the nave of a church or basilica, separated from it by an arcade or colonnade.

Side gable See **Gable**

Side lap
The overlap required for two adjacent building components to prevent the penetration of rain.

Sidelight
A framed area of fixed glass, usually comprising a number of small panes; commonly one of pair of such lights, set vertically on each side of a door.

Sidewalk
Walkway along the side of a road, or leading to a building, usually constructed of flagstone, brick, or concrete.

Sidewalk bridge See **Bridge**

Siding See **Wood**

Signature stone
A stone, found on many eighteenth and nineteenth century dwellings, carved with the date of completion and the name or initials of the owner, usually embedded in the wall over an entry door or in a gable.

Sikhara
The spire or tower over the shrine of an Indian temple.

Sill
The horizontal exterior member at the bottom of a window or door opening which is usually sloped away from the bottom of the window for drainage of water, and overhanging the wall below.

Sill plate
A heavy timber plate at the bottom of the frame of a wood structure resting directly on the foundation.

Sillcourse
In stone masonry, a stringcourse set at the windowsill level; commonly differentiated from the wall by its greater projectlon, finish, or thickness.

Silo
A tall, enclosed structure used primarily to store grain or chopped plants, commonly constructed of wood, masonry, or concrete.

Siloe, Diego de (c. 1495–1563)
Spanish architect and sculptor who introduced Italian Renaissance forms to Spain and played a major role in the development of the distinctive Plateresque style. Work includes the Granada Cathedral (1549).

Similarity
The state or quality of being alike in substance, essentials, or characteristics.

Simple beam See **Beam**

Simulated architecture
An architecture that would consist of holographic images of forms and monuments projected into space by laser beams.

Simulation
The process of representing or modeling a situation.

Sinan, Koca (1489–1578)
One of the greatest Turkish architects, and chief architect to the Ottoman court; brought to full development the classic Ottoman domed mosque, including the Suleymaniye Mosque, Istanbul (1551–1581).

Single-family dwelling
House that is usually detached and designed to shelter a group of related individuals.

Single-hung window See **Window**

Single-pitched roof See **Roof**

Sinking groove
The incised groove that separates the shaft from the capital in the Doric order.

Siras
In Indian architecture, the capital of a column or pillar.

Site
An area or plot of ground with defined limits on which a building, project, or part is located or proposed to be located; the specific location of a building or buildings.

SITE (Sculpture In The Environment)
American group launched by James Wines, and best known for the designs for the Best Products chain of stores, where unique manipulation of architectural elements made the buildings notorious. One of the most unique, but never realized, was the "highrise of houses." wherein a neighborhood of complete single-story residences were stacked within a steel superstructure. The later work includes the exhibits at Expo '92, Seville, Spain (1992).

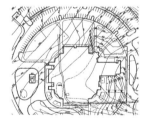

Site plan
A plan of a construction site showing the dimensions and contours of the lot and the dimensions of the building or portion thereof to be erected.

Site relationship
The plot of land where something was, is, or will be located; the situation or position of a place, town, or building, especially with reference to the surrounding locality.

Site relationship

Site work
Construction outside of a building, including earthwork, utilities, paving, and landscaping.

Skeletal frame
Refers to a structural framework of members, originally concealed within a building, or as a self-supporting grid of timber, steel, or concrete.

Skeleton construction
Construction in which the loads are transmitted to the ground by a frame, as opposed to construction with load-bearing walls.

Sketch See **Design drawing**

Skew corbel
A stone built into the bottom of a gable to form an abutment for a wall cornice or eaves gutter.

Skewback
The sloping surface of a member that receives the component materials of an arch.

Skewed
Having an oblique position, or twisted to one side.

Skidmore, Louis (1897–1962)
Founded Skidmore, Owings and Merrill (SOM) in Chicago in 1936, which was organized on teamwork, and used other ideas incorporated from business practice. SOM won fame for Lever House in New York City (1951). Later work included the John Hancock Center, Chicago (1968); projects in Saudi Arabia (1982) and the Canary Wharf developments in London (1990).

Skin
A non-load-bearing exterior wall.

Skintled bond See Bond

Skirt roof See Roof

Sky lobby
An elevator lobby at an upper floor; the sky lobby is served by express lifts only, thus saving an appreciable amount of space.

Skylight
An opening in a roof which is glazed with a transparent or translucent material used to admit natural or diffused light to the space below.

Skyscraper
A building of extreme height containing many stories, constructed of a steel or concrete frame that supports the exterior walls, as opposed to a load-bearing structure.

Skyscraper construction
The method of construction developed in Chicago in which all building loads are transmitted to a metal skeleton, so that any exterior masonry is simply a protective cladding.

Skywalk See Bridge

Slab
The upper part of a reinforced concrete floor, which is carried on beams below; a concrete mat poured on subgrade, serving as a floor rather than as a structural member.

Slab-on-grade
Concrete floor that is supported directly on the earth or fill.

Slat
A thin, narrow strip of wood, often one of a series used within a framework to regulate the passage of light and air into an area.

Slate See Stone

Sleeper
A horizontal timber laid on a slab or on the ground and to which the subflooring is nailed; any long horizontal beam, at or near the ground, which distributes the load from the posts to the foundation.

Sliding door See Door

Sliding sash window See Window

Smithson, Peter (1923–)
Husband to partner Alison (1928–1993), member of CIAM, and leader of the Modern Movement in Britain in the 1950s and 1960s. The use of exposed raw concrete earned Smithson the nickname "Brutus."

Snow guard
A board or other device that prevents snow from sliding off the roof.

Snow load
The superimposed load assumed to result from severe snowfalls in any particular region.

Soane, Sir John (1753–1837)
Designed Number 3 Lincoln's Inn Fields, London.

Society of Architectural Historians
A society dedicated to the encouragement of scholarly research in the field of architectural history.

Socle
A low, plain base course for a pedestal, column, or wall; a plain plinth.

Sod roof See **Roof**

Soffit
A ceiling or exposed underside surface of entablatures, archways, balconies, beams, lintels or columns.

Softwood See **Wood**

Solar collector
A device designed to absorb radiation from the sun and transfer this energy to air or fluid passing through a collector.

Solar heating: active
A solar heating system using mechanical means such as solar collectors, fans, or pumps, to collect, store, and distribute the solar energy.

Solar heating: passive
A solar heating system using a building's site orientation, design, and construction to collect, store, and distribute heat with a minimal use of fans or pumps, relying on the natural flow of heat.

Solar heating system
An assembly of subsystems and components which converts solar energy into thermal energy and uses it for heating.

Solar house
A building so designed that the sun's rays are used to maximum advantage in heating, supplementing or replacing other heating methods.

Solar orientation
The placing of a building in relation to the sun to maximize the amount of heat gained during the coldest months and minimize the amount of heat gained during the warmest months.

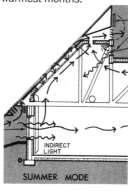

INDIRECT LIGHT

SUMMER MODE

WINTER MODE

Solarium
In ancient architecture, a terrace on top of a flat-roofed house or over a porch, surrounded by a parapet wall but open to the sky; a sunny room with more glass than usual, and often used for therapy.

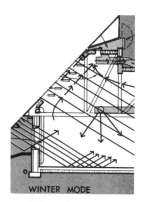

Soldier See **Bond**

Soleri, Paolo (1919–)
Italian-born American architect, who worked for Frank Lloyd Wright in 1947 before returning to Italy to build the Ceramics Factory, in Salerno (1953). He later established the Cosanti Foundation in Scottsdale (1955), and evolved the concept of Arcology, in which architecture and ecology are merged. Arcosanti, near Scottsdale, was commenced in 1970, representing the development of a city along his visionary ideas.

Solid-core door See **Door**

Solid-web joist
A conventional joist with a solid web formed by a plate or rolled section, as opposed to an open-web joist.

Solomonic column See **Column**

Sopraporta
Means "above the door" in Italian; an illustrative painting above a doorway, typically framed by a continuation of the door moldings, is an example.

Sorin
The crowning spire on a Japanese pagoda, usually made of bronze.

Sottsass, Ettore (1917–)
Italian architect working in Milan; he designed artifacts, exhibitions, and interiors. He has been classified as a Postmodernist Kitsch, merging consumer and popular culture with high design; Memphis furniture is an example.

Soufflot, Jacques (1713–1780)
One of the greatest French Neo-classical architects, combining the monumentality of ancient Roman models with the structural lightness admired in Gothic architecture. Work includes the Pantheon, Paris.

Sound
The sensation stimulated in the auditory organs by a vibratory disturbance.

Sound barrier
Any solid obstacle which is relatively opaque to sound that blocks the line of sight between a sound source and the point of reception of the sound.

Sound-insulating glass See **Glass**

Sound insulation
The use of structures and materials designed to reduce the transmission of sound from one room or area of a building to another, or from the exterior to the interior of the building

Sound lock
A vestibule or entranceway that has highly absorptive walls and ceiling and a carpeted floor: used to reduce transmission of noise into an auditorium, rehearsal room or studio, or from the area outside.

Space
The unlimited continuous three-dimensional expanse in which all material objects exist; all the area in and around a structure, or volume between specified boundaries, and the interval between two objects.

Space allocation
The process of generating spatial designs by allocating units of functional spaces to physical space locations.

Space audit
A physical survey and record of the space that is occupied and its functional use.

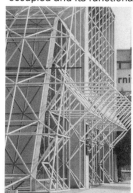

Space frame
A three-dimensional structural framework made up of interconnected triangular elements that enclose a space; as opposed to a frame where all the elements lie in a single plane.

Space planning
The definition of space in terms of size, type, activity and adjacency for particular types of space.

Space utilization
The ratio of the number of people using a space to its potential use capacity, multiplied by the ratio of hours of actual usage to the total available hours, and expressed as a percentage.

Spackle
A paste to fill holes, cracks and defects in the surfaces of various materials.

Spall
A small fragment or chip dislodged from the face of a stone or masonry unit by a blow or by the action caused by the elements, such as a freezing and thawing cycle.

Span
The interval between any two consecutive supports of a beam, girder, or truss or between the opening of an arch.

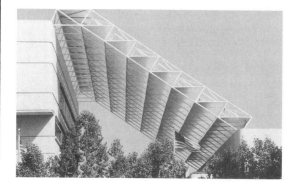

Spandrel

The triangular space that is formed between the sides of adjacent arches and the line across their tops: in a skeletal frame building, the walls inside the columns and between the top of the windows and the sill above.

Spandrel bracket

A pair of curved brackets that form an arched shape.

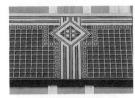

Spandrel panel

A panel covering the spandrel area between the head of a window on one level and the sill of the window immediately above.

Spandrel wall See **Wall**

Spanish Colonial Revival style

A unique feature of this revival style (1915–1940) is the ornate low-relief carvings highlighting arches, columns, window surrounds, cornices and parapets. Red-tiled hipped roofs and arcaded porches are typical. Exterior walls are left exposed or finished in plaster or stucco. Iron window grilles and balconies are prevalent. A molded or arcaded cornice highlights the eaves, and large buildings have ornamental parapets and a symbolic bell tower.

Spanish Colonial style

Adobe-brick wall construction covered with a lime wash or plaster characterized this style (1650–1840). Rounded roof beams were extended over porches, which were covered with tile roofs. Missions of the southwestern United States were richly ornamented vernacular interpretations of this Baroque-like style.

Spanish roof tile See **Tile**

Specifications
A written document accompanying the drawings, describing the materials and workmanship required to carry out the works for each particular trade.

Spherical
Refers to a three-dimensional surface, all parts of which are equidistant from a fixed point.

Sphinx See **Ornament: animal forms**

Spindlework
A Queen Anne decoration, featuring short, turned parts, similar to balusters.

Spiral
Refers to forms that are generated by a continuous curve, traced by a point moving around a fixed point in a fixed plane, while steadily increasing the distance from that point.

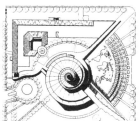

Spiral stair See **Stair**

Spire
A slender pointed element on top of a building, generally a narrow octagonal pyramid set above a square tower.

Spire

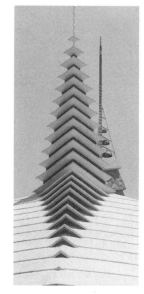

Splay
A sloped surface that makes an oblique angle with another at the sides of a door or window, with the opening larger on one side than the other; a large chamfer; a reveal at an oblique angle.

Splayed arch See **Arch**

Splayed jamb
Any jamb whose face is not at right angles to the wall in which it is set.

Splayed lintel
A horizontal lintel above a window or doorway which slants downward toward the centerline; often containing a keystone at its center.

Splayed mullion
A mullion that joins two glazed units which are at an angle to each other, such as the mullion of a bay window.

Splayed window See **Window**

Splice
To connect, unite, or join two similar members, wires, columns or pieces; usually in a straight line, by fastening the lapped ends with mechanical end-connectors, or by welding.

Splice

butt splice
A butt joint, which is further secured by nailing a piece of wood to each side of a butt joint.

lap splice
A splice made by placing one piece on top of another and fastening them together with pins, nails, screws, bolts, rivets, or similar devices.

Split-level house
A house with a kitchen, dining, and living room area on the main floor, with stairs leading up to the bedrooms at a half-story higher; other stairs may lead downward from the main floor to a family room or utility room.

Spout
A short channel or tube used to spill storm water from gullies, balconies, exterior galleries, so that the water will fall clear of the building; a gargoyle.

Sprayed fireproof insulation
A mixture of mineral fiber with other ingredients, such as asbestos, applied by air pressure with a spray gun; used to provide fire protection or thermal insulation.

Spread footing See Footing

Spreckelsen, Johan Otto von (1929–1987)
Danish architect, who used pure forms in his work, such as the cylinder and sphere. He was (with Paul Andrew) winner of the competition for the design of the Grande Arche de la D'efense, Paris (1983), a huge trapezoidal structure with a hollow center, which terminates the axis that runs from the Tuileries Gardens in the east through the Arc de Triomphe to La D'efense.

Springer
The impost or place where the vertical support for an arch terminates and the curve of the arch begins; the lower voussoir, or bottom stone of an arch, which lies immediately on an impost.

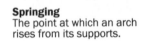

Springing
The point at which an arch rises from its supports.

Springing line
The imaginary horizontal line at which an arch or vault begins to curve; the line in which the springers rest on the imposts.

Sprinkler system
A system, usually automatic, for protection against fire; when activated, it sprays water over a large area in a systematic pattern.

Spur
A decorative appendage on the corners of the base of a round column resting on a square or polygonal plinth, in the form of a grotesque, a tongue, or leafwork.

Square
A regular four-sided figure with equal sides and four equal right angles; may be subdivided along the diagonals or oblique lines connecting the corner angles and the lines that connect the center of each side.

Square billet molding See **Molding**

Square roof See **Roof**

Square rubble masonry See **Masonry**

Squared stone See **Stone**

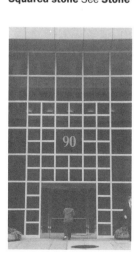

Square-headed
Cut off at right angles, as an opening with upright parallel sides and a straight horizontal lintel, as distinguished from an arched opening.

Square-headed

Square-headed window See **Window**

Squinch
Corbeling built at the upper corners of a structural bay to support a smaller dome or drum; a small arch across the corner of a square room which supports a superimposed octagonal structure above.

Squinch arch See **Arch**

Stabilization
The process of temporarily protecting a historic building until restoration or rehabilitation can begin; typically includes making the building weathertight, structurally stable, and secure against intrusion.

Stack bond See **Bond**

Stadium
A sports arena, usually shaped like an oval, or in a horseshoe shape.

Staff
Ornamental plastering, made in molds and reinforced with fiber, usually nailed or wired into place.

Staggered
Two or more rows of objects that are offset from one another in such a manner as to form a zigzag pattern.

Stained glass See **Glass**

Stained glass window See **Window**

Stainless steel See **Metal**

Stair
A series of steps or flights of steps for going between two or more successive levels with connecting landings at each level, either on the exterior or in the interior.

box stair
An interior staircase constructed with a closed string on both sides, often enclosed by walls or partitions with door openings at various floor levels.

circular stair
A stair having a cylindrical shape.

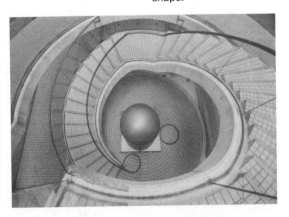

Stair

closed-string stair
A staircase whose profile of treads and risers is covered at the side by a string, or sloping member which supports the balustrade.

dogleg stair
Two flights of stairs parallel to each other with a half-landing in between.

elliptical stair
Winding stair in which the plan of its inside edges is in the shape of an ellipse.

geometrical stair
A winder stair in which the outside of the winders is supported by walls forming three sides of a rectangle, and the inner side is unsupported and without a newel post.

hanging stair
A stair supported by individual hanging steps projecting horizontally from a wall on one side, sometimes with corbels or brackets.

helical stair
Stair whose treads are wrapped around a helix: commonly called a spiral stair.

open stair
A stair or stairway, whose treads are visible on one or both sides and open to a room in which it is located.

Stair

open-string stair
A staircase whose profile of treads and risers is visible from the side; the treads support the balusters.

open-well stair
A stair built around a well, leaving an open space.

service stair
A stairway that is not used for general purposes; it provides access to specific areas such as the roof and equipment rooms.

spiral stair
A flight of stairs, circular in plan, whose treads wind around a central newel, or post.

straight stair
A stair with a single straight flight of steps between levels.

straight-flight stair
A stair extending only in one direction, without turns or wedge-shaped steps.

Stair

winding stair
Any stair constructed chiefly or entirely of winders.

Stair flight
Continuous series of steps without intermediate landings.

Stair landing
Horizontal platform at the end of a flight of stairs: or between two flights of stairs.

half-landing
A landing located halfway up a flight of stairs.

Stair rail
A bar of wood or other material that connects the balusters on a stair.

Stair riser
Vertical portion of a stair step; may be open or closed.

Stair tower
A part of a structure containing a winding stair which fills it exactly; a stair enclosure which projects beyond the roof of a building.

Staircase
A vertical element of access in a structure for ascending or descending from one level to another. The form of the staircase is often expressed on the exterior of the building, if it is located adjacent to an exterior wall.

Stairwell
A vertical space in a building that encloses a staircase.

Stalactite work
An Islamic decorative design consisting of multiple corbeling that resembles natural stalactites, in either plaster, marble or wood.

Stamped metal
Sheet metal that has been shaped by stamping or pressing it with dies to form a raised or recessed decorative design on the surface.

Stanchion
A column, particularly of structural steel; an upright bar placed between the mullions to strengthen a leaded light.

Standby lighting
A lighting system that supplies adequate illumination if the normal system should fail; usually supplied by an emergency generator.

Standby power
The power that is available within one minute of a power failure to operate life safety equipment and continuously operating equipment; emergency power is the power available within ten seconds.

Standing seam joint See **Joint**

Standpipe
A vertical pipe riser with multiple interior connections for fire hoses, terminated at the building facade with a fitting for a fire engine hose; may also have a connection to the main water supply.

Stark, Philip (1949–)
French-born architect whose unusual interiors are his specialty, including the Paramount Hotel interior, New York (1990),

Statehouse
Capitol building of a state government.

Station point See **Perspective projection**

Statuary
Free-standing sculpture, as opposed to relief work.

Statue

A form of likeness sculpted, modeled, carved, or cast in material such as stone, clay, wood, or bronze.

Statuette

Diminutive statue, especially one that is less than life size.

Stave

Wedge-shaped timber.

Stave church

A Scandinavian church of the twelfth and thirteenth centuries constructed entirely of wood with few windows and a steep roof; highly original in structure with fantastic semi-pagan decorative features.

Steamboat Gothic style

A richly ornamental mode of Gothic Revival building (1850–1880) in the Ohio and Mississippi River Valleys characterized by the gingerbread and ornamental construction found on riverboats of the Victorian period.

Steel See Metal

Steel frame

A skeleton of steel beams and columns providing all that is structurally necessary for the building to stand.

Steel stud

A bent steel sheet-metal stud; typically with punched-out holes in the widest face; used in interior framing for drywall construction

Steeple

A tall ornamental structure terminating in a spire and surmounting the tower of a church or public building.

Steiner, Rudolf (1861–1925)

An Austria-Hungarian philosopher, artist, scientist, and architect. His Geotheanum, Dornach, Switzerland (1913), was the epitome of Expressionism, with a strong Symbolist and Jugendstil flavor. It was built of reinforced concrete.

Stele

An upright stone slab or pillar with a carved or inscribed surface, used as a monument or marker, or as a commemorative tablet in the face of a building.

Stellar vault See Vault

Stenciling

Decorative painting on interior walls, consisting of repetitive patterns applied by brushing paint onto the surface through openings cut in the stencil.

Step

A stair unit that consists of one tread, the horizontal upper surface, and one riser, the vertical face.

bull-nosed step

A step, usually the lowest in a flight, having one or both ends rounded to a semicircle and projecting beyond the face of the stair string. The projection extends beyond and around the newel post.

Step

cantilever step
Step built into the wall at one end, but supported at the other end only by the steps below.

curtail step
A step, usually the lowest in a flight, of which one or both ends are rounded into a spiral or scroll shape which projects beyond the newel.

riser
The vertical face of a stair step.

tread
The horizontal upper surface of a step; includes the rounded edge or nosing which extends over the riser.

Stepped
Refers to forms that are increased or decreased by a series of successive increments or modulated by incremental stages or steps.

Stepped

Stepped arch See **Arch**

Stepped flashing
Individual pieces of flashing used where a sloped roof abuts a vertical masonry wall or chimney; each piece is bent and inserted into a mortar joint.

Stepped gable See **Gable**

Stepped pyramid
An early type of pyramid having a stepped and terraced appearance.

Stepped window See **Window**

Stepped-back chimney
Any exterior brick chimney that is wide enough at the base to enclose a large fireplace in the kitchen, then decreasing in area in several steps, possibly collecting other flues from the upper floor.

Stereobate
The substructure, foundation, or solid platform upon which a building is erected. In a columnar building, it includes the uppermost step or platform upon which the columns stand.

Stern, Robert A.M. (1939–)
Worked with Richard Meier before setting up his own practice in 1977. He is seen as one of the influences in Post-modernism, advocating a study of history and the eclectic use of forms. Among his later works are the Walt Disney Casting Center, Lake Buena Vista (1989), Banana Republic Store, Chicago (1991).

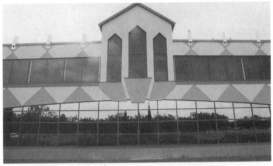

Stiacciato See **Relief**

Stick style
An eclectic wooden-frame style of the late 1800s that was usually asymmetrical in plan and elevation. It had wood trim members applied as ornamentation on the exterior that expressed the structure of the building, as corner posts and diagonal bracing; also featured porches and towers ornamented in the same manner, and ornamented gable apexes.

Stile
One of the upright structural members of a frame, such as at the outer edge of a door or a window sash.

Stilted arch See **Arch**

Stirling, James (1926–1992)
Scots architect; influenced by Le Corbusier. Fell into the category of Brutalism in the Engineering Block building, University of Leicester, England (1959). His later work became increasingly eclectic and expressive and contained illusions to historical themes. Works include the engineering building, Leister University (1959), Olivetti Building Haslemere, Surrey (1972), and Braun Headquarters, Melsungen, Germany (1991).

Stoa
A covered colonnade in ancient Greek and Roman cities, flanking the agora, or open market and meeting place; one- or two-storied, with an open front and shops or offices built into the rear wall.

Stockade
A defensible space that is enclosed by a fence or palisade with loopholes.

Stone
Native rock that has been processed by shaping, cutting or sizing for building or landscaping use. It is fire-resistant and varies according to type, from fairly porous to impregnable. There are three basic types of stone: igneous, such as granite, is long lasting and durable; sedimentary, such as limestone, is made up of organic remains; metamorphic rock is either igneous or sedimentary transformed by pressure and heat or both.

alabaster
A fine-grained, translucent variety of very pure gypsum: white or delicately shaded, and used for ornamental work.

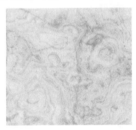

basalt
A dense, dark gray volcanic rock, often full of small cavities, used as a building stone.

belgian block
A hard paving stone, typically granite, roughly cut to the shape of a truncated pyramid, where the top is slightly smaller than the base.

bluestone
A dense fine-grained sandstone that splits easily along bedding planes to form thin slabs.

brownstone
A dark brown or reddish-brown sandstone, used extensively for building in the United States during the middle and late nineteenth century.

Stone

cobble
Stone that is smaller than a boulder, larger than gravel.

cobblestone
A natural stone rounded by water; used for paving and sometimes for walls: decorative designs could be achieved by using different colored stones.

dolomite
Limestone consisting principally of the mineral dolomite.

fieldstone
Loose stone found on the surface or in the soil, flat in the direction of bedding and suitable for use as drywall masonry.

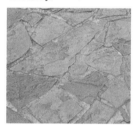

flagstone
A naturally thin flat stone, normally used as a stepping stone or as outdoor paving; sometimes split from rock that cleaves easily.

gneiss
A coarse-grained, dark metamorphic rock; composed mainly of quartz, feldspar, mica, and other minerals corresponding in composition to granite, in which the minerals are arranged in layers.

granite
An igneous rock having crystals or grains of visible size; consists mainly of quartz and mica or other colored minerals.

limestone
Rock of sedimentary origin composed principally of calcite, dolomite or both; used as a building stone or crushed-stone aggregate, or burnt to produce lime.

Stone

marble
Metamorphic rock made up largely of calcite or dolomite; capable of taking a high polish, and used especially in architecture and sculpture; numerous minerals account for the distinctive appearance.

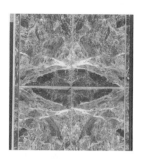

natural stone
Stone that has been quarried and cut, but not crushed into chips and reconstituted into cast stone.

obsidian
A natural volcanic glass, usually black with a bright luster, that is transparent in thin slabs.

quartzite
A variety of sandstone composed largely of granular quartz cemented by silica, forming a homogeneous mass of very high tensile and crushing strengths; used as a building stone and as an aggregate in concrete.

sandstone
Sedimentary rock that is composed of sand-sized grains naturally cemented by mineral materials.

serpentine
A group of minerals consisting of hydrous magnesium silicate or rock largely composed of these minerals; commonly occurs in greenish shades; used as decorative stone.

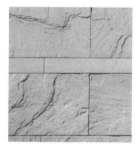

slate
A hard, brittle metamorphic rock characterized by good cleavage along parallel planes; used as cut stone in thin sheets for flooring, roofing, panels, and in granular form as surfacing on composition roofing.

squared stone
Roughly dressed stone blocks with rectangular faces.

travertine
A variety of limestone deposited by springs, usually banded, commonly coarse and cellular, often containing fossils; used as building stones, especially for interior facing or flooring.

Stone

undressed stone
Not trimmed or rendered smooth.

verde antique
A dark green serpentine rock marked with white veins of calcite which takes a high polish; used for decorative purposes since ancient times; sometimes classified as a marble.

volcanic stone
A low-density, high-porosity rock composed of volcanic particles, ranging from ash size to small pebble size, which are compacted or cemented together; used as a building stone or as a thermal insulation material.

Stone Age
The earliest known period of human culture, characterized by the use of stone tools and weapons.

Stone house
A house constructed entirely of stone.

Stone, Edward Durrell (1902–1978)
Absorbed the Modern movement working on Rockefeller Center, and designed the interior of Radio City Music Hall. His U.S. Embassy, New Delhi, India (1954), and the Kennedy Center for the Performing Arts, Washington, D.C. (1961), were axial and symmetrical, and paraphrased the Classical movement.

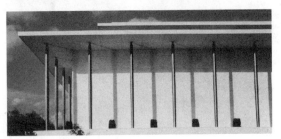

Stonemason
An artisan skilled in dressing and laying stone for buildings and other purposes.

Stool
The flat piece upon which a window closes, corresponding to the sill of a door.

Stoop
A platform or small porch at the entrance to a house, usually up several steps.

Stop
The molding or trim on the inside face of a door or window frame against which the door or window closes.

Stopped flute
A column flute that stops approximately one-third of the shaft height above its base.

Storefront
Ground-level shop employing large sheets of glass display windows with minimal-sized mullions; often having a recessed entrance.

Storeroom
A room set aside for the storage of goods and supplies.

Storm door See **Door**

Storm porch
Enclosed porch that protects the entrance to a house from severe weather.

Storm window See **Window**

Story
The space in a building between floor levels; in some codes a basement is considered a story, generally a cellar is not; a major architectural division even where no floor exists, as a tier or a row of windows.

Straight joint See **Joint**

Straight stair See **Stair**

Straight-flight stair See **Stair**

Straight-line gable See **Gable**

Strap hanger
Metal bars with a rectangular cross section that is bent into a channel shape and used to attach beams to purlins; also called a stirrup.

Strap hinge
A surface-mounted hinge having two leaves; one is fastened to the door and the other is secured to the frame or post.

Strapwork ornament See **Ornament**

Streamline Modern
A phase of Art Deco that emphasizes the horizontal aspects of design, usual elements include curved end walls, rounded corners, horizontal stainless-steel railings, flush windows, round windows, and glass block.

Street furniture
Manufactured elements, such as benches, street-lights, fire hydrants, and light fixtures, found in public spaces.

Streetlight
One of a series of lamps at the top of a post along a street or similar public location.

Streetscape
A diminutive version of the cityscape, relating elements on the ground plane to the viewer; some of the elements consist of building setbacks, trees, parks and open areas, street furniture and signage.

Stress
Internal forces per unit area; when the forces are tangential to the plane they are shear stresses; when they are perpendicular they are called either tensile of compressive stresses, depending on whether they act toward or away from the plane of separation. The deformation caused by stress is called strain.

Stressed skin panel See **Wood**

Stressed-skin construction
A form of construction in which the outer skin acts within the framework to contribute to the membrane and strength of the unit, instead of just a cladding to protect the inside from the weather.

Stretcher
A masonry unit laid horizontally with its length in the direction of the face of the wall.

Striation
Fine narrow ridges or grooves parallel to each other.

Strickland, William (1788–1854)
American architect, a pupil of Latrobe; designed mostly in the Greek Revival style, as well as the Egyptian Revival style.

String
In a stair, an inclined board that supports the end of the steps; also called a stringer.

face string
An outer string, usually of better material or finish than the rough string which it covers; may be part of the actual construction or applied to the face of the supporting member.

outer string
The string at the outer and exposed edge of a stair, away from the wall.

Stringcourse
A horizontal band of masonry, extending across the facade to mark a division in a wall, often encircling decorative features such as pillars or engaged columns; may be flush or projecting, molded or richly carved.

Stringer
A horizontal piece of timber or steel that connects the uprights in a framework and supports the floor; the inclined member that supports the treads and risers of a stair.

Struck molding See **Molding**

Struck mortar joint See **Mortar joint**

Structural engineering
A branch of engineering concerned with the design and construction of structures to withstand physical forces or displacements without danger of collapse or without loss of serviceability or function.

Structural glass See **Glass**

Structural lumber See **wood**

Strut
A bracing member, or any piece of a frame which resists thrusts in the direction of its own length, whether upright, horizontal or diagonal.

Stuart style
A style (1603–1688) typifying the late English Renaissance.

Stubbins, Hugh (1912–)
In 1939, became assistant to Walter Gropius at Harvard, established his own practice in Cambridge (1940), and succeeded Gropius as chairman of the Department of Architecture. He designed the Congress Hall in Berlin (1957), and Citicorp Center in New York City (1978).

Stucco
An exterior fine plaster finish composed of portland cement, lime, and sand mixed with water, used for decorative work or moldings, and usually textured.

Stud
One of a series of upright posts, or vertical structural members, that acts as the supporting element in a wall or partition.

Stud partition
An interior partition with stud framing, normally covered with various materials, such as plaster or drywall.

Studio
Working space of an artist, photographer, or craftsperson; may have special lighting provisions, such as skylights.

Studio apartment
An apartment with a single living space that includes a galley kitchen, plus an enclosed bathroom.

Study See Design

Stupa
A Buddhist memorial site, consisting of an artificial mound on a platform, surrounded by an outer ambulatory with four gateways, and crowned by a multiple sunshade, erected to enshrine a relic.

Style
The overall appearance of the design of a building including form, space, scale, materials, including ornamentation; it may be either a unique individual expression or part of a broad cultural pattern.

Stylobate
The single top course of the three steps forming a foundation of a classical temple upon which the columns rests; any continuous base, plinth, or pedestal upon which a row of columns rests directly.

Subbasement
A story one or more levels below the basement level.

Subcontractor
Specialized building contractor; typically works for the general contractor performing work in a particular trade, such as electrical, masonry, or millwork.

Subdivision
A tract of land divided into residential lots.

Subfloor
Structural floor that supports the finish floor, such as a concrete floor or rough wood floor.

Suborder
A secondary architectural order, introduced chiefly for decoration, as distinguished from a main order of a structure.

Suburb
An outlying neighborhood or town near a city center, used primarily as a residential community, with single-family homes.

Sullivan, Louis H. (1856–1924)
Leader of the Chicago School of Architecture and a pioneer in skyscraper design. The Auditorium Building, Chicago (1887), was his first major work, followed by the Getty tomb, Chicago (1890), Wainwright Building, St Louis (1890), Schiller Theater Building, Chicago (1892), and the Guaranty Building, Buffalo (1895), notable for its rich terra-cotta ornamentation and an early use of Art Nouveau interior decoration. The Carson Pirie Scott Department Store, Chicago (1900), was designed with a horizontal emphasis, and demonstrated his interest in organically inspired facade ornament. His many bank buildings include the National Farmer's Bank, Owatonna, Minnesota (1908).

Louis H. Sullivan

Sullivanesque
A term descriptive of the architectural style and ornamentation of Louis H. Sullivan, from about 1890 to 1924.

Sullivanesque style
A style (1890–1920) named after Louis Henry Sullivan, noted for his stylized ornamentation and simple multi-story forms, designed as uninterrupted elements to express height, much the same as fluting in Classical columns. The windows were separated by ornamental terra-cotta panels, and the massive decorative cornice resembled the capital.

An intricate weaving of linear forms with stylized foliage was highlighted in the cornice with low-relief ornamentation in terra-cotta.

Sumerian architecture
An architecture (5000–2000 B.C.) made of locally available materials: clay-tied bundles of reeds used as structural framing for huts and halls, with sun-dried bricks for the walls between these buttresses.

Monumental temples and palaces were built around a series of courtyards; the ziggurat of Ur is the most famous. Large cities had well-developed drainage and sewer systems, and were protected by strong ramparts.

Summerbeam See Beam

Sun deck
A roof area, balcony, or open porch that is exposed to the sun.

Sun disk
A disk representing the sun with wings, especially used in Egyptian antiquity as emblematic of the sun god.

Sunk draft
A margin cut into a building stone that is sunk below the face of the stone to give it a raised appearance.

Sunk molding See Molding

Sunk panel
A panel recessed below the surface of its surrounding framing or carved into solid masonry or timber.

Sunk relief See **Relief**

Superimposed orders
Use of one order on top of another on the face of a building of more than one story. Usually in the following sequence: Doric (first story), Ionic, and Corinthian (top). The upper order is usually lighter in form than the lower ones.

Suspended forms

Supermarket
A large, self-service, retail market which sells food, household goods, and household merchandise.

Superstructure
Structure above the main supporting level; as opposed to the substructure or basement.

Surbase
The molding or cornice at the top edge of a pedestal.

Surbased arch See **Arch**

Suspended luminaire
A lighting fixture hung from the ceiling by rigid or flexible supports, leaving an air space above the luminaire.

Surround
An encircling border or decorative frame around a door, window or other opening.

Suspended roof See **Roof**

Suspension bridge See **Bridge**

Survey
A boundary or topographic mapping of a site: a compilation of the measurements of an existing building; an analysis of a building for use of the interior space.

Swag
A festoon, hung between rosettes or other terminals.

Suspended ceiling See **Ceiling**

Suspended forms
Refers to forms that are hung so as to allow free movement and appear to be supported without any attachment to objects underneath.

Swan's-neck pediment See **Pediment**

Sway brace See **Brace**

Swing bridge See **Bridge**

Swiss Chalet Style
An architectural house style loosely based on the Swiss Chalet prototype; typical elements include two stories with a front gable, low-pitched roof, front balcony or porch with scroll-work railings, stick work or board-and-batten siding, or stucco with painted ornamentation or scenery.

Symbol
Something that stands for or represents something else by association, resemblance, or convention, deriving its meaning chiefly from the structure on which it appears.

Symmetry
The exact correspondence of forms of similar size and arrangement of parts, equidistant and on opposite sides of a dividing line or plane about the center line or axis.

bilateral symmetry
A balanced arrangement of identical similar elements about a central axis.

radial symmetry
Balanced elements that radiate from a central point.

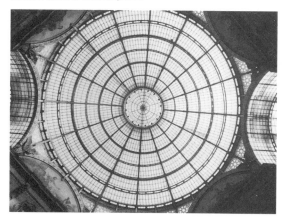

Synagogue
A place of assembly, or a building for Jewish worship and religious instruction.

Syrian arch See **Arch**

System furniture
Modular office furniture with provision for integrated electrical and data connections, including desktops, shelving, and drawers; they can be interconnected in a variety of combinations to create individual or linked workstations.

Systems Design
Three definitions characterize this approach to problem solving. The first is the design of a range of components to be prefabricated in factories and combined in different ways to yield different types of structures. The second is the application of analysis to the supply of materials and assembly processes. The third is a conceptual overview of design where each building is regarded as part of a greater whole and each project is seen in its social, cultural and economic context.

Tt

Tabernacle
A free-standing ornamental canopy above an altar, tomb, or ornamental niche.

Table
Applied generally to all horizontal bands of moldings, base moldings and cornices.

Tablero
A rectangular framed panel which is cantilevered over an outward sloping apron with which it is always used; characteristic of the temples at Teotihuacan In Mexico.

Tablet
A rectangularly shaped separate panel or flat slab, often bearing an inscription or carving of an image.

Takamatsu, Shin (1948–)
Japanese architect, exploring high-tech forms, such as the Kirin Plaza Building, Osaka, Japan (1987).

Talus
Sloped architectural feature, such as a battered wall or an inclined retaining wall against an embankment.

Tange, Kenzo (1913–)
He came from Kunio Mayekawa's office and was influenced by Le Corbusier, but drew on Japanese themes. The Hiroshima Peace Center and Museum (1955) was his first major project, followed by St. Mary's Cathedral, Tokyo (1961). Later work includes the gymnasium for the Tokyo Olympics (1964), covered by a gigantic tensile catenary roof structure, and Tokyo City Hall (1991).

Tapering
Forms exhibiting a gradual diminution in thickness, or reduction in cross section, as in a spire or column.

Tapestry
A large woven illustration hung as a wall decoration.

Tapestry brick See Brick

Tatami
A thick straw floor mat in a Japanese house covered with finely woven reeds and bound with plain or decorated bands of silk, cotton, or hemp; its size of 3 feet by 6 feet is used as a standard unit of measurement.

Tatlin, Vladimir (1885–1953)
Designed the Memorial to the Third International. It was a Constructivist architectural fantasy, a spiral leaning tower. Constructivism was a short-lived ideal in Russia.

Taut, Bruno (1880–1938)
German architect and advisor to the German Garden City Movement. His glass pavilion, Werkbund Exposition, Cologne (1914), is his most celebrated work, a paradigm of Expressionism. He also published many books.

Teahouse
A Japanese garden house used for the tea ceremony.

Teak See Wood

Tectiforms
Shapes resembling man-made structures found painted on the walls of Paleolithic caves.

Tee
A finial in the form of a conventionalized umbrella: found in Japanese architecture on stupas and pagodas.

Tepee
A tent of the American Indians, made usually from animal skins laid on a conical frame of long poles and having an opening at the top for ventilation and a flap door.

Telescope house
A house comprised of several sections, each one of descending height, giving the appearance of fitting together like a collapsible telescope.

Tempera
A rapidly drying paint consisting of egg white, gum, pigment, and water, used in painting murals.

Tempera painting
A mural painting technique used widely in the Middle Ages and the Renaissance, which uses transparent colors on gesso.

Tempered glass See **Glass**

Template
A pattern of sheet material, used as a guide for setting out work and in repeating patterns of painted ornamentation.

Temple
An edifice dedicated to the service of a deity or deities, and connected with a system of worship; an edifice erected as a place of public worship.

Tendril
A long, slender, coiling extension, such as a stem, serving as an ornamental device; used mainly by Art Nouveau architects.

Tenement
A building with multiple dwelling units accessed by a single stairway, with two or more apartments on each floor.

Tenon
The projecting end of a piece of wood or other material, reduced in cross section so that it may be inserted into a corresponding mortise in another piece to form a secure Joint.

Tensile structures
Those that stretch or extend a member or other ductile material such as a fabric or membrane; some forms express this quality even if the material is not fabric, such as thin concrete shells.

Tension column See **Column**

Tepidarium
Room of moderate heat in a Roman bath.

Terminal
A terminus occurring at the end of a series of incidents, as a resting point; a point of emphasis, as in an object situated at the end of an element.

Terminal figure
A carving in the form of a pedestal that tapers outward at the top and merges into an animal, human, or mythological figure; used for columns, statues, and consoles.

Terminal pedestal
A tapered pedestal for a bust, with both objects forming a terminal figure.

Termination
An ornamental element that finishes off an architectural feature.

Terminus
A bust or figure of the upper part of the human body, terminated in a plain rectangular block, sometimes attached to a wall as a pillar, or found springing out of a column.

Terrace
A flat roof or raised space or platform adjoining a building, paved or planted, especially one used for leisure enjoyment .

Terrace roof See Roof

Terra-cotta
A hard-burnt glazed or un-glazed clay unit, either plain or ornamental, machine-extruded or hand-molded, usually larger in size than a brick or facing tile, used in building construction.

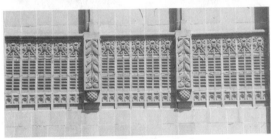

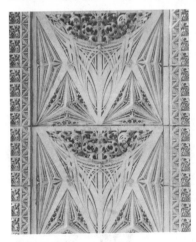

Terrazzo
Marble-aggregate concrete that is cast in place, or precast and ground smooth; used as a decorative surface for walls and floors.

Terry, Quinlan (1937–)
British architect, whose most well known projects include the Howard Building, Downing College, Cambridge (1989), Kansai International Airport, Osaka, Japan (1994).

Tesselated
Formed of small square pieces of marble, stone, or glass in the manner of an ornamental mosaic.

Tessera
A small square piece of colored marble, glass, or tile, used to make geometric or figurative mosaic patterns.

Tetrahedron
A polygon with four plane surfaces.

Tetrastyle
A portico having four columns in front.

Textile mill
A factory in which woven fabrics are manufactured; many early mills were of timber and masonry construction, and were sometimes operated by water power to run the machinery.

Texture
The tactile and visual quality of a surface as distinct from its color or form; as showing a grainy, coarse, tactile or dimensional quality, as opposed to smooth.

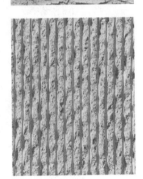

Thatch
A roof covering made of straw, reed, or similar materials fastened together to shed water and sometimes to provide thermal insulation; in tropical countries palm leaves are widely used.

Thatched roof See Roof

The Architects Collaborative (TAC)
A firm started by Walter Gropius in Cambridge. They designed the American Institute of Architects National Headquarters Building, Washington, D.C. (1973).

Theater
A building or outdoor structure providing a stage and associated equipment for the presentation of dramatic or musical performances and seating for spectators.

Theme
An idea, point of view, or perception embodied in a work of art; an underlying and essential subject of artistic expression.

Theme

theme development
To disclose by degree or in detail; to evolve the possibilities by a process of growth; to elaborate with the gradual unfolding of an idea.

theme variation
Repetition of a theme with embellishments in rhythm, details and materials while keeping the essential characteristics of the original.

Thermae
Ancient Roman buildings for public baths; incorporating places for sports, discussions and reading.

Thermal barrier
An element of low heat conductivity placed on an assembly to reduce or prevent the flow of heat between highly conductive materials; used in metal window or curtain wall designs in cold climates.

Thermal conduction
The process of heat transfer through a material medium, in which kinetic energy is transmitted by particles of the material without displacement of the particles.

Thermal expansion
The change in length or volume which a material or body undergoes on being heated.

Tholos
Domed building with a circular plan, such as the Jefferson Memorial in Washington, DC.

Thompson, Benjamin (1918–)
Noted architect/developer; he designed the Design Research Building, Cambridge, (1969), the large retail complex Harbor Place, Baltimore, (1980), and Faneuil Hall Marketplace and Quincy Market Restoration, Boston (1977), for the Rouse Company.

Thomson, Alexander (1817–1875)
Scots Neo-classical architect, an original designer influenced by Schinkel, who worked mostly in Glasgow. His buildings drew on a variety of sources, including ancient Egyptian, Persian, and Indian architecture.

Three-centered arch See **Arch**

Three-dimensional graphics
The process of drawing and displaying objects in three dimensions, using computer graphics programs.

Three-dimensional modeling
The process of producing three-dimensional objects using constructive geometry and rendering them as solids in computer graphics programs.

Three-hinged arch See **Arch**

Three-pinned arch See **Arch**

Three-point perspective See **Perspective projection**

Threshold
A strip fastened to the floor beneath a door, to cover the joint where two types of floor materials meet or to provide weather protection.

Throat
A groove which is cut along the underside of a member, such as a stringcourse or coping on a wall, to prevent water from running back toward the wall.

Thrust
The force exerted by beams against a wall; or the outward force of an arch, dome or vault, counterbalanced if necessary by buttresses.

Tie beam See **Beam**

Tie rod
A rod in tension, used to hold parts of a structure together.

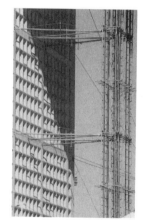

Tier
One of a series of rows arranged one above the other.

Tierceron
An intermediate rib between the main ribs of a Gothic vault.

Tiffany, Louis Comfort (1864–1933)
American designer, best known for his designs in the Art Nouveau style, developing interiors for McKim, Mead & White. He also designed many fine artifacts and light fixtures in stained glass.

Tigerman, Stanley (1930–)
American architect, who opened his office in 1964; where the early work was reminiscent of SOM and Mies Van der Rohe, his growing eclecticism produced many controversial structures.

Tile
A ceramic surfacing unit, usually thin in relation to the facial area; made from clay or a mixture of clay and other ceramic materials; has either a glazed or an unglazed face.

acoustic tile
Rectangular sound-absorbing tile, normally used as a ceiling, whether glued to a backing or used in a grid as a suspended ceiling.

ceramic mosaic tile
An unglazed tile, usually mounted on sheets to facilitate setting; may be either composed of porcelain or natural clay.

Tile

clay tile
A roofing tile of hard, burnt clay. In flooring it is called a quarry tile.

crest tile
Tile which fits like a saddle on the ridge of a roof.

encaustic tile
A tile for pavement and wall decoration, in which the pattern is inlaid or incrusted in clay of one color in a ground of clay of another color.

floor tile
A ceramic tile that can be used as a floor finish: such as encaustic tile, quarry tile, and glazed tile.

glazed tile
Ceramic tile having a fused impervious glazed surface finish, composed of ceramic materials fused into the body of the tile; the body may be nonvitreous, semivitreous, or impervious.

Tile

hollow tile
A structural clay tile unit with vertical hollow cells; used to build interior masonry partitions and as a backup block for brick veneer.

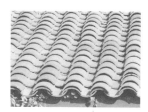

mission tile
A clay roofing tile, approximately semi-cylindrical in shape; laid in courses with the units having their convex side alternately up and down.

paving tile
Unglazed porcelain or natural clay tile, formed by the dust-pressed method; similar to ceramic mosaic tile in composition and physical properties, but thicker.

quarry tile
A dense, unglazed, ceramic tile, used most often for flooring.

ridge tile
A tile that is curved in section, often decorative, used to cover the ridge of a roof.

spanish roof tile
An interlocking terra-cotta roof tile with a convex, curved top that adjoins a narrow flat valley.

Tile

unglazed tile
A hard, dense ceramic tile for floor or walls; of homogeneous composition, and deriving its color and texture from the materials and the method of manufacture.

vinyl-asbestos tile
A resilient, semi-flexible floor tile; composed of asbestos fibers, limestone, plasticizers, pigments, and a polyvinyl-chloride resin binder; has good wearing qualities, high grease resistance, and relatively good resilience.

Tile hanging
Slate or tile shingles that are hung nearly vertically on a wall or roof for weatherproofing.

Tilt-up construction
Construction of concrete wall panels which are cast horizontally, adjacent to their final positions, and then tilted up into a vertical position when hardened.

Timber
Uncut trees that are suitable for construction or conversion to lumber.

Timber connector
One of several types of steel devices, used in conjunction with a bolt, that makes a connection between timber members that overlap each other.

Timber-framed building
A building having timbers as its structural elements, except for the foundations.

Tin See **Metal**

Tin ceiling
Embossed metal panels nailed to furring strips or ceiling beams, and painted as a finished ceiling.

Tinted glass See **Glass**

Toltec architecture
An austere geometric architecture (750–1200) that formed the basis for the Aztec style and others. It was characterized by the use of colonnades, square carved roof supports, monumental serpent columns, and narrative relief panels set in plain wall surfaces.

Tula was one of the major sites in this style, which featured colossal statues of warriors and stone panels carved with human-headed jaguars and carved symbols of Quetzalcoatl.

Tomb
In architecture, a memorial structure over or beside a grave.

Tombstone light
A small window with lights in the shape of an arched tombstone, usually in the transom above a doorway.

Tongue-and-groove joint See **Joint**

Tooled mortar joint See **Mortar joint**

Tooth ornament See **Ornament**

Top plate
Continuous horizontal piece of lumber across the top of an exterior wall that supports the foot of the rafters, or other framework above it.

Topcoat
The final coat of paint or plaster applied to a surface over a primer or undercoat.

Top hung window See **Window**

Topiarium opus
A wall painting representing trees, shrubs, and trellis work, as at Pompeii.

Topographic map
A map that indicates the shape of the surface of the ground, and other salient physical features such as buildings and roads; typically with a series of contour lines that indicate the elevation above sea level.

Topography
Physical features of a particular location, including the shape of the surface of the ground.

Torana See **Gate**

Torii See **Gate**

Torroja, Eduardo (1899–1961)
Spanish architect, and engineer of concrete shells, who studied civil engineering. Most of his designs employed folded, undulating, or warped shapes.

Torsion
The force tending to twist an architectural member.

Torus molding See **Molding**

Totem
The emblem of an individual family or clan, usually represented by an animal.

Totem pole
A wooden post carved and ornamented with the emblem of a clan or family, and erected in front of the homes of the Indians of north-western America.

Tou-kung
A cantilevered bracket in traditional Chinese construction; tiers or clusters of brackets are used to carry rafters that support purlins far beyond the outermost columns of a building.

Tourelle
A small projecting turret with a conical roof, especially one located at an outside corner of a building.

Tower
A tall structure designed for observation, communication, or defense.

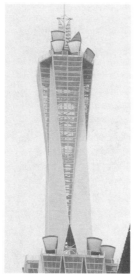

Tower crane
A crane in which the lifting mechanism is mounted on top of a tower that is structurally independent of the structure it is working on.

Town
A concentration of residential and related buildings surrounded by countryside; typically smaller than a city and larger than a village.

Town hall
A public hall or building, belonging to a town, where public offices are established, the town council meets, and the people assemble for town meetings.

Town house
An urban building, without sideyards; containing one residence on one or more floors.

Town plan
A large-scale comprehensive map of a town or city that delineates its streets, important buildings and other urban features.

Townscape
A view of a town or city from a single vantage point; the planning and construction of buildings within a town or city with the objective of achieving overall aesthetically pleasing relationships.

Township
Political and geographic area within the boundaries of a municipal government, sometimes separate from a larger county.

Trabeated
Descriptive of construction using beams or lintels, following the principle of post-and-lintel construction, as distinguished from construction using arches and vaults.

Tracery

The curvilinear ornamental branch-like shapes of stone or wood, creating an openwork pattern of mullions; so treated as to be ornamental; found within the upper part of a Gothic window or opening of similar character.

bar tracery
A pattern formed by the interlocking of branching mullions within the arch of Gothic windows.

blind tracery
Tracery that is not pierced through to openness.

branch tracery
A form of Gothic tracery in the late fifteenth and early sixteenth century made to imitate rustic work with boughs and knots.

fan tracery
Tracery on the soffit of a vault whose ribs radiate like the ribs of a fan.

geometric tracery
Gothic tracery characterized by a pattern of geometric shapes, as circles and foils.

Tracery

intersecting tracery
Tracery formed by the upward curving, forking and continuation of the mullions, springing from the alternate mullions, or from every third mullion and intersecting each other.

panel tracery
Gothic style window tracery in sections within a large opening.

perpendicular tracery
Tracery of the Perpendicular style with repeated perpendicular mullions, crossed at intervals by horizontal transoms, producing repeated vertical rectangles which often rise to the full curve of the arch.

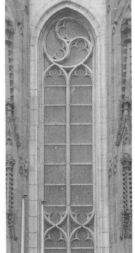

plate tracery
Tracery whose openings are pierced through thin slabs.

Tracery

reticulated tracery
Gothic tracery consisting mainly of a net-like arrangement of repeated geometrical figures.

y-tracery
Tracery where the head of the mullions split into a Y-shape pattern.

Tracery vaulting See Vault

Trajanic column
A large commemorative single free-standing column, with an internal winding stair, spiral bands of relief sculpture winding around the shaft, a large pedestal base, and a commemorative statue on top; named after the antique column of the Emperor Trajan in Rome (C. A.D. 112).

Transept
The space that crosses at a right angle to the nave of a building; may be the same size as the nave in a cruciform building, or larger.

Transfer column See Column

Transformation
The metamorphosis that occurs where primary shapes and forms are changed into additive or subtractive forms.

Transitional style
An architectural style characterized by elements of an older style blended with elements of a more modern style in the same building, such as the evolution of Romanesque into Gothic.

Translation
The movement of a point in space without any rotation.

Translucency
The quality of a material that transmits light sufficiently diffused to eliminate any perception of distinct images beyond.

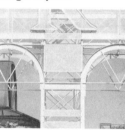

Transom bar
A horizontal bar of wood or stone across a door or window; the crossbar separating a door from the fanlight above it.

Transom light
A glazed light above the transom bar of a door.

Transparency
The quality of a material that is capable of transmitting light so that objects or images may easily be seen on the other side.

Transverse arch See **Arch**

Transverse loading
Loading that is perpendicular to a structural member, such as a vertical loading on a horizontal beam.

Transverse section See **Projection drawing**

Trap
A bend in a soil drain, arranged in such a manner that it is always full of water, which provides a water seal and prevents odors from entering back through the pipes.

Trapdoor
A door that is flush with the surface; located in a floor, roof, or ceiling, or in the stage of a theater.

Trapezoid
A four-sided figure with unequal sides: a parallel trapezoid has two unequal parallel sides, and two equal nonparallel sides; a symmetrical trapezoid has two pairs of adjacent equal sides.

Travertine See **Stone**

Tread See **Step**

Trefoil ornament See **Ornament**

Trefoil arch See **Arch**

Trellis
A structural frame supporting an open latticework or grating constructed of either metal or wood, used to support plants or vines or left exposed.

Trellis

Tresse
Flat or convex bandelets that are intertwined: especially such interlocking ornamentation used to adorn buildings.

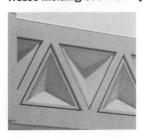

Tresse molding See **Molding**

Triangle
A plane geometrical figure with three sides and three angles; the equilateral triangle has both equal sides and equal angles.

Triangle

Triangular arch See **Arch**

Triangulated
Refers to any construction based on a continuous series of triangles for stability: particularly evident in designs for atrium skylights and space frames.

Triangulation
A method used in the design of space frames to ensure that they are static.

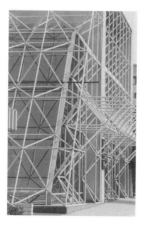

Tribunal
In an ancient Roman basilica, a raised platform for the chair of the magistrates; a place of honor.

Triforium
The space above the vaulting, below the roof, and under the clerestory windows, on the side isle of a church; typically containing three arched openings in each bay forming an arcade into the nave space.

Triglyph
A characteristic ornament of the Doric frieze, consisting of raised blocks of three vertical bands separated by V-shaped grooves, alternating with plain or sculptured panels called "metopes".

Trilith
A monument, or part of a monument, consisting of two upright stones supporting a horizontal stone, as at Stonehenge and other ancient sires.

Trim
The visible woodwork on moldings, such as baseboards, cornices, casings around doors and windows; any visible element, which covers or protects joints, edges, or ends of another material.

Trimetric projection See **Projection drawing**

Trimmer
A piece of timber in a roof, floor, or wooden partition, to support a header which in turn supports the ends of the joists, rafters, or studs; a small horizontal beam, into which the ends of one or more joists are framed.

Tripartite scheme
A type of design for a multistory commercial building often associated with the work of Louis Sullivan. The building's facade is characterized by three major divisions; a base, consisting of the lower three stories; a cap, of one-to-three stories; and a shaft, consisting of the floors between the base and the cap.

Triple-hung window See **Window**

Triton
A sea monster, half man and half fish; often used in classical and Renaissance ornamentation.

Triumphal arch
An arch commemorating the return of a victorious army, usually located along the line of march during a triumphal procession.

Trompe l'oeil
A phrase meaning "that which deceives the eye"; it was originally used to describe precisely rendered views of earlier architectural styles, wherein painters produced a convincing illusion of reality. This has been applied to exterior and interior mural design where architectural elements and entire facades have been painted on blank expanses of buildings, indicating a particular architectural style, period, or design.

Trompe l'oeil

Trophy
A sculptural composition of arms and armor as an emblem of, or a memorial to, victorious battles or triumphant military figures.

Trumeau
A stone mullion supporting the middle of a tympanum.

Truncated
Forms that have been cut off at one end, usually the apex, often with a plane parallel to the base.

Truncated roof See **Roof**

Truss

A composite structural system composed of straight members transmitting only axial tension or compression stresses along each member, joined to form a triangular arrangement.

arched truss

A truss with an arched upper chord and a straight bottom chord, with vertical hangers between the two chords.

bollman truss

A bridge truss with tension rods that radiate from the top of the two end posts to the bottom of the evenly spaced vertical chords; the roadbed is supported between the bottoms of two such trusses.

bowstring truss

A truss with one curved member in the shape of a bow and a straight or cambered member, which ties together the two ends of the bow.

fink truss

A commonly used roof truss, suitable for spans up to 50 feet, composed of two trussed rafters, each divided into four parts by purlins, using a tie across the bottom chord.

howe truss

A truss having upper and lower horizontal members, between which are vertical and diagonal members; the vertical web members take tension, and the diagonal web members are under compression.

king truss

A triangular truss with a single vertical king post that connects the apex of the triangle with the middle of the horizontal tie beam.

lattice truss

A truss consisting of upper and lower horizontal chord connected by web members which cross each other, usually stiffened by joining at the intersection of the braces.

panel truss

A structural truss having rectangular divisions with diagonal braces between opposite corners.

pratt truss

A statically determinate truss, consisting of straight top and bottom chords, regularly spaced vertical compression members, and diagonal tension members; used for medium-to-long span in buildings and for small bridges.

scissors truss

A type of truss used to support a pitched roof; the ties cross each other and are connected to the opposite rafters at an intermediate point along their length.

warren truss

A truss having parallel upper and lower chords with connecting members which are inclined, forming a series of approximately equilateral triangles

vierendeel truss

A steel open web truss composed of rectangular panels without diagonals, and with rigid joints between all the members.

Trussed

Facades with decorative forms derived from truss that support the structure either horizontally or vertically; featuring triangular patterns or diagonal bracing, expressed in exterior materials, either subtly or boldly.

Trussed arch See **Arch**

Trussed beam See **Beam**

Trylon
A tall, narrow, three-sided pyramid; the term was used to describe the symbol of the 1939 New York World's Fair, the Trylon and Perisphere.

Tschumi, Bernard (1944–)
Swiss-born American architect, one of seven identified with Deconstructivism. His best-known work is the Parc de La Villette, Paris (1990), a series of red toylike sculptural forms set into the intersection points of a large grid that covered the entire site.

Tube structure
Structural system for a tall building, which considers the columns and spandrels on the facade as forming a pierced tube, cantilevered from the ground.

Tubular scaffolding
Scaffolding that is built up from galvanized-steel or aluminum tubes, which are held together with clamps.

Tudor arch See **Arch**

Tudor Revival style
A typically asymmetrical style, with the exterior clad in brick or stucco and employing a false half-timbering treatment. Typically employed steeply pitched gables with little overhang at the eaves, bargeboards on the gables, and tall massive elaborate chimneys; narrow casement windows, usually set with a number of small, diamond-shaped panes, often within a Tudor arch.

Tudor style
The final development of English Perpendicular Gothic architecture (1485–1547), during the reign of Henry VI and Henry VIII, preceding Elizabethan architecture and characterized by the use of four-centered arches.

Tulipwood See **Wood**

Tumbling course
A sloping course of bricks that are set perpendicular to a straight-line gable in Dutch Colonial architecture, in imitation of a similar brick construction found in medieval houses in Flanders.

Turkish dome See **Dome**

Turnkey system
A complete system supplied by a single supplier.

Turret
A diminutive tower, characteristically projecting out on corbels from a corner of the structure.

Tuscan order
One of the five classical orders, which is a simplified version of the Roman Doric order, with fewer and bolder moldings, unfluted columns, a plain frieze, and without triglyphs.

Twist
A feature with a curve or turn, specifically a curved stair railing that makes a radial turn with the change of direction.

334

Twisted column See **Column**

Two-centered arch See **Arch**

Two-dimensional graphics
The process of drawing and displaying graphical objects in two dimensions, using elements such as lines and circles.

Two-hinged arch See **Arch**

Two-point perspective See **Perspective projection**

Two-tiered porch
A porch whose first and second stories are similar; each floor is supported by a separate row of columns.

Two-way switch
An electrical switch used to control a light or lights from two locations; two two-way switches are required, one in each location.

Tympanum
The triangular space between the horizontal and sloping cornices immediately above the opening of a doorway or a window, or the space between the lintel above a door and the arch above.

Tympanum

U u

Umbrella shell roof See **Roof**

Unbraced frame
A structural framework in which the resistance to lateral load is provided by the bending resistance of its structural members and their connections.

Undercoat
A coat of paint applied on new wood or over a primer or over a previous coat of paint; improves the seal and serves as a base for the top coat, for which it provides better adhesion.

Undercut
In stonework, to cut away a lower part, leaving a projection above that serves the function of a drip. To rout a groove or channel back from the edge of an overhanging member.

Underfloor heating
Heating provided below the finished floor by electric cables or hot-water pipes; they are usually cast into a concrete slab.

Underlayment
A layer of roofing felt, composition board, or other thin sheet material that covers the subfloor as a base for a finish floor.

Underpinning
The rebuilding or deepening of the foundation of an existing building to provide additional or improved support, as the result of an excavation in adjoining property that is deeper than the existing foundation.

Undressed stone See **Stone**

Undulating
Forms that have a wave-like character or depict sinuous motion with a wavy outline or appearance.

Undulating

Ungers, Oswald M. (1926–)
German architect: whose own house was comprised of simple, blocky, geometric forms. He was a proponent of Modernism, and the context in which buildings are combined with historical references. Work includes the Architecture Museum, Frankfurt (1979), and the German Embassy, Washington, D.C. (1995).

Unglazed tile See **Tile**

Uniform load
Load that is evenly distributed over an area.

Uniformity
The state of being identical, homogeneous, or regular.

Unity
A oneness and absence of diversity; a combination or arrangement of parts and the ordering of all the elements in a work so that each one contributes to a total single aesthetic effect.

Upjohn, Richard (1802–1878)
English-born American architect remembered primarily as a church architect and as a Gothic Revivalist. His most well known building is Trinity Church, New York (1841). He was the first president of the American Institute of Architects, which he helped to found.

Urbahn, Max
Designed the Vehicle Assembly Building at the JFK Space Center, Cape Canaveral, Florida (1966).

Urban design
Design of public urban environments.

Urban renewal
The improvement of a slum, or a deteriorated or under-utilized area of a city; the rehabilitation of relatively sound structures, and the conservation measures to arrest deterioration.

Urn
A vase of varying size and shape, usually having a footed base or pedestal, and used as a decorative device; originally to contain ashes from the dead.

Usable floor area
Space that can actually be occupied by a user.

Utopian architecture
A style of architecture (1960–1993) called "fantastic" or "visionary," produced without the constraints of clients, budgets, materials, or building and planning regulations. It is produced in the form of drawings or models that transcend limitations but are unlikely to be constructed, at least in the foreseeable future.

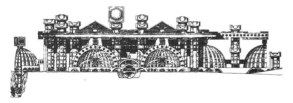

Utopian architecture

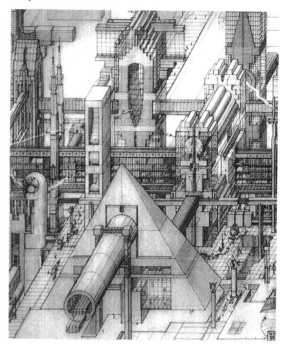

Utzon, Jorn (1918–)
Danish architect; won the competition for the Sydney Opera House in Sydney, Australia (1957–1973), a controversial building with a sail-like roofline. It is architecture as sculpture, but strongly influenced by function. Other work includes the National assembly Building, Kuwait (1972).

V v

Valley
The lower trough or gutter formed by the intersection of two inclined planes of a roof.

Valley rafter See **Rafter**

Value
The amount of light reflected by a hue. The greater the amount of light, the higher the value.

Value analysis
A technique used to examine the evolving design in order to achieve design objectives as economically as possible; it usually involves critiques of the design and subsequent analysis of alternative ideas.

Van Alen, William (1883–1954)
American architect who designed the Chrysler Building, New York City (1930), in a Moderne style, which combined massive forms, inspired by ancient architecture, with Art Deco motifs and streamlined shapes. He used steel and aluminum to celebrate the machine age. The Art Deco upper part incorporates eagle-head and radiator-cap gargoyles, as well as a series of semicircular forms recalling the design of hubcaps.

Van de Velde, Henri (1863–1957)
Dutch Art Nouveau artist and architect.

Van der Rohe, Ludwig Mies (1886–1969)
Designed the German Pavilion, Barcelona Exhibition (1929), built on one level with carefully articulated space, all in high-quality materials. The Tugendhat House, Brno Switzerland (1930), had the living space divided only by screen walls. Mies moved to the United States. in 1938, designing Crown Hall, the architecture school of the Illinois Institute of technology (1956). Many tall glazed office buildings in the world bear his influence, such as the Lake Shore Drive Apartments, Chicago (1948), and the Seagram Building, New York (1958), designed with Philip Johnson, It was considered the culmination of Mies's streamlined style; it was a rectangular slab of bronze, marble, and gray-tinted glass.

Vanbrugh, Sir John (1664–1726)
An architect with no formal training, who designed England's largest and most flamboyant Baroque country houses, with bold massing and dramatically varied skylines. Works include Blenheim Palace, Oxfordshire.

Vane
A metal banner that turns around a pivoted point, moving with the prevailing wind, to indicate the direction of the wind; the banners often have elaborate decorative scrollwork attached to the rod above and below the banner.

Vanishing point See **Perspective projection**

Vapor barrier
Airtight skin of polyethylene of aluminum: which prevents moisture from warm damp air in a building from passing into a colder space, causing condensation.

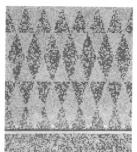

Variegated
Said of a material or surface that is irregularly marked with many different colors.

Variety
The state or quality of having varied or diverse forms, types, or characteristics.

Varnish
A resin dissolved in oil or spirit, which dries to a brilliant, thin, protective film.

Vasari, Giorgio (1511–1574)
The Uffizi Palace, his only significant work, is Mannerist in style.

Vase
A decorative vessel, usually higher than it is wide; used as an architectural ornament, usually on a pedestal, balustrade, or an acroteria on roofs.

Vault
An arched roof or ceiling or a continuous semicircular ceiling that extends in a straight line over a hall, room, or other partially enclosed space.

barrel vault
A masonry vault resting on two parallel walls having the form of a half cylinder: sometimes called a tunnel vault.

barrel-and-groin vault
A vault formed by two identical tunnel-shaped vaults that intersect in the middle.

compound vault
Any vault formed by the intersection of two or more vaults; types include cloister vault, domical vault, groin vault, and segmental vault.

Vault

conical vault
A vault having a cross section in the form of a circular arc, which is larger at one end than the other.

corbel vault
A continuous corbel arch over a space, used by the ancient Mayas of Yucatan; also known as a Mayan arch.

cross vault
A vault formed by the intersection of two barrel vaults which meet at right angles.

domical vault
A dome-shaped vault, where the ribs or groins are semicircular, causing the center of the vaulted bay to rise higher than the side arches.

double vault
A vault, usually domical, consisting of an inner shell separated from a higher outer shell.

fan vault
A concave conical vault, whose ribs, of unequal length and curvature, radiate from the springing like the ribs of a fan.

Vault

groined vault
One covering a square bay where two barrel vaults, of equal diameter and height, intersect.

hemispherical vault
Masonry dome with a semicircular cross section.

intersecting vault
Where two vaults, of either semicircular or pointed form, meet at right angles.

net vault
Vault where the ribs form a network of lozenges.

panel vault
A rib vault having a central square panel connected with diagonal ribs to the corners of the larger square it covers.

polygonal vault
A vault with more than four intersecting vault surfaces; typically octagonal in plan.

ribbed vault
A vault in which the ribs support, or seem to support, the web of the vault .

rampant vault
A vault whose two abutments are located on an inclined plane, such as a vault supporting or forming the ceiling of a stairway; the impost on one side is higher than the impost on the other side.

Vault

stellar vault
A vault where the ribs are so arranged as to form star shapes.

tracery vault
A type of solid vaulting with decorative ribs forming patterns on the surface.

Vault capital
The capital of a pier that supports a vault or a rib thereof.

Vault rib
An arch under the soffit of a vault, appearing to support it.

Vaulted
Constructed as a vault.

Vaulting course
A horizontal course made up of abutments or the springers of a vaulted roof.

Vaulting shaft
A colonette in a membered pier that appears to support a rib in a vault.

Velarium
A large tentlike arrangement drawn up over an amphitheater to protect spectators from the sun.

Veneer
The covering of one material with thin slices of another to give an effect of greater richness.

Venetian arch See Arch

Venetian blind
A window shading device, composed of a series of thin slats, which can be turned at an angle to block out the view; they can be raised and lowered very easily.

Venetian door See Door

Venetian molding See Molding

Venetian mosaic See Mosaic

Venetian window See Window

Ventilator
In a room or building, any device or contrivance used to provide fresh air or expel stale air.

Venturi, Robert (1925-)
An American Postmodernist who set up practice with John Rausch (1930–) and later with wife Denise Scott Brown (1930–), and later still with Steven Izenour (1930–). Early work included the Vanna Venturi House, Philadelphia (1963), Franklin Court, Philadelphia (1976), Gordon Wu Hall, Princeton University (1983), Seattle Art Museum (1991), and the Museum of Contemporary Art, San Diego (1996).

Veranda
Similar to a balcony but located on the ground level; it can extend around one, two or all sides of a building.

Verdigris
The green copper carbonate formed on copper roofs and statues that are exposed to the atmosphere; the patina it produces can be carefully controlled.

Verge
Edge of a sloping roof that overhangs a gable.

Vergeboard
An ornamental board hanging from a projecting roof; a bargeboard

Vermiculated
Ornamented by regular winding, wandering, and wavy lines, as if caused by the movement of worms.

Vermiculite
A generic name for treated minerals which are used for insulation and fire protection, and often as an aggregate in plaster or concrete.

Vernacular architecture
Architecture that makes use of common regional forms and materials at a particular place and time; usually modest and unpretentious, and a mixture of traditional and more modern styles, or a hybrid of several styles.

Vernacular architecture

Vertical pivoting window See **Window**

Vertical sliding window See **Window**

Vestibule
An intermediate chamber or passage located between the entrance and interior or court of a building that serves as a shelter or transitional element from exterior to interior space.

Vest-pocket park
A miniature park, usually in an urban area, that is built on a small plot of land.

Vestry
Attached building to a church, where the vestments and sacred vessels are kept; also called a sacristy.

Victorian
Any style used during the reign of Queen Victoria (1837–1901): typical styles of the period include Eastlake, Gothic Revival, Italianate, Queen Anne style, and Richardsonian Romanesque.

Victorian Gothic style
A colorful style (1860–1890), wherein materials of different colors and textures are juxtaposed, creating decorative bands and highlighting corners, arches and arcades. Materials most often used are ornamental pressed bricks, terra-cotta tile and incised carvings of foliated and geometric patterns. Openings have straight heads as well as pointed Gothic arched heads. In timber-framed buildings, the gable, porch and eave trim are massive and strong.

Victorian Romanesque style

A polychromatic exterior combined with the semicircular arch highlight this style (1870–1890). Different colored stone or brick for window trim, arches, quoins and belt courses contrasts with the stone wall surface. Decorative bricks and terra-cotta tiles are also used. Round arches are supported by short polished stone columns. Foliated forms, including grotesques and arabesques, decorate the capitals and corbels. Windows vary in size and shape.

Victory

A female diety of the ancient Romans or the corresponding deity the Greeks called Nike; representation of the deity, usually a woman in wind-blown draperies, holding a laurel wreath, palm branch, or other symbolic object.

Vierendeel truss See **Truss**

Vignette

A French design for an iron balconet, used as a protection at window openings.

Vignette

Vignola, Giacomo Barozzi de (1507–1573)

Born in Vignola, Italy, he became a leading architect in Rome following Michelangelo's death. He wrote the *Rules for the Five Orders of Architecture* in 1562.

Vihara

A Buddhist or Jain monastery in Indian architecture.

Village

A small group of houses and related facilities surrounded by countryside; typically smaller than a township.

Vinoly, Rafael

Argentine-born American architect; whose early project was the John Jay College of Criminal Justice in New York (1988). He was winner of the competition for the Tokyo International Forum, Tokyo, Japan (1996).

Vinyl See **Plastic**

Vinyl-asbestos tile See **Tile**

Viollet-Le-Duc, E. Emmanuel (1814–1879)
Architect and medievalist; appointed to head the Ecole des Beaux-Arts in 1863; wrote a _Dictionary of Architecture_ in 1854.

Virtual
Pertaining to conceptual rather than physical

Virtual office
A workplace that is determined by where the employee happens to be engaged in carrying out work at any particular time; usually remote from the main workplace.

Virtual Reality
The simulation of the real world in virtual space by computer programs, allowing for the virtual interaction of users, such as walking through a computer-generated environment.

Visionary architecture
A term which originally described the work of certain Neoclassical architects, notably Boullee and Ledoux; later applied to any imaginary scheme featuring fantastic or futuristic structures.

Vision-proof glass See **glass**

Visor roof See **Roof**

Visualization
The process of displaying realistic visual images of an object for evaluation.

Vitruvian scroll
A series of scrolls connected by a stylized wavelike continuous band; also called a wave scroll.

Vitruvius, Marcus Pollio (46–30 B.C.)
A Roman architect, engineer, and architectural theorist. His treatise, _De Architectura,_ the only one from antiquity To survive, was published in Italy and became a basic Renaissance sourcebook.

Volute
A spiral, scroll-like ornament having a twisted or rolled shape, found most often on the capital of the Ionic column.

Vomitory
An entrance or opening, usually one of a series, piercing a bank of seats in a theater or stadium, permitting entry or egress by large numbers of people.

Voussoir
A wedge-shaped block whose converging sides radiate from a center forming an element of an arch or vaulted ceiling.

Voussoir

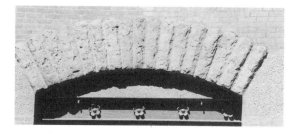

stepped voussoir
A voussoir that is squared along its upper surfaces so that it fits horizontal courses of masonry units.

Vries, Hans Vredeman de (1526–1606)
Flemish architect and painter whose engravings, derived from Serlio, and architectural pattern books were very influential on northern Europe.

W w

Waffle slab
A two-way ribbed slab.

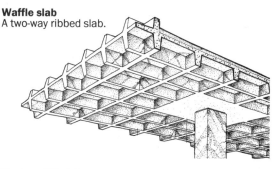

Wagner, Otto (1841–1918)
Austrian architect whose architecture predated the Art Deco style. He designed the Majolika Haus, Vienna (1898), an original Art Noveau building in which a floral design covers the facade. He designed the Sezession Exhibition Building, Vienna (1899); and also the Postal Savings Bank, Vienna (1904), which had a high vaulted central hall with tapering metal supports.

Otto Wagner

Wainscot
A protective or decorative facing applied to the lower portion of an interior partition or wall, such as wood paneling or other facing material.

Walker, Ralph (1889–1973)
An American architect who was best known for his Art Deco skyscrapers, including the Barclay-Vesey Telephone Building (1923) and the Irving Trust Building (1929), both in New York City.

Walker, Thomas (1804–1887)
American architect of German descent, pupil of William Strickland and John Haviland, and the second president of the American Institute of Architects. Work includes the Capitol, Washington, D.C.

Walk-up apartment
Apartment without an elevator: usually five stories or less.

Walkway
A passage or lane designated for pedestrian traffic.

Wall
A structure that encloses or subdivides a space with a continuous surface: except where fenestration or other openings occur.

balloon frame wall
A system of framing a wooden building wherein the exterior bearing walls and partitions consists of single studs that extend the full height of the frame from the top of the soleplate to the roof plate.

bearing wall
Supports any vertical load in addition to its own weight.

cant wall
A wall canted in elevation from true vertical.

cantilever retaining wall
A wall retaining soil that acts as a cantilevered beam as opposed to one acting as a continuous beam spanning between supports.

cavity wall
An exterior wall, usually of masonry, consisting of an outer course and an inner course separated by a continuous air space connected by metal ties.

curtain wall
A method of construction in which all building loads are transmitted to a metal skeleton frame, so that the non-load-bearing exterior walls of metal and glass are simply a protective cladding.

346

Wall

exterior wall
A wall that is part of the envelope of a building thereby having one face exposed to the weather or to earth.

fire wall
Any fire-resistant wall that separates one building from another or subdivides a large building into smaller spaces; usually continuous from the foundations extending above the roof.

foundation wall
A wall below, or partly below grade, to provide support for the exterior walls or other parts of the structure.

gable wall
Wall which continues to the roofline on the gable end of a structure.

gravity retaining wall
Retaining wall that relies on the weight of the masonry or concrete for its stability.

half-timbered wall
Descriptive of buildings of the sixteenth and seventeenth centuries, which were built with strong timber foundations, supports, knees, and studs, and whose walls were filled in with plaster or masonry materials such as brick.

interior wall
Any wall within a building; entirely surrounded by exterior walls.

load-bearing wall
A wall capable of supporting an imposed load in addition to its own weight.

Wall

masonry wall
A load-bearing or non-load-bearing wall consisting of hollow masonry units.

non-load-bearing wall
A wall subject only to its own weigh and wind pressure.

partition
An interior wall dividing a room or part of a building into separate areas: may be either non-load-bearing or load-bearing.

party wall
A wall used jointly by two parties under an easement agreement, erected upon a line dividing two parcels of land, each one a separate real estate entity; a common wall.

retaining wall
A wall, either freestanding or laterally braced, that bears against earth or other fill surface and resists lateral and other forces from the material in contact with the side of the wall.

screen wall
A movable or fixed device, especially a framed construction designed to divide, conceal, or protect, but not to support.

serpentine wall
A wall with a plan in the shape of a wavy line with alternating arcs of circles.

shear wall
A wall that resists shear forces in its own plane due to wind or earthquake forces.

spandrel wall
A wall built on the extrados of an arch, filling the spandrels.

Wall column See **Column**

Wall cornice
Cornice at the top of a masonry wall.

Wall dormer See **Dormer**

Wall gable See **Gable**

Wall plate
A horizontal piece of timber, laid flat along the top of the wall at the level of the eaves, which carries the rafters.

Wall shaft
Engaged column or colonnette that is supported by a corbel or bracket, and appears to support a vault rib or clustered ribs above it.

Wall tile
Thin tile used as a wall finish, it is glued to the wall with mastic, then the joints are grouted. Types include glazed ceramic, terra-cotta, glass, mosaic, or plastic; may be square, rectangular, or other geometric shape.

Warehouse
A building designed for the storage of various goods.

Warm color
Red, orange, and yellow; optically they tend to advance.

Warnecke, John Carl (1919–)
Successor to his father's firm of the same name; he designed the Hennepin County Government Center, Minneapolis (1976), consisting of twin 24-story towers with an enclosed atrium.

Warp
Distortion in the shape of a plane timber surface, due to moisture movement; may be caused by improper seasoning.

Warren truss See **Truss**

Warren, Whitney (1864–1943)
American architect trained in Paris at the Beaux Arts. He designed the New York Yacht Club (1898) and Grand Central Terminal, New York, with Charles A. Reed (1857–1911) and Allen Stem (1856–1931).

Watch tower
An elevated structure of any type used as a lookout; may be a separate structure or rise above the other portions of a building or wall.

Waterproofing
A coating or membrane applied to a surface, such as a foundation wall, to prevent the intrusion of water under pressure; materials may include asphalt, felt, tar, or various synthetic membranes.

Water table
A horizontal offset in a wall sloped on the top to throw off water running down the wall.

Watertight
An enclosure or barrier that does not permit the passage of moisture.

Wattle-and-daub
A primitive construction consisting of a coarse basketwork of twigs woven between upright poles, and plastered over with mud.

Wavy
Refers to forms that are arranged into curls or un-dulations, or any graphic representation of curved shapes, outlines or patterns that resemble such a wave.

Weather vane
A metal form, fixed on a rotating spindle that turns to indicate the direction of the wind, usually located on top of a spire, pinnacle or other elevated position on a building.

Weatherboarding
Wood siding commonly used as an exterior covering on a frame building consisting of boards with a rabbeted upper edge that fits under an overlapping board above.

Weathered
Descriptive of a material or surface that has been exposed to the elements for a long period of time; having an upper surface that is splayed so as to allow water to drain off.

Weathered

Weathering
An inclination given to the surface of horizontal joints in masonry construction to prevent water from collecting in them.

Weatherproof
A general term indicating the ability to withstand natural elements.

Weep hole
A small opening in a wall or window member, through which accumulated condensation or water may drain to the building exterior, such as from the base of a cavity wall flashing, or a skylight.

Weese, Harry (1919–)
Principal of the Chicago-based firm which designed office buildings for Chicago. They also designed the metro subway stations for Washington, D.C.

Welded beam See Beam

Western Stick style
This adaptation of the Stick style (1890-1920) was characterized by a gently pitched gable roof that extended well beyond the wall and by projecting balconies. A unique feature is the exposed stick-like rafters that project along the roof eaves.

Wheel Window See **Window**

White oak See **Wood**

White pine See **Wood**

White, Stanford (1853–1906)
Partner in the firm of McKim, Mead & White. The buildings produced by the firm were the most appreciated of their time. He designed the Washington Square Arch in New York City, and houses for Louis Comfort Tiffany, Charles Dana Gibson, and Joseph Pulitzer.

Wide-flange section
A structural section whose cross section resembles the letter H rather than the letter I; used for columns due to its capacity to avoid rotation or buckling.

Widows' walk
A rooftop platform or narrow walkway, used originally as a lookout for incoming ships in colonial coastal houses.

Wigwam
Eastern native American dwelling, round or oval in plan, with a rounded roof consisting of a bent pole framework covered by pressed bark or skins.

Wind brace
Any brace, such as a strut, which strengthens a structure or framework against the wind; a diagonal brace that ties rafters of a roof together to prevent racking.

Wind load
The positive or negative force of the wind acting on a structure; wind applies a positive pressure on the windward side of buildings and a negative suction to the leeward side.

Winding stair See **Stair**

Windmill
A tower structure with wind-powered vanes connected by a rotating shaft to a pump or generator; common on ranches and farms for pumping water and generating electricity.

Window
An opening in an exterior wall of a building to admit light and air, usually glazed; an entire assembly consisting of a window frame, its glazing, and any operating hardware.

angled bay window
A bay window that protrudes out over a wall and is triangular in plan.

awning window
A window consisting of a number of top-hinged horizontal sashes one above the other, the bottom edges of which swing outward; operated by one control device.

bay window
A window forming a recess in a room and projecting outwards from the wall either in a rectangular, polygonal or semicircular form. Some are supported on corbels or on projecting moldings.

bent window
A window that is curved in plan, typically with a bent sash; the jambs are typically parallel or radial.

Window

blank window
A recess in an exterior wall, having the external appearance of a window; a window which has been sealed off but is still visible.

bow window
A rounded bay window projecting from the face of a wall; in plan it is a segment of a circle.

box-head window
A window constructed so that the sashes can slide vertically up into the head to provide maximum opening for ventilation.

bungalow window
A double-hung window with a single light in the bottom sash and rectangular divided lights in the upper sash.

cabinet window
A type of projecting window or bay window for the display of goods in shops.

Window

camber window
A window arched at the top.

cant window
A bay window erected on a plan of canted outlines; the sides are not at right angles to the wall.

casement window
A window ventilating sash, fixed at the sides of the opening into which it is fitted, which swings open on hinges along its entire length.

Chicago window
A horizontal window consisting of a large square fixed central pane with narrow vertical sliding sashes on either side, typically the full width of the bay, as in the Carson Pirie & Scott store by Louis Sullivan.

circular window
A window in the shape of a full circle, often with decorative elements, and arranged in a radial manner.

circular window

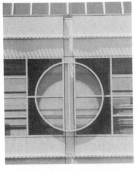

compass window
A rounded bay window that projects from the face of a wall: also a window having a rounded semicircular member at its head.

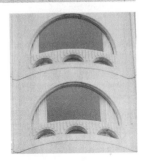

coupled window
Two closely spaced windows which form a pair.

crippled window
A dormer window.

dormer window
A vertical window that projects from a sloping roof, placed in a small gable.

double window
Two windows, side by side, which form a single architectural unit.

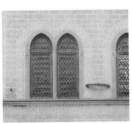

Window

double-hung window
A window having two vertically sliding sashes, each closing a different part of the window; the weight of each sash is counterbalanced for ease of opening and closing.

double lancet window
A window having mullions shaped to form two lancet windows that are side by side; found in Carpenter Gothic, Collegiate Gothic, and Tudor revival styles.

eyebrow window
A bottom-hinged, inward-opening sash in the window of an eyebrow dormer.

false window
The representation of a window that is inserted in a facade to complete a series of windows or to give the appearance of symmetry.

folding casement
One of a pair of casements, with rabbeted meeting stiles, which is hung in a single frame without a mullion and hinged together so that it can open and fold in a confined space.

French window
A type of casement window, similar to a door, where the sash swings from the jamb of the opening.

frieze-band window
One of a series of small windows that form a horizontal band directly below the cornice; usually continuing across the main facade.

gable window
A window in a gable; a window shaped like a gable.

high-light window
A window or row of windows set high up in the wall; also called a clerestory window.

Window

hopper window
A window sash which opens inward and is hinged at the bottom; when open, air passes over the top of the sash.

jalousie window
A window consisting of a series of overlapping horizontal glass louvers, which pivot simultaneously in a common frame and are actuated by one or more operating devices.

lancet window
A narrow window with a sharp pointed arch that is typical of English Gothic architecture; one light shaped in the form of a lancet window.

landscape window
A double-hung window whose upper sash is highly decorated with small panes of colored glass; the lower sash contains a larger pane of clear glass.

lattice window
A window casement, fixed or hinged, with glazing bars set diagonally.

loop window
A long narrow, vertical opening, usually widening inward, cut in a medieval wall, parapet, or fortification, for use by archers.

lozenge window
A window composed of lozenge-shaped panes set on the diagonal.

lucarne window
A small dormer window in a roof or spire.

operable window
A window which may be opened for ventilation, as opposed to a fixed light.

oriel window
A bay window corbeled out from a wall of an upper story; a projecting bay that forms the extension of a room, used extensively in medieval English residential architecture.

oval window
A window in the shape of an ellipse, or in a shape between an ellipse and a circle.

ox-eye window
A round or oval aperture, open, louvered, or glazed; an occulus or oeil-de-boeuf.

ox-eye window

peak-head window
A window with a triangular head, most often found in Gothic Revival church architecture; also called a lancet window.

picture window
A large fixed pane of glass, often between two narrower operable windows, usually located to present the most attractive view to the exterior.

pivoting window
A window having a sash which rotates about fixed vertical or horizontal pivots, located at or toward the center, in contrast to one hung on hinges along an edge.

ribbon window
One of a horizontal series of windows, separated only by mullions, which forms a horizontal band across the facade of a building.

rose window
A large, circular medieval window, containing tracery disposed in a radial manner.

roundel
A small circular panel or window; an oculus, a bull's eye or circular light like the bottom of a bottle.

Window

sash window
A window formed with glazed frames that slide up and down in vertical grooves by means of counterbalanced weights.

shed dormer window
A dormer window whose eave line is parallel to the eave line of the main roof instead of gabled to provide more attic space.

single-hung window
A window with two sashes, only one of which opens.

sliding sash window
A window which moves horizontally in grooves or between runners at the top and bottom of the window frame.

splayed window
A window whose frame is set at an angle with respect to the face of the wall.

square-headed window
Window that has a straight horizontal lintel above it.

stained-glass window
A window whose glass is colored.

stepped windows
A series of windows, usually in a wall adjacent to a staircase, arranged in a stepped pattern that generally follows the step's profile.

Window

storm window
An auxiliary window: usually placed with the existing window in the same frame, to provide additional protection against severe weather.

top-hung window
A casement window hinged horizontally.

triple-hung windows
A window with three vertical sliding sashes that allow the window to open to two-thirds of its height.

Venetian window
A large window, characteristic of Neo-classical styles, divided by columns or piers resembling pilasters into three lights, the middle one of which is usually wider that the others, and sometimes arched at the head,

vertical pivoted window
A window having a sash which pivots about a vertical axis at or near its center; when opened, the outside glass surface is conveniently accessible for cleaning.

vertical sliding window
A window having one or more sashes that move only in the vertical direction; they are held in various open positions by means of friction or a rachet device instead of being supported by a counterweight.

wheel window
A large circular window in which the tracery radiates from the center; a variety of the rose window.

Window casing
The finished frame surrounding a window; the visible frame; usually consists of wood, metal, or stone.

Window crown
The upper termination of a window; such as a hood or pediment; also called a window cap.

Window frame
The fixed, non-operable frame of a window, consisting of two jambs, a head and a sill, designed to receive and hold the sash or casement and all necessary hardware.

Window head
The upper horizontal cross member or decorative element of a window frame.

Window light
A pane of glass which has been installed in a window frame.

Window mullion
A vertical member between the lights of a window.

Window muntin
A rabbeted member for holding the edges of windowpanes within a sash.

Window pane
One of the divisions of a window or door, consisting of a single unit of glass set in a frame.

Window seat
A seat built into the inside bottom of a window.

Windowsill
The horizontal member at the base of a window opening.

Windward
On the side exposed to the wind; the opposite of leeward.

Wines, James (1932–)
American architect who founded SITE (Sculptures In The Environment) in 1969. Their work includes Best Products Showrooms (1972–1984), and Avenue Five, Seville Expo (1992), and Tennessee Aquatorium, Chattanooga (1993).

Wing
Projection on the side of a building that is smaller than the main mass; often one of a symmetrical pair.

Winged bull
A winged human-headed bull of colossal size, usually in pairs, guarding the portals of ancient Assyrian palaces as a symbol of force and domination.

Wire-cut brick See **Brick**

Wire glass See **Glass**

Wireframe model
In computer graphics, a three-dimensional display consisting of lines or polygons without any surface rendering.

Witches' cap
Conical roof of a tower.

Wivern See **Ornament: animal forms**

Wood
The hard, fibrous substance that composes the trunk and branches of a tree, lying between the pitch and the bark. ·

artificial wood
Any of the various mixtures that are molded to simulate wood; often using sawdust, paper, or other wood fiber as a major ingredient mixed with glue.

bald cypress
A deciduous softwood tree resistant to decay and often used in contact with the soil and for exposed elements such as shingles; also used for flooring and trim.

balsam fir
A softwood tree with coarse grained wood, used for interior trim.

balsam poplar
A large hardwood tree, with soft straight-grained wood used for painted millwork.

beveled siding
Tapered boards used as siding, installed with the thinner part at the top.

birch
A moderately strong, high-density wood, yellowish to brown in color; its uniform texture is well suited for veneer, flooring, and turned wood products.

burl
A decorative pattern in wood caused by adjacent knots.

Wood

cedar
A highly aromatic, moderately high-density, fine-textured wood of a distinctive red color with white streaks; widely used for fence posts, shingles, and mothproof closet linings.

cherry
An even-textured, moderately high-density wood, rich red- brown in color; takes a high luster, and is used for cabinet- work and paneling.

chestnut
A light, coarse-grained, medium-hard wood, used for ornamental work and trim.

clapboard
One of a series of boards used for siding, with a tapered cross section, most commonly called beveled siding.

conifer
A tree belonging to the botanical group which bears cones; it includes all the softwoods used in building, particularly the pines and firs.

cypress
A moderately strong, hard, and heavy softwood; its heart-wood is naturally decay-resistant, and is used for exterior and interior construction where durability is required.

dimension timber
Rough-sawn wood with a rectangular or square cross section that exceeds the standard nominal dimensions of 4 by 5 inches.

douglas fir
A strong, medium-density, medium-textured softwood; widely used for plywood and as lumber and timber in construction.

ebony
Wood of a number of tropical species, usually distin-guished by its dark color, durability, and hardness; used for carving ornamental cabinetwork.

elm
A tough, strong, moderately high-density hardwood of brown color; often has a twisted interlocked grain; used for decorative veneer, piles and planks.

fir
A softwood of the temperate climates including douglas fir, white fir, silver fir, balsam fir; used for framing and interior trim.

folded plate
A thin skin of plywood reinforced by purlins to form structures of great strength.

glue-laminated arch
An arch made from layers of wood that are joined with adhesives. The glued joints transmit the shear stresses, so the structure acts as one piece capable of use as structural arches and long-span beams.

gum
A moderately high-density hardwood, whitish to gray-green in color and of uniform texture; used for low-grade veneer, plywood, and rough cabinet work.

Wood

hardboard
A dense smooth-surfaced composition board composed of highly compressed fibers; one such type is called Masonite.

hardwood
Timber from all trees except the conifers, which are called softwood.

heartwood
The center portion of a tree trunk that is no longer growing or carrying the sap; often harder, denser, and of a different color.

hemlock
Wood of a coniferous tree; moisture-resistant, soft, coarse; uneven-textured, splinters easily, inferior for construction use.

hickory
A tough, hard, strong wood; has high shock resistance and high bending strength.

laminated timber
Timber beam or arch manufactured from four or more layers of wood, usually about one inch thick, bonded together with waterproof adhesive.

larch
A fine-textured, strong, hard, straight-grained wood of a coniferous tree; heavier than most softwoods.

lath
One of many narrow strips of wood that serve as a base for plaster, usually nailed at regular intervals to studs in walls or rafters in ceilings.

locust
Wood of the locust tree; coarse-grained, strong, hard, decay-resistant, and durable.

mahogany
A straight-grained wood of intermediate density, pinkish to red-brown in color; used primarily for interior cabinetwork and decorative paneling.

maple
A hard, tough, moderately high-density wood: light to dark brown in color, with a uniform texture; used for flooring and wood trim.

Masonite
Trade name of a brand of tempered pressed board.

oak
A tough, hard, high-density wood; coarse-textured, ranging in color from light tan to pink or brown; used for both decorative and structural and applications, such as framing timbers, flooring, and plywood.

particleboard
A large class of building boards made from wood particles compressed in a binder; often faced with a veneer.

pine
A wood of a number of species of coniferous evergreens; may be divided into two classes, soft pine and hard pitch pine; an important source of construction lumber and plywood.

Wood

plastic wood
A paste of wood flour, synthetic resin, and a volatile solvent; used for filling holes and cracks in wood, it dries soon after application.

plywood
An engineered panel composed of an odd number of thin sheets permanently bonded together, sometimes faced with a veneer.

redwood
A durable, straight-grained, high-strength, low-density softwood; especially resistant to decay and insect attack; light red to deep reddish-brown; used primarily for construction, plywood, and millwork.

satinwood
A hard, fine-grained, pale to golden yellow wood of the acacia gum tree; used in cabinetwork and decorative paneling.

shake
Any thick hand-split, edge-grained shingle or clapboard; formed by splitting a short log Into tapered sections.

shingle
A roofing unit of wood, asphalt, slate, tile, concrete, asbestos cement, or other material, that is cut to stock dimensions and thicknesses and used as an overlapping covering over sloping roofs and side walls.

shiplap siding
Wood sheathing whose edges are rabbeted to make an overlapping joint.

siding
A finish covering on the exterior walls of a wood-framed building; may be wood, aluminum, or asbestos-cement material.

softwood
Wood from trees with needles which produce cones, typically evergreen; includes cedar, cypress, douglas fir, hemlock, pine, spruce, and tamarack.

spruce
A white to light brown or red-brown, straight and even-grained wood; moderately low density and strength; relatively inexpensive; used for general utility lumber.

stressed-skin panel
A panel constructed of plywood and seasoned lumber; the simple framing and plywood skin act as a total unit to resist loads.

structural lumber
Lumber that is used for framing that has dimensions larger than a 2 by 4.

teak
A dark golden yellow or brown wood with a greenish or black cast, moderately hard, coarse-grained, very durable; immune to the attack of insects; used for construction, plywood and decorative paneling.

tulipwood
A soft, close-textured durable wood that is yellowish in color; used for millwork and veneer.

Wood

veneer
A thin sheet of wood that has been sliced, rotary-cut, or sawn from a log; used as one of several plies in plywood for added strength or as facing material on less attractive wood.

white oak
A hard, heavy, durable wood, gray to reddish-brown in color; used for flooring, paneling, and trim.

white pine
A soft, light wood which works easily; does not split when nailed; does not swell or warp appreciably; is widely used in building construction.

yellow pine
A hard resinous wood of the longleaf pine tree, having dark bands of summerwood alternating with lighter-colored springwood; used as flooring and in general construction.

Wood joint
A joint formed by two boards, timbers, or sheets of wood that are held together by nails, fasteners, pegs, or glue.

Wood shingle See **Wood**

Wood siding See **Wood**

Wood veneer See **Wood**

Wood, John (1704–1754)
Planned Bath, England, in the form of a Palladian-style Roman city, using crescent-shaped terraces.

Wood, John (the younger) (1767–1775)
Planned the Royal Crescent, Bath, England, on a circular plan.

Wood-frame construction
Construction in which the exterior walls, bearing walls and partitions, floor and roof constructions, and their supports are of wood or other combustible material; that is, when it does not qualify as heavy-timber construction.

Woodwork
Work produced by the carpenter's and joiner's art, applied to parts or objects in wood rather than to the complete structure.

Working drawings
Drawings, intended for use by a contractor, subcontractor, or fabricator, which forms part of the contract documents for a building; contains the necessary information to manufacture or erect an object or structure.

Workmanship
The quality of work executed by a craftsman or a contractor.

Wreath ornament See **Ornament**

Wreathed column See **Column**

Wren, Sir Christopher (1632–1723)
One of England's greatest scientists and architects, he was active in rebuilding London after the fire of 1666. He rebuilt St. Paul's Cathedral, London (1673).

Wright, Frank Lloyd (1867–1959)
Originator of the Organic style, as demonstrated in many innovative works. Unity Temple, Oak Park, Illinois (1906), was a concrete church with a complex interior space on several levels. The Millard house, Pasadena, California (1923), was built of decorative precast concrete blocks.

Fallingwater, Bear Run, Pennsylvania (1937), was cantilevered out over a waterfall in horizontal sections. It was not unlike the European International Style in elevation but was three-dimensional in actuality.

The Johnson Wax Building, Racine, Wisconsin (1937), features the innovative use of materials, such as glass tubes for skylights.

He built a second home, office, and school in the desert at Taliesin West, Scottsdale, Arizona (1938).

The Guggenheim Museum, New York City (1943–1960), is one of his best-known works, with the exterior expressing the interior arrangement.

Frank Lloyd Wright

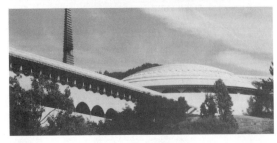

Wright, Lloyd (1890–1978)

American architect, and elder son of Frank Lloyd Wright. Trained in his father's studio, he helped prepare drawings for the *Wasmuth Portfolio* (1918). He worked on several houses including the Barnsdall Residence in Los Angeles. Later work included the Swedenborg Memorial Wayfarer's Chapel, Palos Verdes, California (1946).

Wrought-iron work

Iron that is hammered or forged into shape, either when hot or cold, usually decorative.

Wurster, William (1895–1973)

As principal of Wurster, Bernardi and Emmons he produced many works in what was called the Bay Region style. He designed many university buildings in California, and Ghiradelli Square in San Francisco (1962).

X x

X-brace See **Brace**

Y y

Yamasaki, Minoru (1912–1986)
An American architect of Japanese descent; he and his partner George Hellmuth made their mark with the TWA Terminal at Lambert Airport, St. Louis. The Pruitt-Igoe public housing project, also in St. Louis (1954), won several awards, but was detested by its inhabitants and later demolished. He used aluminum grille screens and other intricate detailing in high-rise structures, such as the Michigan Gas Company Building in Detroit (1963).

Minoru Yamasaki

The twin towers for the World Trade Center in New York City (1972) were his landmark structures. They were to him a "monument to world peace." Both structures were completely destroyed in a terrorist attack (2001).

Yard
An area of uncultivated ground adjacent to a dwelling, in urban sites, they are often paved with brick, stone, or tile.

Y-tracery See **Tracery**

Yurt
A circular tent-like dwelling, usually movable, used by nations of northern and central Asia; constructed of skins stretched over a wooden framework.

Z z

Zapotec architecture
This eclectic architecture (700–900) is found in Oaxaca, Mexico. The Zapotecs assimilated influences from the Olmecs (700–300 B.C.) and especially from Teotihuacan (30–900 A.D.). It culminated in a recognizable regional style, characterized by pyramids having several stepped terraces, accented with balustrades whose tops were decorated. One of the most notable sites is Monte Alban, a carefully planned ceremonial complex.

Zeidler, Eberhard (1926–)
German-born architect; trained at the Bauhaus and later settled in Canada. Best known for the enormous Eaton Center, Toronto (1969), Ontario Place, Toronto (1968), and Queens Quay Terminal Warehouse, Toronto (1981), and the Vancouver Convention Center (1997).

Zevi, Bruno (1918–1999)
Italian architectural theorist; he studied at Harvard University before returning to Italy. He published many books, including *Towards an Organic Architecture* (1945) and the *Modern Language of Architecture* (1973). He was opposed to International Modernism, Postmodernism, classicism and Neo-classicism, advocating an organic approach instead.

Ziggurat
A Mesopotamian temple having the form of a terraced pyramid rising in three-to-seven successively receding stages in height; built of mud brick, featuring an outside staircase and a shrine at the top.

Zigzag
A line formed by angles that alternately project and retreat; occurring in bands, on columns, and in larger patterns on cornices.

Zodiac
The imaginary band of the celestial sphere on either side of the yearly path of the sun moon and stars, divided since Babylonian times into twelve segments, named after the twelve constellations, and each with its own symbol.

Zone
A number of floors which are adjacent, that are served by the same elevators; also applies to spaces that have different requirements for heating or cooling.

Zoning
Political jurisdictions divided into geographic zones with different mixtures of allowable use, size, siting, and form of real property; typically applied in conjunction with a zoning code or review of permit applications for developments and variances.

Zoomorph
Boulders carved by the Maya with animals and other forms, as distinct from megaliths cut and carved into the form of a stela.

Zoomorphism
Representation of gods in the form of animals; also, use of animal forms in art or symbolism.

Zoophoric column
A column bearing a figure or figures of one or more men or animals.

Zoophoric column

Zoophorus
A horizontal band bearing carved figures, animals or persons, especlaily a sculptured Ionic frieze.

Zwinger
The protective fortress of a city: the modern name of several German palaces, or parts of palaces.

INDEX

Aalto, Alvar 1
Abacus 1
Abadie, Paul 1
Abat-jour 1
Abat-vent 1
Abbey 1
Abramovitz, Max 1
Absolute architecture 1
Abstraction 1
Abutment 2
Abutment arch 15
Academy 2
Acanthus 2
Accent lighting 2
Accessibility 2
Accolade 2
Accordion door 109
Accouplement 3
Achromatic 3
Acorn ornament 227
Acoustic tile 324
Acoustical door 109
Acoustical plaster 3
Acropodium 3
Acropolis 3
Acroteria 3
Acrylic 4
Acrylic fiber 251
Active solar energy 4
Acute angle 4
Acute arch 15
Adams style 4
Adams, Robert 4
Adaptive use 4
Addition 4
Addorsed 4
Adjacency 4
Adler, Dankmar 4
Adobe 4
Adobe brick 52
Aedlcule 4
Aegricranes 227
Aeolic capital 62
Aerial photo-mosaic 5
Affleck, Raymond 5
Affronted 5
A-frame 5
Aggregate 5
Agora 5
Agraffe 5
Air conditioning 5

Air lock 5
Air-inflated structure 5
Aisle 5
Alabaster 310
Alberti, Leon Battista 6
Alcove 6
Alhambra 6
Alignment 6
Allegory 6
Alley 6
Alteration 6
Alterpiece 6
Alto-relievo 268
Aluminum 207
Aluminum door 109
Aluminum foil 6
Amalaka 6
Ambient lighting 6
Ambulatory corridor 6
Amenities 6
American order 7
American School style 7
Amorini 7
Amorphous 7
Amortizement 8
Amphi-prostyle 8
Amphitheater 8
Anal glyph 268
Anamorphic image 8
Anchor 8
Anchor bolt 8
Anchor plate 8
Anchorage 8
Ancone 9
Ando, Todao 9
Andrews, John 9
Angle brace 50
Angle buttress 57
Angle capital 62
Angle cleat 9
Angle column 80
Angle iron 9
Angle joint 184
Angle niche 221
Angle of incidence 9
Angle of reflection 9
Angle post 256
Angle volute 9
Angled bay window 350
Anglo Saxon architecture 10
Angular 10

Annulet 10
Anshen, Robert 10
Anta 10
Antechamber 11
Antefix 11
Antepagment 11
Anthemion 11
Anthemion band 11
Antic 11
Apadana 11
Apartment 11
Apartment hotel 11
Apartment house 12
Apex 12
Apex stone 12
Apophyge 12
Applied trim 12
Applique 12
Apprentice 13
Apron 13
Apse 13
Apteral 13
Aqueduct 13
Arabesque 13
Arabesque style 13
Arbor 13
Arboretum 13
Arcade 14
Arcaded arch 15
Arcading 14
Arcature 15
Arch 15
Arch order 23
Archaic 23
Arched 23
Arched dormer 112
Arched impost 24
Arched truss 333
Archigram 24
Architect 24
Architectonic 24
Architectural 24
Architectural conservation 24
Architectural design 24
Architectural element 24
Architectural engineering 24
Architectural historian 24
Architectural history 24
Architectural Review Board 24
Architectural significance 24
Architectural style 24

Bead-and-reel molding 212
Beaded joint 216
Beak molding 212
Beam 40
Beam ceiling 40
Bearing pile 40
Bearing plate 40
Bearing wall 346
Beaux-Arts Classicism 40
Beaux-Arts style 41
Becket, Welton 41
Bed molding 212
Bed mortar joint 216
Bedroom 41
Beeby, Thomas H. 41
Beehive tomb 41
Behrens, Peter 41
Belfry 42
Belgian block 310
Bell 42
Bell arch 15
Bell cage 42
Bell chamber 42
Bell gable 141
Bell roof 277
Bell tower 42
Bell turret 42
Bell-cast roof 277
Bell-shaped dome 104
Belluschi, Pietro 42
Beltcourse 42
Belvedere 43
Bench 43
Benchmark 43
Bent 43
Bent sash 43
Bent window 350
Berlage, Hendrik Petrus 43
Berm 43
Bernini, Gianlorenzo 43
Bestiary 228
Bethlehem column80
Beton-brut 44
Bevel 44
Beveled joint 184
Beveled molding 212
Beveled siding 357
Bezant 44
Bibiena, Guiseppe 44
Bidding 44
Bi-fold door109
Bifron capital 62

Bi-lateral symmetry 317
Billet molding 212
Biotecture 44
Birch 357
Birds 228
Birkirts, Gunnar 44
Black-figure technique 44
Blank door 109
Blank window 351
Blemish 44
Blending 44
Blind 45
Blind arcade 14
Blind arch 15
Blind door 109
Blind hinge 45
Blind joint 184
Blind pocket 45
Blind stop 45
Blind story 45
Blind tracery 327
Block 45
Block modillion 211
Blocking 45
Blue print 45
Bluestone 310
Blunt arch 16
Board 45
Board-and-batten 45
Boardwalk 45
Boathouse 45
Bodhika 45
Bofill, Ricardo 45
Boiserie 45
Bolection molding 212
Bollard 45
Bollman truss 333
Bolster 46
Bolster beam 40
Bolt 46
Bolted connection 46
Bond 46
Bond course 48
Bond timber 48
Bonnet 48
Book matched 48
Boom 48
Border 48
Borromini, Francesco 48
Boss 48
Bossage 48
Botanical garden 49

Botta, Mario 49
Bottom chord 49
Boullee,' Etienne-Louis 49
Bouquet 231
Bovine 228
Bow girder 49
Bow knot 231
Bow window 351
Bower 49
Bowstring truss 333
Box beam 40
Box column 80
Box frame 49
Box girder 49
Box stair 304
Boxed cornice 91
Boxed out 50
Box-head window 351
Brace 50
Braced frame 50
Bracket 50
Bracket capital 62
Bracketed cornice 92
Bracketed hood 51
Bramante, Donato 51
Branch tracery 328
Brass 207
Brattice 51
Breast 51
Breezeway 51
Breuer, Marcel 51
Brick 52
Brick bat 52
Brick veneer 52
Bridge 53
Bridging 54
Bridle joint 184
Brise-soleil 54
Broach 54
Broken arch 16
Broken gable 141
Broken joint 184
Broken pediment 241
Broken rangework 199
Bronze 207
Bronze Age 54
Brownstone 310
Bruder, Will 54
Brunelleschi, Filippo 54
Brutalism 54
Bucranium 228
Bud 54

Building 55
Building adaptive reuse 55
Building addition 55
Building alteration 55
Building area 55
Building artifact 55
Building code 55
Building component 55
Building conservation 55
Building construction 55
Building envelope 55
Building environment 55
Building grade 55
Building height 55
Building inspector 55
Building line 55
Building maintenance 56
Building material 56
Building occupancy 56
Building permit 56
Building preservation 56
Building reconstruction 56
Building rehabilitation 56
Building remodeling 56
Building renovation 56
Building restoration 56
Building retrofit 56
Building services 56
Building stone 56
Building subsystems 56
Building survey 56
Built environment 56
Built-up beam 40
Built-up roofing 277
Bulkhead 56
Bull header 52
Bull header bond 46
Bull stretcher bond 46
Bullfinch, Charles 56
Bull-nosed step 308
Bungalow 56
Bungalow door 109
Bungalow style 57
Bungalow window 351
Bunshaft, Gordon 57
Burgee, John 57
Burl 357
Burnham, Daniel Hudson 57
Bush-hammered concrete 57
Bush-hammered finish 57
Butt joint 184
Butt splice 302

Butterfly roof 227
Buttress 57
Byzantine architecture 58
Byzantine Revival style 58
Cabin 59
Cabinet 59
Cabinet window 351
Cabinetmaker 59
Cable molding 212
Cable stays 59
Cable column 80
Cable fluted column 80
Cable molding 212
Calatrava, Santiago 59
Caldarium 59
Calendar 59
Calf's tongue molding 212
Callicrates 59
Camber 60
Camber arch 16
Camber beam 40
Camber window 351
Came 60
Campaniform capital 63
Campanile 60
Campen, Jacob van 60
Canal 60
Canalis 60
Candela, Felix 60
Canephora 60
Canine 228
Canopy 60
Canopy roof 277
Cant 61
Cant bay 39
Cant molding 212
Cant strip 61
Cant wall 346
Cant window 351
Cantilever 61
cantilever retaining wall 346
Cantilevered 61
Cantilevered steps 309
Cap 62
Cap molding 212
Capital 62
Capital improvement 64
Capitol 64
Capstone 64
Cardboard model 64
Cardinal points 64
Cardinal, Douglas 64

Carolingian architecture 64
Carpenter 64
Carpenter Gothic style 64
Carport 65
Carriage House 65
Carriage porch 65
Cartoon 101
Cartouche 65
Carved work 65
Carver 65
Caryatic order 66
Caryatid 66
Cascade 66
Cased frame 67
Cased openings 67
Casement window 351
Casework 67
Casing 67
Casino 67
Cast iron 207
Cast stone 67
Castellated 67
Castellation 67
Cast-in-place concrete 85
Cast-iron façade 67
Cast-iron lacework 68
Castle 68
Castle style 68
Catacombs 68
Catch basin 68
Catenary 68
Catenary arch 68
Cathedral 68
Cathri 68
Catwalk 68
Caudill, William 68
Caulicoli 69
Caulk 69
Caulking compound 69
Cavetto molding 212
Cavity wall 346
Cavity wall masonry 199
Cavo-relievo 268
Cedar 357
Ceiling 69
Ceiling diffuser 69
Ceiling fan 69
Ceiling grid 69
Ceiling joist 185
Ceiling medallion 69
Cell 69
Cella 69

Grout 161
Grouted masonry 161
Gruen, Victor David 161
Guarini, Guarino 161
Guest house 161
Guilloche molding 213
Guimard, Hector 161
Guirgola, Romaldo 161
Gum 357
Gusset 161
Gutta 161
Gutter 162
Gwathmey, Charles 162
Gymnasium 162
Gypsum board 162
Gypsum plaster 162
Hacienda 162
Hadid, Zaha 162
Half arch 19
Half baluster 162
Half column 82
Half door 109
Half-landing 305
Half-round molding 213
Half-space landing 190
Half-timbered 162
Half-timbered wall 347
Hall 163
Hall chamber 163
Hall church 163
Hallway 163
Halprin, Lawrence 163
Hammer beam 40
Hammer brace 163
Hammer-beam roof 278
Handrail 163
Hanger 163
Hanging gable 141
Hanging stair 304
Hankar, Paul 163
Hardboard 358
Hardouin-Mansart, Jules 163
Hardpan 163
Hardwood 358
Hardy, Hugh Gelston 163
Harmika 164
Harmonic proportion 164
Harmony 164
Harrison, Peter 164
Harrison, Wallace Kirkman 164
Hatch 164
Haunch 164

Haunch arch 19
Haviland, John 164
Head 164
Head mortar joint 216
Header 164
Header bond 47
Headroom 164
Hearthstone 164
Heartwood 358
Heat gain 164
Heat loss 164
Heat-absorbing glass 151
Heavy-timber construction 165
Hejduk, John 165
Helical reinforcement 165
Helical stair 304
Helices 165
Helix 165
Hellenic architecture 165
Hellenistic architecture 165
Hellmuth, George 165
Helm 165
Helm roof 278
Hemispherical 165
Hemispherical dome 105
Hemispherical vault 340
Hemlock 358
Henry II style 165
Henry IV style 165
Heptagon 165
Herm 166
Herrera, Juan de 166
Herringbone 166
Herringbone blocking 166
Herringbone bond 47
Herron, Ronald James 166
Hexagonal 166
Hexastyle 166
Hickory 358
Hierarchy 166
Hieroglyph 166
High relief 269
High Renaissance 167
High rise 167
High style 167
High tech architecture 167
High Victorian 167
High Victorian Gothic 167
High-light window 353
Hildebrandt, Johann L. von 167
Hinge 168
Hip 168

Hip knob 232
Hip rafter 265
Hip roof 278
Hip-and-valley roof 278
Hipped dormer 112
Hipped end 168
Hipped gable 141
Hippodrome 168
Historiated 168
Historic district 168
Historic preservation 168
Historic structure 168
Historical freize 168
Historical marker 168
Historical monument 168
Historical research 168
Historical significance 168
Hittite architecture 168
Hoffman, Josef 169
Hoist 169
Holabird, William 169
Holl, Elias 169
Holl, Steven 169
Hollien, Hans 169
Hollow block 169
Hollow core door 109
Hollow masonry unit 200
Hollow molding 213
Hollow square molding 213
Hollow tile 325
Hollow-tile floor 131
Hollyhock ornament 232
Homestead 169
Homesteading 169
Homogeneous 169
Honeycomb 169
Honeysuckle ornament 232
Honnecourt, Villard de 170
Hood 170
Hoodmold 213
Hood, Raymond M. 170
Hopper window 353
Horizon line 245
Horizontal cornice 92
Horn 170
Horse 230
Horseshoe arch 19
Horta, Victor 170
Hospital 170
Hotel 170
Hot-rolled sections 170
House 170

Museum 218
Mushroom column 82
Muslim architecture 218
Mutule 218
Mycenaean architecture 218
Naos 219
Nara 219
Narthex 219
Nash, John 219
National Trust for Historic
    Preservation 219
National Historic Landmark 219
Natural forms 219
Natural stone 311
Natural ventilation 219
Nave 219
Neck 219
Neo-classicism 219
Neo-expressionism 219
Neo-formalism 220
Neolithic Era 220
Neon lamp 220
Nervi, Pier Luigi 220
Net vault 340
Network 220
Neumann, Johann B. 220
Neutra, Richard Josef 220
New Brutalism 220
New Classicism 221
New England Colonial
    style 221
Newel 221
Newel cap 221
Newel post 221
Niche 221
Niemeyer, Oscar 221
Nogging 221
Nominal size of lumber 222
Noncombustible 222
Nonconforming building 222
Non-load-bearing wall 347
Norman architecture 222
Norman cottage 222
Nosing 222
Notched molding 213
Nouvel, Jean 222
Nowicki, Matthew 222
Noyes, Eliot 222
Nursery home 222
Nylon 251
Nympheum 222
Oak 358

Obata, Gyo 223
Obelisk 223
Oblique projection 260
Oblique section 260
Oblong 223
Obscure glass 151
Observatory 223
Obsidian 311
Obtuse angle arch 20
Octagonal 223
Octagonal house 223
Octahedral 223
Octastyle 223
Oculus 223
Office building 224
Offset 224
Ogee 224
Ogee arch 20
Ogee pediment 241
Ogee roof 279
Olhbrich, Joseph 224
Olive leaf cluster 232
Olmec architecture 224
Olmsted, Frederick Law 224
One-point perspective 245
Onigawara 224
Onion dome 105
Opacity 225
Opal glass 151
Opalescent glass 151
Open cornice 92
Open eaves 225
Open pediment 241
Open plan 225
Open space 225
Open stair 304
Open-space easement 225
Open-string stair 305
Open-timbered 225
Open-timbered roof 279
Open-web joist 225
Open-well stair 305
Openwork 225
Openwork grille 225
Opera house 225
Operable transom 225
Operable window 354
Opus incertum 225
Opus quadratum 225
Opus reticulatum 225
Opus spicatum 225
Opus testaecum 225

Orb 225
Orchestra 225
Orchestration 226
Order 226
Orders 226
Organic 226
Organic architecture 226
Organization 226
Oriel window354
Oriental style 227
Orientation 227
Ornament 227
Ornament: animal forms 227
Ornament in relievo 233
Ornamental 233
Ornamental cast iron 233
Ornamental iron 233
Ornamental metal 234
Ornamental plaster 234
Ornamental stone 234
Ornamentation 234
Orthographic projection 260
Ostberg, Ragner 234
Otto, Frei 234
Ottoman style 234
Ottonian architecture 234
Oud, Jacobus J. P. 234
Outbuilding 234
Outlooker 234
Outrigger 234
Oval 234
Oval window 354
Overdoor 234
Overhang 235
Overhanging 235
Overhead door 110
Overlapping 235
Overlapping counterpoint 93
Oversailing 235
Overthrow 235
Ovolo molding 213
Ovum 235
Owings, Nathaniel A. 235
Owl 230
Ox-eye window 354
Ozenfant, Amadee 235
Pagoda 236
Pai-lou 145
Paint 236
Painted glass 151
Painter 236
Paired brackets 236

Sprinkler system 302
Spruce 358
Spur 303
Square 303
Square billet molding 214
Square roof 280
Square rubble masonry 201
Squared stone 311
Square-headed 303
Square-headed window 355
Squinch 303
Squinch arch 22
Stabilization 303
Stack bond 47
Stadium 303
Staff 303
Staggered 304
Stained glass 152
Stained glass window 355
Stainless steel 207
Stair 304
Stair flight 305
Stair landing 305
Stair rail 305
Stair riser 306
Stair tower 306
Stair turret 306
Staircase 306
Stairwell 306
Stalactite work 306
Stamped metal 306
Stanchion 306
Standby lighting 306
Standby power 306
Standing seam joint 185
Standpipe 306
Stark, Phillip 306
Statehouse 306
Station point 246
Statuary 306
Statue 307
Statuette 307
Stave 307
Stave church 307
Steamboat Gothic style 307
Steel 208
Steel frame 307
Steel stud 308
Steeple 308
Steiner, Rudolf 308
Stele 308
Stellar vault 341

Stenciling 308
Step 308
Stepped 309
Stepped arch 22
Stepped flashing 309
Stepped gable 142
Stepped pyramid 309
Stepped roof 280
Stepped voissoir 345
Stepped windows 355
Stepped-back chimney 309
Stereobate 309
Stern, Robert A.M. 310
Stiacciato 269
Stick style 310
Stile 310
Stilted arch 22
Stirling, James Frazer 310
Stoa 310
Stockade 310
Stone 310
Stone Age 312
Stone house 312
Stone, Eward Durrell 312
Stonemason 312
Stool 312
Stoop 312
Stop 312
Stopped flute 312
Store front 312
Storeroom 312
Storm door 110
Storm porch 312
Storm window 355
Story 312
Straight joint 185
Straight stair 305
Straight-flight stair 305
Straight-line gable 142
Strap hanger 313
Strap hinge 313
Strapwork ornament 233
Streamline Moderne style 313
Street furniture 313
Streetlight 313
Streetscape 313
Stress 313
Stressed skin panel 358
Stressed-skin construction 313
Stretcher 313
Striation 313
Strickland, William 313

String 313
Stringcourse 313
Stringer 313
Struck molding 214
Struck mortar joint 216
Structural engineering 313
Structural glass 152
Structural lumber 358
Strut 314
Stuart style 314
Stubbins, Hugh Asher 314
Stucco 314
Stud 314
Stud partition 314
Studio 314
Studio apartment 314
Study 102
Stupa 314
Style 314
Stylobate 314
Subbasement 314
Subcontractor 314
Subdivision 314
Subfloor 314
Suborder 314
Suburb 314
Sullivan, Louis H. 314
Sullivanesque 315
Sullivanesque style 315
Sumerian architecture 315
Summerbeam 40
Sun deck 315
Sun disk 315
Sunk draft 315
Sunk fillet molding 214
Sunk panel 315
Sunk relief 269
Superimposed orders 316
Supermarket 316
Superstructure 316
Surbase 316
Surbased arch 23
Surround 316
Survey 316
Suspended ceiling 69
Suspended forms 316
Suspended luminaire 316
Suspended roof 280
Suspension bridge 54
Swag 316
Swan's-neck pediment 242
Sway brace 50

Triangular arch 23
Triangulated 331
Triangulation 331
Tribunal 331
Triforium 331
Triglyph 331
Trilith 331
Trim 331
Trimetric projection 261
Trimmer 331
Trimming joist 185
Tripartite scheme 331
Triple-hung window 355
Triton 332
Triumphal arch 332
Trompe L'oeil 332
Trophy 332
Troweled joint 216
Trumeau 332
Truncated 332
Truncated roof 281
Truss 333
Trussed 333
Trussed arch 23
Trussed beam 40
Trylon 334
Tschumi, Bernard 334
Tube structure 334
Tubular scaffolding 334
Tudor arch 23
Tudor Revival style 334
Tudor style 334
Tulipwood 358
Tumbling course 334
Turkish dome 106
Turnkey system 334
Turret 334
Tuscan order 334
Twist 334
Two-centered arch 23
Two-dimensional graphics 335
Two-hinged arch 23
Two-point perspective 246
Two-tiered porch 335
Two-way switch 335
Tympanum 335
Umbrella shell roof 281
Unbraced frame 336
Undercoat 336
Undercut 336
Underfloor heating 336
Underlayment 336

Underpinning 336
Undressed stone 312
Undulating 336
Ungers, Oswald Mathias 336
Unglazed tile 325
Uniform load 336
Uniformity 336
Unity 336
Upjohn, Richard 336
Urbahn, Max 336
Urban design 337
Urban renewal 337
Urn 337
Usable floor area 337
Utopian architecture 337
Utzon, Jorn 337
Valley 338
Valley rafter 265
Value 338
Value analysis 338
Van Alen, William 338
Van de Velde, Henri 338
Van der Rohe, Ludwig
    Mies 338
Vanbrugh, Sir John 338
Vane 338
Vanishing point 246
Vapor barrier 339
Variegated 339
Variety 339
Varnish 339
Vasari, Giorgio 339
Vase 339
Vault 339
Vault capital 341
Vault rib 341
Vaulted 341
Vaulting course 341
Vaulting shaft 341
Velarium 341
Veneer 52, 359
Venetian arch 23
Venetian blind 341
Venetian door 110
Venetian molding 214
Venetian mosaic 217
Venetian window 355
Ventilator 341
Venturi, Robert 341
Veranda 342
Verde antique 312
Verdigris 342

Verge 342
Vergeboard 342
Vermiculated masonry 201
Vermiculite 342
Vernacular architecture 342
Vertical pivoting window 355
Vertical sliding window 355
Vestibule 342
Vest-pocket park 342
Vestry 342
Victorian 342
Victorian Gothic style 342
Victorian Romanesque 343
Victory 343
Vierendeel truss 333
Vignette 102
Vignola, Giacomo Barozzi 343
Vihara 343
Village 343
Vinoly, Rafael 343
Vinyl 251
Vinyl-asbestos tile 325
Viollet-Le-Duc, Emmanuel 344
Virtual 344
Virtual office 344
Virtual reality 344
Visionary architecture 344
Vision-proof glass 152
Visor roof 281
Visualization 344
Vitruvian scroll 344
Vitruvius, Marcus Pollio 344
Volcanic stone 312
Volute 344
Vomitory 344
Voussoir 344
Vries, Hans Vredeman de 345
Waffle slab 345
Wagner, Otto 345
Wainscot 346
Walker, Ralph Thomas 346
Walker, Thomas U. 346
Walk-up apartment 346
Walkway 346
Wall 346
Wall column 83
Wall cornice 348
Wall dormer 112
Wall gable 142
Wall plate 348
Wall shaft 348
Wall tile 348